KB275122

MAGNUS
서술형 시리즈

도서 출판 오스틴북스

고등영어 서술형

기본편

8주완성

박지성 이진희 공저

수능영어가 절대평가로 바뀐 지 얼마 지나지 않아 다시 입시에 변화가 생기면서 고등학교 1학년 내신의 중요성이 강조되고 있다. 그런 의미에서 서술형 문제 대한 중요도는 더욱 커지고 있는 느낌이다.

최근 chatGPT의 활용이 높아지면서 기존에 출제된 문제를 응용•변형 하거나 참신한 신유형의 서술형 문제가 출제되는 현실에서 기출 유형에 문제 뿐 아니라 신유형 문제에 철저히 대비할 필요가 있다.

본서는 전국 200개 이상의 고등학교 내신에 출제된 서술형 문제 유형을 분석•정리하고, 총 100개의 구문에 맞춰 기출과 신유형 문제를 모두 담아 어떠한 유형의 문제라도 당황하지 않고 대처할 수 있도록 구성했다.

객관식 문제와 달리 서술형은 오랜 시간 투자를 바탕으로 한 탄탄한 기본실력이 뒷받침되지 않는다면 결코 좋은 성적을 기대할 수 없다. 책의 구성과 특징에서 밝힌 본서의 활용법에 따라 믿음을 가지고 책을 마무리한다면 고등영어 내신에서 좋은 성적을 받을 수 있음을 확신한다.

저자 박지성

※ 구문 학습 병행의 필요성

구문은 문장을 형성하는 수많은 규칙들 가운데 특별한 형태로 자주 활용되는 언어적 패턴을 말한다. 예를 들어 "내가 그를 만난 곳은 (다른 아닌) 공원이었다."라는 말을 전달할 때 문장 내 특정 표현을 강조하기 위해 다음과 같은 표현이 활용된다.

> **It** was <u>at the park</u> **that** I met him.

위 예문은 일반적으로 it ~ that강조 구문이라고 부르고, 부사구인 at the park의 내용을 강조하고 있다.

| 구문학습의 필요성 |

① 해석 속도 극대화

문법이 문장이란 퍼즐을 구성하는 조각들을 어떻게 맞추는지 이해하는 것이라면, 구문학습은 특정 형태로 맞춰진 "맞춤형 퍼즐"이라고 볼 수 있다. 특정 형태를 취한다는 말은 그 형태의 변화가 없고, 반복적으로 사용된다는 의미이므로 학습을 통한 체득은 곧 문장해석 속도의 극대화와 동일한 말이 된다.

② 해석의 정확성

특정 구문에 대한 학습은 문장해석의 정확성으로 이어진다.

> **It follows that** he is a good man

위 문장에서 It follows that S V의 구문을 몰랐다면, "그것은 그가 착한 사람이라는 것이 따른다." 또는 "그가 착한 사람이라는 것이 따른다"와 같이 오역할 수 있다. 이 표현은 앞서 전개된 내용을 바탕으로 "(당연히) ~라는 결론이 따른다"는 의미로 위 문장은 "(결과적으로) 그는 착한 사람이다"로 해석해야 한다. 구문학습은 문법 학습만으로 메울 수 없는 특정 문장에 대한 해석의 정확성을 높여준다.

③ 내신 서술형과 수행평가 에세이

특정 문법 또는 구문의 활용을 묻는 영작 문제가 주를 이루는 서술형 문제뿐 아니라 에세이 작문과 같은 수행평가에서 좋은 점수를 받기 위해서는 구문학습은 그 어느 때보다 중요하다. 덧붙여, 눈으로 보는 영어가 아니라 "이해 → 암기 → 영작"으로 이어지는 "쓰는 영어"에 대한 대비가 필수이다.

④ 착실한 내신준비는 곧 수능영어 고득점

수능영어는 기본적으로 1단락 1문항을 기본 골격으로 삼다보니, 당연히 제시한 시간에 상당히 많은 지문을 소화해 내야 하는 시간압박(time pressure)이 높은 시험이다. 문장해석 속도를 극대화시키는 구문학습은 내신영어뿐 아니라 수능영어에 필요하며, 특히 어법문제와 직결된다. 이뿐만 아니라 주제, 제목, 요지, 문단요약과 같은 대의파악 문제의 핵심내용은 일반적으로 강조, 도치, 최상급, 가정법, 상관등위접속사와 같은 특수구문으로 표현되기에 수능고득점을 위해선 구문학습은 필수이다.

✼ 본서의 구성

본서의 구성과 특징은 다음과 같다.

1. 구문

본서는 강별로 아래와 같은 Key Point를 통해서 각 구문에 대한 핵심을 추려 간단·명료하게 설명했다.

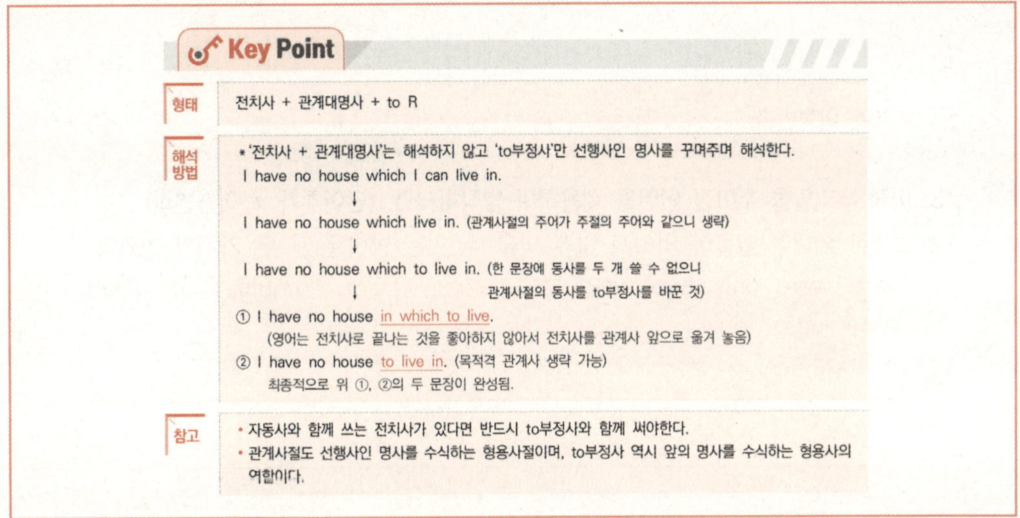

2. 미리 Voca

각 장에서 나오는 어휘를 미리 학습함으로써 문제 접근성을 높였다.

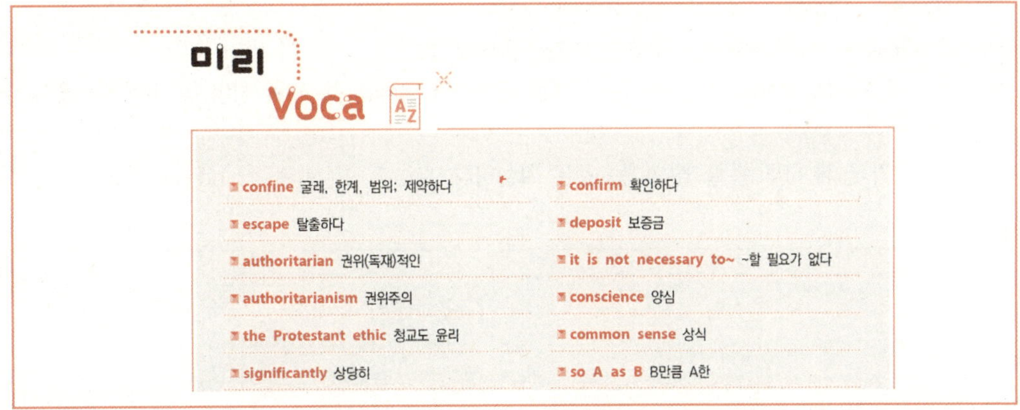

구성과 특징

3. 다양한 유형의 서술형 문제 단계적 구성

① 제시된 단어만을 활용한 영작

> **연습문제 2. 아래 우리말을 괄호 안에 주어진 단어만을 활용하여 영작하시오.**
>
> ✤ 당신이 멍청한 짓을 하지 않기 위해서는 두려워할 줄 알아야 한다.
> You need some fears (foolish / things / to / you / from / keep / doing).
>
> ➜ ____

② 단어추가와 어형변화

> **3. 아래 우리말을 주어진 단어를 활용하여 영작하시오. (단어추가 + 어형변화)**
>
> ✤ 발생한 위대한 일들이 잊히지 않게 막을 수 있는 방법은 단 두 가지가 있었다.
> There were only two ways (forgotten / from / could / in which / great happenings / being / people / hinder).
>
> ➜ ____
>
> ____

③ 조건부 영작

> • 조건 •
> • it is ~ that(whether) S V의 구문을 활용할 것
> • 각 문장의 해석을 보고, 제시된 단어를 활용하여 영작할 것. 추가 단어 및 어형변화 있음.
>
> 1. 그가 집에 하루 종일 있었다는 것은 확실하다. (certain / stay at home / all day long)
>
> ➜ ____

④ 문장전환

※ 아래 지문을 읽고, 밑줄 친 ⓑ의 문장을 해석하고 빈칸에 알맞은 단어를 넣으시오.

ⓐ The roadside is crowded with locals, and (그들의 두뇌는 지역의 지식으로 가득 차 있다.) but ⓑ <u>we are too arrogant and embarrassed to ask the way.</u> So we drive around in circles, ⓒ (   ) and ⓓ (   ) successive hypotheses ⓔ (그림 같은 전망을 어디서 찾아야하는지에 관하여) that would entertain and enlighten the tourists.

해석 ➡ ____

We are (   ) arrogant and embarrassed (   ) (   ) (   ) ask the way.

⑤ 빈칸 채우기

유형 1. 내용정리

※ 아래 지문을 읽고, 물음에 답하시오.

It depends on their concentration than on a high IQ (학생들이 좋은 성적을 얻는지 못 얻는지는). Students with high grades often prepare for exam in advance by regularly reviewing their notes. In contrast, students with poor grades wait until the last minute and then quickly try to catch up.

✿ 본문의 내용을 바탕으로 아래 빈칸에 들어갈 표현을 적으시오. (동사의 어형변화에 주의)

Students with good grades	Students with poor grades
start studying _______ _______	wait _______ _____ _______ _______, hardly _______ _______

구성과 특징

유형 2. 본문에 나온 표현을 활용한 빈칸 채우기

I once said to a first date "Should I kiss you goodnight?" She looked confused for a moment and said "Yes". I went to kiss her on the cheek, and there was a moment of (a) c____________ about whether (b) (내가 그녀의 입술에 키스를 할 것인지 볼에 할 것인지를), and (c) 그녀는 머리를 어느 방향으로 틀어야하는지 몰랐다.).

⑥ 문단요약

유형 1. 우리말 제시형

Leaders and manager are basically different types of people. Every organization structures itself to accomplish its goal in a way that is in tune with or responsive to its environment. <u>Once the efficiency of the organization is established, people to about simply maintaining the system, assuming that the environment will stay the same.</u> Managers, then, take the leading role in sustaining the business. But the environment for any organization is always changing, thus the organization becomes less able to cope with the situation, creating more management problems. Times like this require organizations to think more in terms of leadership. Leaders seek to bring their organization more in line with the realities of their environment, which often necessitates changing the very structure, resources, and relationships of their organization. As they do, leaders can bring renewed vitality to their people.

Q. 위 본문의 내용을 한 문장으로 요약하려고 한다. 빈칸에 들어갈 표현을 순서대로 쓰시오.
　(단, 첫 철자가 제시된 경우 해당 철자로 시작하는 단어로 표현할 것)

When the environment of their organization changes and causes problems, leaders are expected to take more a__________(적응을 돕는) measures to resolve them compared to managers who are usually involved in __________ the e__________(기존의) system

유형 2. 구문 활용

※ 아래 지문의 내용을 한 문장으로 요약하려고 한다. 빈 칸에 들어갈 표현을 본문에서 찾아 쓰시오.

The best equipment a young man can have for the battle of life is a conscience, common sense and good health. There is no friend so good as a good conscience. There is no enemy so dangerous as a bad conscience. Conscience makes us either kings or slaves.

For a young man to go through the battle of life, it is _______ great importance to keep __________.

⑦ 이어질 내용 추론

※ 아래 지문을 읽고, 물음에 답하시오.

If you're faced with a complicated problem, (그것을 잘라서 많은 단순한 문제들로 만들고, 그리고 그것들을 하나씩 하나씩 처리하고 싶은 마음이 생길 것이다.). It is sometimes claimed that if you have solved all the simple problems you've solved the whole thing. That's reductionism in a nutshell. And as a methodology it works extremely well. In my discipline, which is physics, it's had some amazing successes. Look at the world about us, just see how complicated it is, the richness and diversity of nature. How are we ever to come to understand it? Well, a good way to start is by breaking it up into small bite-sized pieces. One example is atomism. The belief that the entire universe is made up of atoms, or some sort of fundamental particles, and that everything that happens in nature is just the rearrangement of these particles, have proved extraordinarily fruitful. Once you focus down to the level of individual atoms you can work out all the laws and principles that govern them. You can figure out in detail what they are doing.

Q. 위 본문의 마지막 내용이 이어지는 문장이다. 빈칸에 적절한 표현을 쓰시오.

It's then tempting to believe that if you understand individual ______ and the way they interact, you understand __________.

구성과 특징

⑧ 패러프레이즈

❖ 문맥을 고려하며, 밑줄 친 (가)의 문장과 같은 뜻의 다른 문장으로 표현하려고 한다. 빈칸에 들어갈 적절한 단어를 쓰시오.
   It would be misleading to suggest that Piaget is oblivious to the limitations.
   = Piaget was fully ________ of the limitations.

⑨ 지칭추론

The latest studies indicate that (사람들이 정말 원하는 것은 자신의 부모와 같은 특징을 가진 배우자이다). Women are after a man who is like their father and men want to be able to see their own mother in the woman of their dreams. Cognitive psychologist David Perrett studies what makes faces attractive. He has developed a computerized morphing system that can endlessly adjust faces to suit his needs. Perrett suggests that we find our own faces charming because they remind us of the faces we looked at constantly in our early childhood years.

❖ 위 본문의 내용으로 보아 밑줄 친 the faces를 지칭하는 대상은?

이외에도 다양한 유형의 서술형 문제를 담아 기출유형과 신유형에 모두 대비할 수 있도록 만전을 기했다.

Contents

MAGNUS
서술형 시리즈

MAGNUS

서술형평가 고등영어
unit 01~36

미리

Voca 

☐ **clever** 영리한	☐ **earn** 벌다(make)
☐ **width** 폭, 너비	☐ **the majority of** 대부분의
☐ **prehistoric** 선사시대의	☐ **quip** 비꼬다
☐ **commercialize** 상업화하다	☐ **estimate** 추정하다, 추정
☐ **origin** 기원	☐ **rate** 속도, 비율, 요금
☐ **slave** 노예	☐ **cooperation** 협력, 협동
☐ **chance** 가능성, 기회	☐ **craft** 공예, 기술, 공들여 만들다
☐ **object** 물건, 목표, 반대하다	☐ **policy** 정책
☐ **surface** 표면	☐ **personnel** 인원, 직원
☐ **draw** 그리다, 끌어당기다	☐ **tinsmith** 양철, 양철공
☐ **lead** 이끌다, 지휘하다, 납	☐ **millwright** 기계설치공
☐ **various** 다양한	☐ **unbolt** 빗장을 벗기다
☐ **hammer** 망치[해머]로 치다	☐ **mount** 오르다, 시작하다, 끼우다
☐ **metal** 금속	☐ **a feeling of fullness** 포만감
☐ **well-known** 잘 알려진	☐ **strategy** 전략, 계획
☐ **seashore** 해안	☐ **raisins** 건포도
☐ **suffer** 겪다	☐ **content** 내용물
☐ **latitude** 위도	

형태	배수사 as 원급 as/ 배수사 비교급 than

해석방법	She / has / <u>twice</u> as much as much money / as you. 　그녀는 / 두 배나 많은 돈을 / 가지고 있다/ 너보다 He / has / <u>three times</u> more money / than she. 　그는 세 배나 많은 돈을 가지고 있다/ 그녀보다

참고	• 배수사가 생략될 수도 있다. I paid double the price. 　나는 그 가격 보다 두 배나 많은 돈을 지불했다.

Exercise 01 배수사 표현에 주의하여 아래 우리말을 주어진 단어를 사용하여 영작하시오.

1 그 땅의 가격은 10년 전의 금액보다 두 배가 올랐다.

(of / 10 years ago / as / as / risen / high / twice / have / the land / the prices).

➜ ____

2 그 레슬링 선수는 나보다 두 배나 무겁다.

(is / heavier / than / times / I / three / wrestler / the).

➜ ____

3 당신은 당신이 생각하는 똑똑한 것보다 반 정도도 똑똑하지 않다.

(half / you / clever / are / as / not / you / are / you / think / as).

➜ ____

4 유미는 내 책의 두 배 이상의 책을 가지고 있다.
(number / of / books / Yumi / has / my / twice).

→ ____

5 이 거리는 저 거리의 폭의 반 정도 된다.
(the / is / one / half / that / width / street / of / this).

→ ____

도전

6 노예 제도는 선사 시대의 기원을 가지지만, 로마인에 의해 상업화되었으며 일부 로마인은 노예를 10,000명이나 보유했습니다.
Slavery is (was / commercialized / but / origin, / of / a / the Romans / by / prehistoric), (many / some / slaves / 10,000 / as / as / whom / had / of).

→ ____

→ ____

고난도

7 부유한 샌프란시스코에서 하위 20%에서 태어난 아이는 성인이 되어 상위 20%에 들 가능성이 디트로이트에서 태어난 비슷한 아이보다 두 배 더 높습니다.
A child born in the bottom 20% in wealthy San Francisco (ending up / as / of / has / much chance / a similar child / in the top 20% / as an adult / twice / as / in Detroit / as).

→ ____

  제시된 우리말에 맞게, 괄호 안의 단어를 바르게 배열하시오.

1 인도는 중국을 제외하고 세상에서 가장 사람들이 많은 나라이다. 인도는 미국보다 약 세 배 이상의 사람들이 있다. 비록 인도는 미국에 비해 땅덩어리는 반 정도 되더라도.

India has more people than any other country in the world except China. (the United States / times / it / three / has / people / as / many / about / as), although (it / only / has / land / as / half / much).

→ ____

→ ____

2 지구는 그 표면이나 주위에 있는 어떤 물건보다 수백만 배는 더 무겁다. 그래서 모든 것들을 지구로 끌어당길 수 있는 것이다.

(of / times / the earth / than / heavier / millions / any object / is) near to or upon its surface; so it draws every such object toward it.

→ ____

3 납으로 만들어진 파이프는 거의 2000년 전에 만들어 졌다. 납은 물보다 11배정도 무겁다. 그것은 너무 부드러운 금속이라서 다양한 모양으로 만들어질 수 있다.

(lead / made / of / pipes / the) were made almost 2.000 years ago. (as / heavy / times / water / lead / is / as / eleven). (various shapes / into / be / it / it / so soft / is / hammered / can / that / a metal).

→ ____

→ ____

→ ____

도전

4 해안에 있는 마을은 같은 위도에 있는 내륙의 마을만큼 극심한 추위를 겪지 않는다는 것은 잘 알려진 사실입니다. (as V S의 도치를 활용할 것)

It is well-known that (from / as / do / those / much / cold / not / towns / the seashore / suffer / on / as / do / extreme) in the same latitude further inland.

→ ____

Exercise 03 각 지문을 읽고, 물음에 답하시오.

1

Would you rather earn $50,000 a year while other people make $25,000, or would you rather earn $100,000 a year while other people get $250,000? Prices of goods and services are the same. Similarly Ⓐall other things being equal, would you rather make twice as much as other people or twice as much as yourself but less than half of other people? Surprisingly, research shows that the majority of people select the first option: they would rather make twice as much as others even if that meant Ⓑ_________(earn) half as much as they could have. Ⓒ_____ _____ _____ _____ _____! But as H. L. Mencken quipped, Ⓓ "A wealthy man is one who earn $100 a year more than his wife's sister's husband."

* quip: 비꼬다

1 밑줄 친 Ⓐ를 접속사를 넣어 완전한 부사절로 바꾸시오.

> All other things being equal, would you rather make twice as much as other people?

→ ____

2 괄호 안의 단어를 문맥에 맞게 변형하여 빈칸 Ⓑ에 넣으시오.

→ ____

3 빈칸 ⓒ에 들어갈 감탄문을 아래 제시된 단어만을 사용하여 문맥에 맞게 영작하시오.

→ ____

4 밑줄 친 ⓓ에서 어법상 <u>틀린</u> 부분을 찾아 알맞게 고치시오.

→ ____

5 밑줄 친 ⓓ의 문맥적 의미를 작성한 것이다. 빈칸에 들어갈 한 단어를 쓰시오.

> The quote by H.L. Mencken emphasizes that people's perception of wealth is often based on being slightly better off than their peers, thus reinforcing the importance of ________ status in shaping human satisfaction and behavior.

2

Cost estimates follow from time estimates simply by Ⓐ<u>multiplying</u> the hours required by the required labor rates. Beware of coordination problems Ⓑ<u>which</u> multiple crafts are involved. Ⓕ__________, one major company has a policy ⓒ<u>that</u> requires the following personnel in order to remove an electric motor: a tinsmith to remove the cover, an electrician to disconnect the electrical supply, a millwright to unbolt the mounts, and one or more laborers to remove the motor from its mount. That situation ⓓ<u>fraught</u> with inefficiency and high labor costs, since all four trades must Ⓔ<u>be scheduled</u> together, Ⓖ(적어도 세 명은 넋 놓고 지켜만 봐야하기에) while the fourth is at work. Ⓗ(비용은 가능한 것의 최소 4배가 될 것이며), and is often greater if one of the trades does not show up on time.

＊ fraught: ~으로 가득 찬

1　위 글의 내용과 일치하지 <u>않은</u> 것은?

① The cost estimate means the time estimate multiplied by the required time and required labor.

② Attention must be paid to cooperation issues that require a large number of people.

③ It takes four people to remove an electric motor at one company.

④ A situation where multiple people work together is full of inefficiency and high labor force.

⑤ If five people make a schedule and one person does not show up on time, the cost goes up five times.

2　Ⓐ~Ⓔ 중에서 어법상 틀린 것을 두 곳 찾아 바르게 고치시오.

틀린 번호	틀린 표현	바른 표현
＿＿＿ :	＿＿＿＿＿＿＿＿	＿＿＿＿＿＿＿＿
＿＿＿ :	＿＿＿＿＿＿＿＿	＿＿＿＿＿＿＿＿

3　위 글의 Ⓕ에 들어갈 알맞은 연결사를 고르시오.

① On the other hand　　② Similarly

③ Moreover　　④ Nonetheless

⑤ For instance

4　괄호 Ⓖ의 우리말을 아래 제시어를 사용하여 영작하시오. (단, 필요시 어형변형 할 것)

제시어

watch / three / people / at / least / with

→ ＿＿＿＿＿＿＿＿＿＿＿＿＿＿＿＿＿＿＿＿＿＿＿＿＿＿＿＿

5 밑줄 친 ㉯의 우리말을 아래 제시어를 활용하여 영작하시오.

what / be / the / could / could / cost / times / be / it / four

→ ____

Exercise **04** 아래 지문을 읽고, 물음에 답하시오.

(가)Water has no calories, but it takes up a space in your stomach, which creates a feeling of fullness. Recently, a study found that people who drank two glasses of water before meals got full sooner, ate fewer calories, and lost more weight. You can put the same strategy to work by choosing foods that have a higher water content over those with less water. For example, the only difference between grapes and raisins is that (나)Grapes have about 6 times as much water in them _______ _______ ______. (다)(그 물은 그것들이 당신을 얼마나 배부르게 할지에 큰 차이를 만듭니다.).

1 다음은 밑줄 친 (가) 문장을 재진술한 것이다. 제시된 철자로 시작하는 단어를 빈칸에 쓰시오.

Water has no calories, but it takes up a space in your stomach, which creates a feeling of fullness.

= Water contains zero calories, yet it o_______ space in your stomach, r______ i_____ a sensation of b______ f_____.

2 밑줄 친 (나)의 문장 빈칸을 채우고, 동일한 의미의 재진술 문장을 작성하려고 한다. 빈칸을 채우시오.

Grapes have about 6 times as much water in them _____ _____ _____.
= There is about 6 times more _____ in grapes _____ _____ _____.

3 본문의 내용과 일치하도록 아래 빈칸을 채우려고 한다. 제시어와 함께 빈칸에 들어갈 표현을 본문에서 찾아 넣으시오.

제시어

fill, up

You'll feel much more ________ _____ after eating 100 calories' worth of ______ than you would after eating 100 calories' worth of ______.

4 괄호 (다)의 우리말을 아래 제시어만을 사용하여 영작하시오. (단, 필요한 경우 문맥에 맞게 동사를 변형할 것)

제시어

a big / fill / up / make / they / how much / that water / in / difference / you

→ ____

02 가정법 과거(완료) 구문

미리 Voca 

❑ **embezzle** 횡령하다	❑ **obtain** 획득하다
❑ **devote** 쏟다, 헌신하다	❑ **realize** 깨닫다
❑ **literature** 문학	❑ **strangely** 이상하게
❑ **perseverance** 인내	❑ **neuroscience** 신경과학
❑ **approach** 접근하다	❑ **form** 형성하다
❑ **conventional** 전통적인, 기존의	❑ **process** 처리하다
❑ **critical** 비판적인	❑ **strive for** …을 얻으려고 노력하다
❑ **fundamental** 근본적인	❑ **compensatory** 보상하는, 균형을 맞추는
❑ **prophecy** 예언	❑ **cushion** (충격을) 완화하다, 완충하다
❑ **fulfill** 실행하다, 성취하다	❑ **potential** 잠재적인, 가능성 있는
❑ **enslave** 노예가 되게 하다	❑ **be capable of** ~을 할 수 있다
❑ **debt** 빚, 채무	❑ **be reliant on** ~에 의존하다
❑ **release** 풀어놓다, 면제하다	❑ **opposite** 반대의, 정반대의
❑ **fountain** 분수, 원천	❑ **scale** 척도, 비율
❑ **depth** 깊이	❑ **correspondingly** 그에 따라, 상응하여
❑ **unsophisticated** 소박한, 순진한	❑ **miserable** 비참한, 불행한
❑ **common** 흔한, 공통의	❑ **component** 구성 요소
❑ **aid** 도움, 지원	❑ **in turn** 차례로, 결과적으로
❑ **trait** 특징, 특성	❑ **internal** 내부의

🔑 Key Point

형태
- 가정법 과거 If 주어 + 동사의 과거형, 주어 + would, could, should, might + 동사원형
- 가정법 과거완료 If + 주어 + had + p.p, 주어 + would ,could, should, might + have + p.p

해석방법
- 가정법 과거: 만일~라면 좋았을 텐데
  If I knew the answer, I could help you.
  (만일 내가 정답을 알았다면, 너를 도와줄 수 있을 텐데)
- 가정법 과거완료: 만일~라면 좋았었을 텐데
  If he had been honest, I would have employed him.
  (만일 그가 정직했었더라면, 나는 그를 고용했었을텐데)

참고
- 가정법에서 직설법으로의 전환
- (a) 가정법 과거
  If he were honest, I would employ him.
  ⇒ As he is not honest, I don't employ him.
- (b) (가정법 과거완료)
  If you had taken my advice, you wouldn't have been in trouble.
  ⇒ As you did not take my advice, you were in trouble.
- If의 생략-If를 생략하고, 조동사 were or had가 문두에 위치한다.
  If I were a bird, I would fly to you.
  Were I a bird, I would fly to you.

Exercise 01 다음 우리말을 제시되 단어를 활용하여 영작하시오. (단, 단어 추가와 어형변화 있음)

1 만일 그가 너의 결혼식을 들었다면, 그는 놀랐을 것이다.

of / he / if / hear / surprise / would / he / marriage / your

→ _______________________, _______________________

2 만일 내가 그 소식을 알았었더라면, 나는 너에게 말했어야만 했다.

I / if / tell / should / news / know / the / have / you / I

→ _______________________, _______________________

3 만일 그가 전쟁에서 죽지 않았더라면, 살아있었을 텐데.

not / the / alive / be / he / he / would / kill / if / war / in / been

➜ ________________________________, ________________________________

4 만일 해가 서쪽에서 뜬다고 해도, 나는 결정을 바꾸지 않을 것이다.

the sun / I / my mind / change / if / in the west / to / rise / not / would

➜ ________________________________

🚩도전

5 그녀가 그릿의 중요성을 알았다면, 그녀는 더 많은 인내와 열정으로 자신의 경력에 접근했을 것이다.

(she / of / grit / had / the importance / known), (more / have / would / her / passion / she / and / perseverance / career / with / approached).

➜ ________________________________

➜ ________________________________

Exercise 02 각 문제를 우리말에 맞게, 괄호 안의 단어를 알맞게 배열하시오.

1 만일 전 세계의 사람들이 크리스마스의 정신을 이해할 수 있다면, 우리 모두가 싸우지 않고, 전쟁하지 않고 서로서로 잘 지낼 수 있는 기회가 있을 텐데.

(if / in / could / the world / understand / only people) the spirit of Christmas, (there / a better chance / be / would) for all to get along with each other, without fighting and making wars.

➜ ________________________________

➜ ________________________________

2 만일 내가 그 돈을 횡령했다는 것이 알려진다면, 나는 내 지위를 잃어버릴지도 모른다.

(were / that / known / it) I had embezzled the money, (position / might / lose / my / I).

→ ____

→ ____

3 가끔씩 내가 만일 내 인생전부를 문학에 헌신한다면 좀 더 훌륭한 작가가 될 수 있었을지 아닐지에 대해 내 자신에게 묻는다.

From time to time I have asked myself whether (I / have / should / writer / a / better / been), (devoted / if / my / literature / had / I / whole / to / life)

→ ____

→ ____

도전

4 소크라테스가 기존의 지혜에 의문을 제기하지 않았다면, 우리는 현대 철학에 기본이 되는 비판적 사고 능력을 발달시키지 못했을지도 모른다.

(conventional / had / questioned / Socrates / wisdom / if / not), (the critical thinking skills / are / modern philosophy / developed / we / fundamental / not / to / that / have / might).

→ ____

→ ____

5 모피어스가 네오를 믿지 않았다면, '원(The One)'에 대한 예언은 결코 실현되지 않았을 것이며, 인류
는 기계들에 의해 계속해서 지배당했을 것이다.
(Neo / Morpheus / Had / in / believed / not), (have / been / the One / never / about
/ might / fulfilled / the prophecy), and (enslaved / the machines / have / by /
remained / humanity / could).

→ ____

→ ____

→ ____

Exercise 03 각 지문을 읽고, 물음에 답하시오.

1

He was poor and always in debt. (가)He would have been easily forgotten if he had not
gone mad. But his Ⓐ ___________ released Ⓑ (that / was / the hidden / poet / him / in).
He was born again. A fountain of song rose up from the depth of his spirit.

1 밑줄 친 (가)의 문장을 As로 시작하는 직설법으로 바꾸시오.

He would have been easily forgotten if he had not gone mad.

= As ____ .

2 괄호 Ⓐ 안에 들어갈 단어를 본문에 찾아 쓰시오. (단, 필요 시 어형변화 할 것.)

Ⓐ ___________

3 문맥의 흐름이 자연스럽도록 괄호 Ⓑ 안에 있는 단어를 바르게 배열하시오.

→ ___________

2

The folk songs originate among the <u>unsophisticated</u> people of a nation: they became a part of the everyday life of the people because Ⓐ <u>they</u> express common emotions and interests. If we would study the very heart of a people, Ⓑ (만일 우리가 한 민족의 기본적인 욕구와 특징적인 자질을 안다면), we might be greatly aided in our study by Ⓒ (우리가 민요에서 얻을 수 있는 흔적).

1 밑줄 친 Ⓐ가 지칭하는 단어나 내용을 쓰시오.

→ _______________

2 괄호 Ⓑ의 우리말을 아래 제시어만 사용하여 바르게 영작하시오.

> **제시어**
>
> if / character / basic / we / would / and / desires / traits / know / its

→ ____

3 괄호 Ⓑ의 우리말을 아래 제시어만 사용하여 바르게 영작하고, 생략된 관계대명사를 알맞은 위치에 넣으시오.

> **제시어**
>
> folk / the / we / obtain / evidence / its / from / songs

→ ____

4 본문의 내용과 일치하도록 괄호 안의 조건에 맞게 빈칸에 들어갈 단어를 써 넣으시오.
(단, r로 시작하고 n으로 끝나는 총 11개의 철자로 구성된 단어임)

> Folk songs are a r_______n of the people's core emotions, interests, desires, and character traits.

(가)<u>By the time I started middle school, I realized that most of my fellow students had the idea that we Asian students are all smart</u>. It's true that some are. But what about those of us who aren't? Having to act like a brain can be a pain. My classmates come to me for answers, but I sometimes can't help them. Then they look at me strangely. (나)(만약 내가 천재라면, 나는 천재처럼 대우받는 것을 꺼려하지 않을 거야). But since I am not, I do.

1 밑줄 친 (나)의 문장을 아래 조건에서 제시된 구문을 활용하여 문맥에 맞게 재진술하시오.

• 조건 •
• no sooner ~ than 구문을 활용할 도치문으로 재진술 할 것.
• 시제에 주의할 것.

(가)By the time I started middle school, I realized that most of my fellow students had the idea that we Asian students are all smart.

= ____

2 아래 제시어를 활용하여 괄호 (나) 안의 우리말을 영작하시오.

제시어

genius, mind, treat, like one

→ ____

3 위 지문의 내용을 한 문장으로 표현하려고 한다. 빈칸에 들어갈 표현을 <u>본문에서 찾아</u> 쓰시오. (단, 빈칸의 위치에 따라 <u>단어의 품사는 변형</u>될 수 있음)

The idea that all Asian students are (a) ________ can be (b) _________ to those who are not.

(a) _________   (b) _________

Exercise 05 다음을 읽고, 물음에 답하시오.

Based on discoveries in neuroscience, pain and pleasure are formed and processed in the same area of the brain. Our bodies constantly strive for homeostasis, which is defined as the balance of bodily functions. (가)<u>Without the body's effective compensatory mechanisms</u>, which may cushion potential highs and lows, we would not be capable of surviving. Pleasure and pain are like two sides of the same coin; they seem to work together and are heavily reliant on one another and keep balance. If you imagine pleasure and pain as the two opposite points on a scale, you can easily understand that as one of the two points rises, the other must correspondingly fall. We've all heard the expression, "No pain, no gain." Well, according to psychiatrist Dr. Anna Lembke, there may be some truth to these words. She says that our attempts to escape being miserable are in fact making us even more miserable. This is because pain is actually an essential component of our ability to maintain a neutral state, and allowing it will in turn reset our internal scale back to __________ .

✔ 고난도

1 밑줄 친 (가)의 표현을 바꾸어 표현할 때 빈칸에 들어갈 단어를 채워 넣으시오.

> (가)Without the body's effective compensatory mechanisms,
> = __________ ________ the body's effective compensatory mechanisms,
> = If it ______________________________________ ,
> = If we ____ , (equip을 문맥에 맞게 포함할 것)

2 문맥 상 빈칸에 들어갈 단어는?

미리 Voca 

- **Pacific Ocean** 태평양
- **biodiversity** 생물 다양성
- **theory** 이론
- **species** 종
- **adaptation** 적응
- **relevant** 관련 있는, 적절한, (사람들의 삶 등에) 의의가 있는[유의미한]
- **be indifferent to** ~에 무관심하다
- **cease** 중단하다 유효한, 관련 있는
- **skyscraper** 고층건물
- **the majority** 다수
- **the minority** 소수
- **selfish** 이기적인
- **lift** 해제하다
- **sanction** 제재
- **analyze** 분석하다

- **seek out** ~을 찾다, 찾아내다
- **intense** 강렬한
- **controlled** 통제된
- **chief** 우두머리, 장
- **branch** 나뭇가지, 지점, 갈라지다
- **youthful** 젊은, 초기의
- **attempt** 시도하다
- **refer to** 지칭하다
- **reinforce** 강화하다
- **crucial** 중요한
- **justice** 정의
- **point to** ~을 지칭하다
- **principle** 원칙
- **underlie** (…의) 기저를 이루다
- **establishment** 설립, 수립, 확립, 기관, 시설, (사회) 기득권층, 지배층

🔑 Key Point

형태	If S should V ~, S would (will) V were to V should (shall) V

해석 방법	If it should rain tomorrow,/ we / would (will) not / go on a picnic. 만일 혹시라도 내일 / 비가 온다면, / 우리는 소풍가지 / 않을 것이다.

참고	• 가정법에서 If생략 가능하다. 조동사를 문두에 위치하고, 주어와 동사를 나란히 써 준다. Should it rain tomorrow, we will not go on a picnic.

Exercise 01 보기처럼 다음의 가정법 미래구문을 if를 생략한 문장으로 만들고, 알맞게 해석하시오.

> If I should live in Taiwan, I will have lots of spicy food.
> ⇒ Should I live in Taiwan, I will have lots of spicy food.
> ⇒ 만일 내가 타이완에 산다면, 나는 매운 음식을 많이 먹을 거야.

1 If Bill should call you, tell him he can come at any time.

➜ ____

➜ ____

2 If the Pacific Ocean were to dry up, he would never change his habit of thinking.

➜ ____

➜ ____

1 만일 어떠한 문제가 생기더라도, 나에게 전화해줘

(please / you / find / call / should / me / any / if / problems)

________________________, ________________________________

2 내가 만일 내일 죽는다 해도, 나는 후회하지 않을 거야.

(I / have / I / die / tomorrow / no / regrets / should / will)

________________________, ________________________________

3 만일 그가 가수가 된다면, 그의 어머니 또한 기쁘실 거야.

(his / singer, / he / be / will / well / happy / a / should / mother / as / become / if)

________________________, ________________________________

4 그들이 만약 100점을 받는다면, 그들의 선생님이 상을 주실 거야.

(their / a score of / teacher / they / give / will / prizes / get / them / should / 100)

________________________, ________________________________

도전

5 만약 Buffon이 오늘날의 생물 다양성을 관찰한다면, 그의 종 적응 이론이 여전히 유효하다는 것을 발견할 가능성이 높을 것이다.

(species adaptation / today's biodiversity, / his theories / likely / Buffon / are / If / to / were / find / relevant / he / on / that / still / observe / would).

→ ____

____

Exercise 03 각 문제를 우리말에 맞게, 괄호 안의 단어를 알맞게 배열하시오.

1 만일 네가 달에 착륙한다면, 너는 매우 이상한 장소에 있는 너 자신을 발견할 것이다. 너는 거기에서 어떠한 소리도 듣지 못하며, 어떠한 냄새도 맡을 수 없을 것이다.

(you / should / the moon / if / on / land), (find / would / yourself / you) in a very strange place. (there / hear / would / you / no / sound), (you / smell / anything / nor / could).

→ ____

→ ____

2 엘리베이터는 현대세계에서 중요한 역할을 한다. 고층건물 안의 모든 엘리베이터들이 운행하는 것을 멈춘다면, 끔찍할 것이다.

Elevators play an important part in the modern world. (It / terrible / be / would) (if / the elevators / all) in a skyscraper (running / stop / should).

→ ____

→ ____

3 만약 세상이 다수의 의지에 의해서 돌아가야 한다면, 그리고 그 다수는 이기적이거나 소수의 필요에 있어서 무관심하다면, 그 민주주의는 사실상, 하나가 되기 위해 중지해야한다.

(run / if / the world / be / were / to) by the will of the majority, and the majority were selfish or indifferent to the needs of the minority, (cease / , in fact, / the democracy / would / to be one).

→ ____

→ ____

4 만약 국제 제재가 해제된다면, 이는 국가에 새로운 무역 기회와 경제 성장을 열어줄 것이다.

(lifted / were / be / to / international / sanctions / if), (growth / open / and / opportunities / for / up / it / trade / the / economic / would / new / country).

→ ____

→ ____

고난도

5 만약 David Bordwell이 사람들이 왜 공포 영화를 보는지 분석한다면, 그는 관객들이 통제된 환경에서 강렬한 감정을 경험하기 위해 이러한 영화를 찾는다고 제안할 가능성이 높을 것이다.

(people / Bordwell / watch / to / why / David / were / analyze / movies / horror), (emotions / a / would / seek / suggest / he / experience / intense / environment / viewers / in / controlled / out / to / these films / likely / that).

→ ____

→ ____

Exercise 04 각 지문을 읽고, 물음에 답하시오.

1

There were too many kings in the world, Jefferson thought, and new republics should support each other. (a) (만일 새로운 프랑스 공화국이 실패하면), he said, (b) America's new ideas of freedom and justice would lose their chief support.

1 괄호 ⓐ 의 우리말을 제시된 단어만을 사용하여 알맞게 영작하시오.

> **제시어**
>
> Republic / French / should / new / the / fail

→ ____

2 밑줄 (b) 의 문장을 해석하시오.

→ ____

3 본문의 내용을 분석한 내용이다. 아래 박스 안의 단어만 활용하여 빈칸을 채우시오. (단, 필요시 문맥에 맞게 단어의 형태를 변형할 것)

succeed	reinforce	crucial

Jefferson saw the ________ of the French Republic as ________ not just for France, but for ________ the ideals of democracy and republicanism globally, including in the United States.

4 본문과 일치하도록 다음 빈칸에 들어갈 단어를 채워 넣으시오.

The "new ideas of freedom and justice" that Jefferson refers to specifically point to the principles underlying the American Revolution and the establishment of the United States as a ________.

Ⓐ(만일 누군가가 책 한 권을 쓰려고 한다면) on any branch of science Ⓑ which all discoveries
Ⓒ made by youthful workers Ⓓ left out, Ⓔ there would be Ⓕ very little left to write about.

1 괄호 Ⓐ의 우리말을 제시된 단어만을 사용하여 알맞게 영작하시오.

> **제시어**
> book / attempt / one / to / If / a / write / to / were

→ ____

2 Ⓑ~Ⓕ 중에서 어법상 틀린 것을 <u>두 개</u> 찾고 바르게 고치시오.

번호	틀린 표현	바른 표현
____ :	____________	____________
____ :	____________	____________

미리 Voca 

- **neither** 어느 쪽도 ~아닌, 어느 쪽
- **fortune** 재산, 운
- **determine** 결정하다, 결심하다
- **assassination** 암살
- **focus on** ~에 집중하다
- **conspiracy** 음모
- **sensationalize** 선정적으로 다루다[표현하다], (흥분·충격을 유발하기 위해) 과장하다
- **key to** ~을 여는 열쇠, ~에 핵심
- **thoroughly** 대단히, 철저히
- **soak** 흠뻑 적시다
- **inn** 여인숙, 여관
- **miserable** 비참한
- **figure** 숫자, 인물, 이해하다, 계산하다
- **precisely** 정확히
- **species** 종, 종류

- **evolve** 진화하다, 발전시키다
- **develop** 개발하다, 발전시키다
- **interdependence** 상호의존
- **gradual** 점차적인
- **mutual** 상호 간의, 공동의
- **adaptation** 각색, 적응
- **coarse** 피부나 천이 거친, 굵은, 음탕한
- **nutritious** 영양가가 높은
- **trial** 재판, 시험
- **gratify** 기쁘게 하다, 만족시키다
- **gradually** 서서히, 점차
- **acquire** 얻다, 습득하다
- **digestive** 소화의
- **optimal** 최적의
- **digest** 소화하다

형태	I wish 주어 + 동사의 과거형/ I wish 주어 had + p.p
해석 방법	• 가정법 과거: ~했더라면 좋을 텐데. I wish / I <u>had</u> the interesting book. ⇒ 나는 좋을 텐데/ 내가 재미있는 책이 있더라면.(=현재에 재미있는 책이 없음) I wish / I <u>had had</u> the interesting book. ⇒ 나는 좋을 텐데 / 내가 재미있는 책이 있었더라면.(과거에 재미있는 책이 없었음)
참고	• I wish 구문은 현재 또는 과거에 이루지 못한 소망에 대한 유감스러움을 나타내는 문장이므로, 문맥상 전환이 가능하다. I wish I <u>had</u> the interesting book. ⇒ I am sorry I <u>do not</u> have the interesting book. I wish I <u>had had</u> the interesting book. ⇒ I am sorry I <u>did not</u> have the interesting book.

Exercise 01 보기처럼 I wish 구문을 직설법 I am sorry구문으로 바꾸고, 해석하시오.

> I wish I were an English teacher.
> ⇒ I am sorry I am not an English teacher.
> ⇒ 내가 영어선생님이었으면 좋을 텐데.
>   나는 (현재) 영어선생님이 아니라 유감스럽다.

1 I wish he were here to help us.

→ _______________________________________

→ _______________________________________

2 I wish I had been with you on the train.

→ _______________________________________

→ _______________________________________

3 I wish I could be a little younger.

→ ____

→ ____

4 I wish I had known her phone number.

→ ____

→ ____

5 I wish he had sent me an email.

→ ____

→ ____

Exercise 02 각 문제를 우리말에 맞게, 괄호 안의 단어를 알맞게 배열하시오.

1 우리 중에 아무도 어떠한 말을 하지 않았다. 그때가 내가 그녀를 만난 것이 마지막이었다. 나는 내가 그녀에게 좀 더 친절했었더라면 좋았었을 텐데.

Neither of us said anything. It was the last time I saw her. (been / wish / I / kinder / to / her / had / I).

→ ____

2 나는 내가 이 마을에서 도망칠 수 있다면 좋을 텐데. 만일 내가 쥐들을 없애는 방법을 알 수만 있다면 내가 전 재산을 줬을 텐데.

(wish / I / away / I / run / could) from this town. (would / give / I / fortune / all / my), (if / know / get / I / rid / rats / of / could / to / the / how).

→ ____

→ ____

→ ____

3 당신이 직장을 구할 때, 그 일은 당신이 알고 있는 것 그리고 당신이 얼마나 많이 아느냐에 결정된다. 당신은 사람들이 "나는 내가 학교에서 그것을 배웠었더라면 좋았을 텐데 아니면 나는 내가 교육을 좀 더 받았으면 좋았을 텐데"라고 말하는 것을 들었을지도 모른다.

When you are looking for a job, (job / is / the / often / determined) by (much / know / know / you / how / what / and / you). You may have heard people say, "(had / I / learned / that / I / in school / wish)," or "(had / had / wish / education / I / more / I)."

→ ____

→ ____

→ ____

4 나는 미디어가 트럼프의 암살에 대한 음모론을 선정적으로 다루기보다는 사실 보도에 집중했으면 좋겠다.

I wish (Trump's / on / assassination / focused / about / factual / conspiracy theories / the media / sensationalizing / reporting / rather than).

→ ____

5 나는 정부가 비트코인이 전통적인 명목 화폐에 대한 대안을 제공하고 중앙집권적인 금융 시스템에 대한 의존도를 줄이는 잠재력을 인정했으면 좋겠다.

I wish (provide / an alternative / reliance / traditional / on / Bitcoin / financial systems / and / reduce / governments / recognized / to / of / the potential / centralized / fiat currencies / to).

→ ____

Exercise 03 각 지문을 읽고, 물음에 답하시오.

Four out of every ten students from the fourth to eighth grades worry about what they will be when they grow up. They also (A)(학교에서 공부를 더 잘하고 싶은 것이다), since they know that education is the key to the things they would like to do later on.

1 괄호 Ⓐ의 우리말을 아래 제시어를 활용하여 영작하시오.

> **제시어**
>
> school / better / do / in / they / could / wish

→ ____

2 위 글을 요약하려고 한다. 아래 제시된 조건에 맞게 빈칸을 채우시오.

> **• 조건 •**
> - 제시된 철자로 시작하는 단어를 쓸 것.
> - Ⓒ의 경우 본문에 언급된 표현을 문맥에 맞게 작성할 것.

> ⊙T_______ f_______ of the students from the 4th to 8th grades think that education is what makes their dreams ⓛc_________ t_________ when they are ⓒg_________.

It rained very hard all the day; I Ⓐ <u>was thoroughly soaked</u>, and by noon a good deal tired; so I stopped at a poor inn, Ⓑ <u>which I stayed</u> all night, Ⓒ<u>began now to</u> (가) <u>wish that I had never left home</u>. I cut such a miserable figure, too, that I found, by the questions Ⓓ <u>asked me</u>, I Ⓔ <u>suspected</u> to be a runaway servant, and in danger of being taken up on that suspicion.

1 밑줄 친 Ⓐ~Ⓔ 중 어법상 틀린 것을 <u>세 개</u>를 골라 바르게 고치시오.

틀린 번호	틀린 표현	바른 표현
______ :	______________	______________
______ :	______________	______________
______ :	______________	______________

2 밑줄 친 (가)와 같은 의미의 직설법 문장으로 전환하시오.

I wish that I had never left home.

➜ I am _________________________________.

3 다음은 본문의 내용을 재진술한 것이다. 빈칸에 들어갈 단어를 채워 내용을 완성하시오. (단, 제시된 철자로 시작하는 단어를 쓸 것)

It rained h______ all day. I got completely soaked and was very tired by noon. So, I stopped at a shabby inn and stayed there o______. I started to r______ I______ h______. I looked so pitiful that people asked me questions, thinking I might be a runaway servant. I was worried I might g______ a______ because of that suspicion.

Exercise  04   아래 지문을 읽고, 물음에 답하시오.

(가)(우리가 식품에 대해 그것을 하나의 물건으로 덜 생각하고 하나의 관계로 더 생각한다면 어떻게 될까)? In nature, that is of course precisely what eating has always been: relationships among species in systems we call food chains that reach all the way down to the soil. Species co-evolve with the other species that they eat, and very often there develops a relationship of interdependence. A gradual process of mutual adaptation transforms a coarse plant into nutritious and tasty food for an animal. Over time and through trial and error, the plant becomes tastier in order to gratify the animal's needs and desires, while the animal gradually acquires (나)(그 식물을 최상으로 이용하기 위해 필요로 하는 소화도구는 무엇이나).

1   괄호 (가)의 우리말을 아래 조건에 맞게 영작하시오.

> **• 조건 •**
> • were to 가정법 문장임.
> • less of A and more of B 구문을 활용할 것.
> • 아래 제시어만 사용하여 영작할 것.
> 　제시어 would / less of a thing / about / were / food / and / more of a relationship / if / to / thinking / start / we / happen / as

➜ What ______________________________________

____

2   괄호 (가)의 우리말을 아래 조건에 맞게 영작하시오.

> **• 조건 •**
> • 복합관계형용사가 이끄는 명사절의 구조.
> • 아래 제시어만 사용하여 영작할 것.
> 　제시어 it / needs / make / the plant / digestive tools / optimal use / whatever / of / to

➜ ______________________________________

3 아래 문장은 본문에 이어지는 내용이다. 본문에서 빈칸에 알맞은 표현을 찾아 채우시오. (단, 필요시 단어의 형태를 변형할 것)

> For example, the milk of cows did not start out as a _______ and _______ food for humans; in fact, it made them sick until people who lived around cows _______ the ability to digest milk.

4 본문의 내용을 한 문장으로 요약하려고 한다. 아래 빈칸을 채우시오.

> _______ is a by-product of _________ among species in systems we call food chains.

05 as if 가정법 구문

미리 Voca 

☐ **complex** 복잡한	☐ **cancer cell** 암세포
☐ **narrative structure** 서사구조	☐ **legislation** 제정법, 법률의 제정
☐ **analyze** 분석하다	☐ **debate** 토론하다
☐ **to and fro** 이리저리 움직이는	☐ **shelf** 선반
☐ **lean** 기울다, ~에 기대다	☐ **start** 흠칫[깜짝] 놀라다
☐ **temple** 절, 사원, 관자놀이	☐ **intelligence** 지능, 기밀, 정보
☐ **lad** 남자아이, 청년, 친구들	☐ **present** 현재의, 참석한, 존재하는, 현재, 선물
☐ **furnish** 비치하다, 제공하다	☐ **pale** 창백한, 옅은
☐ **bask** 햇볕을 쬐다, 은혜 따위를 입다	☐ **reverence** 숭배, 존경
☐ **dramatically** 극적으로	☐ **calamity** 재앙
☐ **starve** 굶주리다	

형태	as if 주어 + 동사의 과거형/ as if 주어 had + p.p

해석 방법	• as if 가정법 과거 He speaks/ <u>as if</u> he <u>knew</u> everything. ⇒ 그는 말한다/ 마치 그가 모든 것을 다 아는 것처럼.(=현재 잘 모른다.) • as if 가정법 과거완료 He speaks <u>as if</u> he <u>had read</u> the novel. ⇒ 그는 말한다/ 마치 그가 그 소설을 읽었었던 적이 있는 것처럼.(=과거에 읽은 적이 없다.) • as though He looks <u>as though</u> he <u>were</u> a foreigner. ⇒ 그는 마치 외국인인 것처럼 보인다.

참고	• as if 구문도 직설법으로 문장 전환이 가능하다. He speaks as if he <u>knew</u> everything. ⇒ In fact, he <u>does not</u> know everything. He speaks as if he <u>had read</u> the novel. ⇒ In fact, he <u>did not</u> read the novel.

Exercise  **아래 우리말을 제시된 단어만 사용하여 영작하시오.**

1 그녀는 마치 공주인 것처럼 말한다.

(a / if / were / as / princess / she / she / talks).

2 그 소년은 길을 잃은 것처럼 보인다

(if / he / looks / boy / as / way / his / the / lost).

3 그는 하와이에 많이 다녀온 것처럼 말했다.

(had / as / Hawaii / talked / he / he / there / many / been / if / about / times).

4 그는 모든 것을 알았던 것처럼 말했다.

(known / talked / he / he / had / as / everything / if).

도전

5 그는 마치 복잡한 퍼즐을 풀어야 하는 것처럼 영화의 서사 구조를 분석했다.

(the film's / complex / be / narrative structure / were / he / analyzed / solved / it / puzzle / a / to / as if).

Exercise 02 각 문제를 우리말에 맞게, 괄호 안의 단어를 알맞게 배열하시오.

1 그 길 전체는 인생으로 가득 차 있다. 사람들은 마치 그들이 잃어버릴 만한 시간이 없는 것처럼 서둘렀다.

The whole street is full of life. People hurry to and fro (if / not / to / as / lose / a moment / they / had).

→ ____

2 그는 의자에 기대어 눈을 감았다. 그의 얼굴은 종이처럼 하얗다. 그는 힘들게 숨을 내쉬었고, 그의 관자놀이는 마치 그가 달리던 중이었던 것처럼 땀으로 젖어있었다.

He leant back in his chair and shut his eyes. His face was as white as paper. He breathed hard and his temples were wet with sweat, (been / running / had / he / though / as).

→ ____

3 많은 소년들에게 법정은 대중이 그들을 주목할 수 있는 기회를 제공하기위해 만들어진 것처럼 보였다.

To most lads (it / if / organized / as / seems / the courts / were) to furnish them a chance to bask in the public eye.

→ ____

4 그녀는 마치 그녀가 하는 모든 선택이 암 세포를 기르거나 굶주리게 할 수 있는 것처럼 극적으로 생활 방식을 바꾸었다.

(changed / lifestyle / her / dramatically / she), (she / the / starve / made / as if / could / feed / cancer / either / choice / every / or / cells)

→ ____

→ ____

5 마치 국가의 미래가 이 하나의 쟁점에 달려 있는 것처럼 두 정당이 그 문제에 대해 토론했다.

(of / single / the two parties / the issue / climate change legislation / this / the future / depended / point / on / debated / the nation / as if / of)

Exercise 03 각 지문을 읽고, 물음에 답하시오.

1

Books, it is true, are silent as you see them on their shelves; but when I enter a library, I feel as if the dead were present, and I know if I put questions to these books Ⓐthey will answer me.

1 Ⓐ가 지칭하는 것을 <u>4단어</u>로 쓰시오.

Ⓐthey: ________ ________ ________ ________

2

The death of Nelson was felt in England ⒶＸＸＸ___________________________; men started at (가)the intelligence, and turned pale, (나)(마치 사랑하는 친구를 잃은 소식을 들은 것처럼). ⒷIt seemed as if we had never till then known how deep we loved and reverenced him.

1 위 글을 읽고, 영국 사람들이 Nelson 대통령의 죽음을 어떻게 생각하였는지 아래 제시어를 활용하여 빈칸 Ⓐ를 채우시오.

> **제시어**
> as / than / more / something / a public / calamity

→ ____

2 밑줄 친 (가)와 동의표현을 적으려고 한다. 제시된 철자로 시작되는 단어를 쓰시오.

(가) the intelligence

= the n________

3 괄호 (나)의 우리말을 아래 제시어를 활용하여 영자하시오. (단, 추가단어와 단어의 어형변화 있음)

> **제시어**
> if / hear / a dear friend / they / of / as / of / the loss

→ ____

4 밑줄 친 Ⓑ의 문장에서 어법상 어색한 곳을 골라 알맞게 고치시오.

틀린 표현	바른 표현
___________________	___________________

미리 Voca 

❑ **climb** 오르다	❑ **as it were** 말하자면
❑ **here and there** 여기저기	❑ **sentiment** 정서, 감정
❑ **be made of** ~로 만들어지다	❑ **heartily** 진심으로
❑ **merely** 단지, 그저	❑ **youth** 젊은이, 젊은 시절
❑ **different from** ~와 다른	❑ **sigh** 한숨 쉬다, 한숨
❑ **parcel** 소포	❑ **reflect** 반영하다, 반사하다, 심사숙고하다
❑ **air mail** 항공우편	❑ **profit** 이익, 이익을 얻다, 이익을 주다
❑ **rarely** 좀처럼 ~ 않은	❑ **household** 가정, 가정의
❑ **breakthrough** 돌파구, 획기적인 발전	❑ **task** 과제, 과업
❑ **profound** 깊은, 심오한	❑ **chore** 잡일
❑ **the populace** (전)국민	❑ **direct** 지도하다
❑ **stir** 일으키다	❑ **good sense** 바른 분별력(판단력)
❑ **debate** 논쟁	❑ **reflect on** ~을 곰곰이 생각하다
❑ **division** 분열	❑ **of profit** 유익한
❑ **endeavor** 노력하다, 시도하다, 노력, 시도	❑ **guidance** 지도
❑ **certain** 확실한, 어떤	❑ **disparity** 격차, 불균형
❑ **station** 자리, 위치	❑ **gender-specific** 성별에 따라 특정한, 성별 특유의
❑ **certain** 특정한, 어느 정도의	❑ **advocate** 지지자, 옹호자, 지지하다
❑ **remove** 제거하다	❑ **notable** 주목할 만한, 뛰어난, 유명인
❑ **judgement** 판단	❑ **distribution** 분배, 배포, 분포
❑ **concerning** ~와 관련된	

🔑 Key Point

형태	강조하는 단어가 문두에 위치하여 조동사 + 주어 + 동사의 어순

해석 방법	• 부정 부사구 + 조동사 S V ~ Never / have I seen her. ⇒ 결코 / 나는 그녀를 본 적이 없다. • 장소의 부사구 + 자동사 + 명사 주어 At the summit / stood a castle. ⇒ 정상에 / 성이 서 있다. • 보어 be동사 주어 Happy is / the man who is content with his lot. ⇒ 행복하다 / 본인의 몫에 만족하는 사람은. • 종속절의 주어 동사 도치 He traveled widely / as did most of his friends. ⇒ 그는 널리 여행했다 / 그의 친구들 대부분이 그랬듯이. • 기타 도치 구문 so/neither/nor + 조동사 + 주어 So do I. ↔ Neither do I. ⇒ 나도 그렇다/ 나도 그렇지 않다.

참고	• 주어와 동사의 수 일치할 때 주의한다. Never have he seen me.(x) ⇒ Never has he seen me.(o) At the beach is bananas.(x) ⇒ At the beach are bananas.(o)

Exercise 01 보기처럼 밑줄 친 부분을 강조하기 위해 도치구문을 만들고, 알맞게 해석하시오.

I knew little what he did.
⇒ Little did I know what he did.
⇒ 나는 그가 행동했던 것을 거의 몰랐다.

1 I dreamt little that I should never see her again.

→ ____

[해석] ____

2 High buildings stood <u>here and there</u>.

➜ ____

[해석] ____

3 I knew that she had told a lie <u>only then</u>.

➜ ____

[해석] ____

4 We are going to climb <u>that mountain</u>.

➜ ____

[해석] ____

5 He didn't like music, <u>or</u> I did <u>not</u>.

➜ ____

[해석] ____

Exercise 02 다음 문장의 해석을 참고하여, 괄호 안의 단어를 배열하시오.

1 여러 날이 지났다. 마침내, 눈이 내렸고, 눈이 내린 후, 서리가 되었다. 그 거리는 마치 그것들이 은으로 만들어진 것처럼 보였다.

Many days passed; at last, the snow came, and (after / the snow / the frost / came). (looked / of / streets / they / silver / the / if / as / were / made).

➜ ____

➜ ____

2 낸시는 흑인 소녀이다. 하지만 그녀의 고등학교 반 친구들은 그녀를 다르다고 생각하지 않았다.

Nancy was a black girl. But (did / high / classmates / of / different / her / as / school / think / her / seldom).

→ ____

✅ 고난도

3 내가 비행기를 탔다는 것을 더 이상 여행이라고 볼 수는 없다; 그것은 단지 어떤 장소로 보내지는 것이며, 이는 소포로 보내지는 것과는 거의 다를 바 없다. (단, 영작 시 목적어 도치구문을 포함할 것)

(not / consider / I / going / by / at all / traveling / as / jumbo / do / jet); it is merely being "sent" to a place, and (becoming / by / little / parcel / very / sent / different / air mail / this / is / a / from).

→ ____

🚩 도전

4 의학적 현실이 환자의 생존율에 이렇게 큰 영향을 미친 적은 드물다.
Rarely (a / breakthroughs / medical / had / significant / patient survival rates / have / such / impact / on).

→ ____

✅ 고난도

5 이전에는 한 번의 선거가 국민들 사이에서 이렇게 깊은 논쟁과 분열을 일으킨 적이 없다. (부정 부사구를 문두로 하는 도치로 영작할 것)

(profound / among / election / never / a / the populace / has / and / before / debate / stirred / such / single / division)

1

(a) Unless we remove ourselves, as it were, from our own natural station, and endeavor to view them at a certain distance from us, (b) (우리는 결코 우리 자신의 감정과 동기를 조사해 볼 수 없다.), (c) we can never form any judgement concerning them.

1 〈보기〉처럼 (a) 의 문장을 의미가 같은 다른 문장으로 고치시오.

┤ 보기 ├

Unless it is sunny, take your umbrella.
→ If it is not sunny, take your umbrella.

Unless we remove ourselves from our own natural station

→ _______________________________________

2 괄호 (b) 안의 우리말을 참고하여, 〈보기〉의 단어를 알맞게 배열하시오.

┤ 보기 ├

(and / our / own / can / survey / never / we / sentiments / motives)

→ _______________________________________

3 〈보기〉를 참고하여 밑줄 친 (c) 의 문장을 부정어를 강조하여 도치구문으로 만드시오.

┤ 보기 ├

He never imagined that he would change the world.
→ Never did he imagine that he would change the world.

→ _______________________________________

2

(a) I heartily wish that in my youth I had had someone of good sense to direct my reading.
(b) I sigh when I reflect on the amount of time wasting on books that was of no great profit to me. (c) (그나마 내가 받았던 모든 독서 지도는 그 젊은 남자 덕택이다.) who came to live with the same family in Heidelberg (d) as I was living with.

1 밑줄 친 (a)와 같은 의미의 다른 문장으로 바꿔 쓰시오.

I wish that in my youth I had had someone of good sense to direct my reading.

→ I am sorry ____

2 밑줄 친 (b)에서 어법상 틀린 곳을 두 곳 찾아 바르게 고치시오.

→ ____

★
3 아래 제시어를 활용하여 괄호 (c)의 우리말을 영작하시오.

(a young man / guidance / had / what / owe / to / I / little / I)

→ ____

4 괄호 (d)에 있는 as의 쓰임과 같은 것을 고르시오.
① He sat watching her as she got ready.
② She may need some help as she's new.
③ She's very tall, as is her mother.
④ Happy as they were, there was something missing.
⑤ He is as hard a worker as has ever been employed.

5 다음은 본문의 내용을 재진술한 것이다. 괄호 안의 단어를 바르게 배열하시오.

In my youth, I ⒜(regret / had / not / a / mentor / having / wise) to guide my reading choices. I lament the time I spent on books ⒝(greatly / ultimately / not / benefit / me / did / that). ⒞(only / on / substantial / the / guidance / I / reading / received) was from a young man who lived with the same family in Heidelberg where I resided.

⒜(regret / had / not / a / mentor / having / wise)

: ____

⒝(greatly / ultimately / not / benefit / me / did / that)

: ____

⒞(only / on / substantial / the / guidance / I / reading / received)

: ____

Exercise  **아래 지문을 읽고, 각 물음에 답하시오.**

(가)<u>People have written much of late about</u> sharing household tasks between men and women. Chores once thought to belong only to one sex, for example, fixing cars by men and cooking by women, are sometimes shared now. But there is a gap between what people say should happen and what they actually do. Although most people think chores should be shared, many reports show (a) <u>this</u> is (b) not <u>what happens</u>.

1 (가)의 밑줄 친 문장을 Much를 주어로 하는 문장으로 만들려고 한다. 빈칸을 채우시오. (주어진 빈칸에 맞게 생략 가능한 것은 생략할 것)

(가) People have written much of late about

= Much ____ ____ ______ __ ____ _____

2 밑줄 친 (a)와 (b)를 지칭하는 내용을 영작하려고 한다. 빈칸에 들어갈 표현을 본문에서 찾아 쓰시오.
(본문의 언급된 단어를 활용할 것)

(a) this: ________ ________ being shared between men and women

(b) what happens: a gap between ________ ________ ________ ________ ________ and
________ ________ ________ ________

3 다음은 본문의 내용을 재진술한 것이다. 박스 안의 단어만을 사용하여 빈칸을 채워 재진술을 완성하시오. (단, 필요 시 단어의 형태를 변형할 것)

disparity	gender-specific	advocate
for	reflect	gender
chore	in	reality
notable	ideals	

Despite increasing discussion about sharing household tasks between ______ and the evolving trend of sharing traditionally ________ ______ like car repair and cooking, there remains a ______ ______ between societal ______ and actual practices, with many reports indicating that while people ______ _____ equal chore distribution, this is often not ______ ______ ______.

미리 Voca 

- **pleasure** 기쁨, 쾌락
- **suffering** 고통
- **go fishing** 낚시하러 가다
- **decentralized** 탈중앙화의
- **nature** 속성
- **disrupt** 방해하다, 훼방하다
- **optimist** 낙천주의자
- **pessimist** 비관주의자
- **conceit** 자만심
- **temperance** 금주, 절제
- **volatility** 변동성
- **cosmic** 우주의
- **radiation** 복사
- **support** 지지하다, 부양하다

- **crucial** 중요한
- **respondent** 반응하는, 피고인의, 응답자
- **swallow** 삼키다
- **curiously** 호기심을 갖고
- **psychologist** 심리학자
- **seemingly** 겉보기에는
- **crowd** 군중
- **peer** 또래, 자세히 들여다보다
- **publicly** 공개적으로
- **in the dark** 모르는 상태인, 무지한
- **go with the crowd** 대중을 따르다
- **cave in** 굴복하다, 항복하다
- **group pressure** 집단 압력

🔑 Key Point

형태	중복되는 단어 또는 부사절의 종속절에서 대명사 + be동사는 생략한다.
해석 방법	While (he was) reading a book,/ he fell asleep. 　책을 읽는 동안 / 그는 잠이 들어버렸다.
참고	• 주어와 동사의 생략 　They worked harder than (they had worked) before. • 반복어구의 생략 　While one makes me happy, the other (makes me) unhappy. • 접속사의 생략 　I know (that) he is honest.

Exercise 01  다음 생략구문에 주의하여 생략되는 부분에 괄호를 치고, 알맞게 해석하시오.

> I have a book (which) Tom gave me.
> ⇒ 나는 Tom이 나에게 주었던 책 한권을 가지고 있다.

1 To some life is pleasure, and to others life is suffering.

→ ____

2 When I was young, I used to go fishing with her.

→ ____

3 Look at the pictures which were painted in different colors.

→ ____

4 I do not care if they go or they do not go.

➜ ____

5 I believe that Bitcoin's decentralized nature could potentially disrupt global financial systems.

➜ ____

Exercise 02 각 문제를 우리말에 맞게, 괄호 안의 단어를 알맞게 배열하시오.

1 한국 사람들은 프랑스인들이 프랑스를 사랑하는 만큼, 미국인들이 미국을 그러는 것처럼 그들의 나라를 사랑한다.

The Koreans love their country as much as (France / and / the / love / America / the / Americans / French).

➜ ____

2 나는 거울이 세상에서 최악의 발명품이라고 확신한다. 낙관주의자는 거울 속을 들여다보면서 더 낙관적이 되고, 비관주의자들도 마찬가지이다. 그러므로, 거울은 자만감을 키우거나 자신감을 파괴하기도 한다.

I am sure that the mirror is the world's worst invention. The optimist (and / a / becomes / mirror / too / optimistic / looks / into); the pessimist too pessimistic. Thus mirrors increase conceit or destroy confidence.

➜ ____

3 잃어버린 부는 산업과 경제로 다시 얻을 수 있을지 모른다. 잃어버린 지식은 학습에 의해 다시 얻을 수 있고, 잃어버린 건강은 금주와 약에 의해 다시 얻을 수 있다. 하지만, 잃어버린 시간은 영원히 사라진다.

(by / Lost / regained / industry / economy / and / be / may / wealth), lost knowledge by study, (health / by / and / medicine / temperance / lost), but lost time is gone forever.

→ ____

🚩 도전

★
4 비트코인 가격 상승은 투자자들을 흥분시키는 반면, 시장 변동성은 그들을 불안하게 만듭니다.

(rise / while / prices / in / excited / the / makes / Bitcoin / investors), (the / anxious / volatility / market)

→ ____

→ ____

✅ 고난도

5 과학자들이 우주 배경 복사를 조사하는 동안, 그들은 빅뱅 이론을 지지하는 중요한 증거를 발견했습니다.

(cosmic / microwave / examining / background / the / radiation / while), (supporting / crucial / evidence / the / discovered / Big Bang theory / scientists)

→ ____

→ ____

1

(a) <u>When asked in the survey what would make them happier in the year of 2010</u>, respondents listed more time with family, good health, job challenge and opportunity all far ahead of money.

1   〈보기〉처럼 밑줄 친 (a) 에서 생략된 두 단어를 넣어 문장을 완성하시오.

┤ 보기 ├

As watching TV, he ate popcorn.
→As (he was) watching TV, he ate popcorn.

→ ____

2   위 글을 요약했을 때, 빈칸에 알맞은 단어를 쓰시오.

__________ it comes to happiness, people __________ family and health __________ money.

2

Some books are to be tasted, (a) <u>others to be swallowed</u>, and some to be chewed and digested; (b) __________, some books are to be read only in parts; <u>others to be read, but not curiously, and some little to be read wholly, and with diligence and attention.</u>

– Francis Bacon, Of Studies

1   (a) 의 문장을 생략된 단어를 포함하여 온전한 문장으로 다시 쓰시오.

→ ____

2 괄호 (b) 안에 들어갈 알맞은 연결어를 고르시오.

① for instance   ② on the other hand   ③ that is

④ therefore   ⑤ nonetheless

3 밑줄 친 (c) 에서 어법상 어색한 것을 골라 알맞게 고치시오.

틀린 표현   ⇨   바른 표현

___________________   ___________________

4 본문의 내용의 주제에 대한 설명이다. 아래 조건에 맞게 괄호 안의 단어를 바르게 배열하여 내용을 완성하시오.

> • 조건 •
> • Ⓐ의 경우 [전치사 + 관계대명사 S be p.p]의 구문을 포함하고, 추가단어는 없되 필요시 동사의 형태를 변형할 것.
> • Ⓑ의 경우 3형식 구조의 문장이며, 추가단어나 어형변화 없이 괄호 안의 단어만을 사용하여 영작할 것.

The topic of the passage is Ⓐ(ways / which / and / can / books / the / different / appreciate / read / in / be). The passage metaphorically compares reading books to the processes of tasting, swallowing, chewing, and digesting, emphasizing that Ⓑ (attention / levels / books / different / of / different / and / require / engagement).

In 1951 social psychologist Solomon Asch performed an experiment with groups of twelve people. (그들은 동일하지 않은 길이의 네 개의 선이 제시된 방으로 인도되었다). They had to decide which two were the same length and publicly vote for their choice. Person after person (11 in all) voted for the wrong line — because they had all been told <u>to</u> ahead of time. The one individual who was in the dark couldn't imagine how in the world all these seemingly normal people could all choose the wrong line. When it was his turn to vote, he had to decide, "Do I go with what I know my senses are telling me, or do I go with the crowd?" One third of those tested caved in to group pressure and changed their vote to agree with their peers.

1　괄호 안의 우리말을 아래 조건에 맞게 영작하시오.

> **• 조건 •**
>
> • be p.p의 수동태와 [N where S be p.p]의 관계부사 표현을 포함할 것.
> • 아래 제시어를 활용하되 단어를 추가하고, 필요시 단어의 형태를 변형할 것.
> 　제시어　 bring / room / where / line / unequal length / display / into

➡ ____

2　밑줄 친 to뒤에 생략된 표현을 쓰시오.

3　위 본문의 내용을 한 문장으로 요약하려고 한다. 빈칸에 들어갈 표현은 쓰시오. (단, 제시된 철자로 시작하는 단어를 쓸 것)

> Solomon Asch experiment showed how p______ p______ to conform can influence people into m______ w______ d________.

현재완료 + since 구문

미리 Voca 

mere 한낱 ~에 불과한	**philosophy** 철학, 인생관
give up 포기하다	**poverty** 빈곤
desire 욕망	**honor** 존경하다, 기리다
regret 후회하다	**master** 대가, 거장
approach 접근, 다가옴	**mock** 조롱하다
introduce 도입하다	**geometrical** 기하학의
sail (배의) 돛	**due** 적절한
ridicule 조롱하다, 비웃다	**observance** 준수
significantly 크게, 상당하게	**proportion** 비율, 균형
reduce 줄이다	**fixed** 고정된, 변하지 않는
breakthrough 돌파구, 급격한 발전	**universal** 보편적인
natural language 자연어	**reasonable** 합리적인, 적정한
processing 처리	**assume** 가정하다, 맡다
fluency 유창성	**application** 적용, 지원
generate 생성하다, 만들다	**religious** 종교의, 신앙심이 깊은
contemporary 동시대인	**veneration** 존경, 숭배

🔑 Key Point

형태	have(has) + p.p 부사 since, for, how long, recently, lately와 함께 쓰인다.

해석 방법	I have taught English / for 10 years. ⇒ 난 영어를 가르쳐 왔다 / 10년 동안 She has swum since she was young. ⇒ 그녀는 수영을 해 왔다 / 그녀가 어렸을 때 이후로 쭉.

참고	• 현재완료시제(have⟨has⟩ + p.p는 뚜렷한 과거를 나타내는 시제와 쓰이지 않는다.
	  They have learned English 10 years ago.(x)
	  ⇒ They learned English 10 years ago.(o)
	• 현재완료와 함께 쓰이는 since 절에는 보통 과거형을 써 준다.
	  She has swum since she was young.

Exercise 01 다음 문장의 해석에 유의하여 괄호 안의 동사를 변형하여 빈칸을 채우시오.

1 It (   ) (   ) three years since we (   ) there. (be / part).
우리가 거기를 떠나온 지도 3년이 흘렀다.

2 Seven years (   ) (   ) since I (   ) to write these books. (pass / begin)
내가 이 책들을 쓰기 시작한 이후로 7년이 지났다.

3 I (   ) (   ) her since she (   ) a mere girl. (know / be)
나는 그녀가 겨우 어린 소녀였을 때부터 그녀를 알아왔다.

4 They (   ) (   ) for the company for 3 years. (work)
그들이 그 회사에서 3년 동안 함께 일을 해 왔다.

5 She (   ) (   ) here since she (   ) born. (live / be)
그녀는 태어난 이후로 쭉 여기에 살아왔다.

Exercise 02 두 문장의 의미를 합하여 한 문장으로 쓰시오.

1 I began to play the piano 3 years ago. + I still play it.

→ ____

2 It started to rain a week ago. + It still rains.

→ ____

3 She started to learn Spanish in 2012. + She still learns it.

→ ____

4 He began to make the special chair last year. + He is still making it.

→ ____

Exercise 03 각 문제를 우리말에 맞게, 괄호 안의 단어를 알맞게 배열하시오.

1 내가 흡연을 끊은 이후로 이미 1년이 지나왔고, 나는 더 이상 담배에 대한 어떠한 욕구도 없다.
(one / already / it / been / year / has) (since / I / smoking / gave / up), and I no longer have any desire for cigarettes.

→ ____

____

2 내가 서울에서 살게 된 지 약 4년이 흘렀다. 그 도시는 내가 점점 더 많이 살고 싶어지는 도시이다. 나는 2년 동안 한국을 떠나와야 한다는 것에 다만 유감이다.

(years / passed / have / about / four) (since / I / live / in / came / Seoul / to), a city which (to / love / come / I / have) more and more. I only regret that I am going to have to be away from Korea for two years.

→ ____

____

3 윈드서핑이 도입된 이후로 27년 이상이 되어왔다. 여름이 다가오면서, 윈드서핑을 하는 사람들의 화려한 돛이 물 위에 종종 보인다.

(than / has / been / more / years / it / twenty-seven) (since / introduced / was / windsurfing). With the approach of summer, colorful sails of windsurfers are often seen on the water.

→ ____

____

4 의료 기술이 최근에 발전하여 로봇 수술이 일상화되고 있으며, 환자의 회복 시간을 크게 줄이고 있습니다. (N + where S V의 구조 포함)

(robotic / advanced / technology / surgeries / has / are / routine / to / the / where / recently / becoming / point / Medical), significantly reducing recovery times for patients.

→ ____

____

✓ 고난도

5 AI 연구자들은 최근에 자연어 처리에서 중요한 돌파구를 이루어 기계가 인간의 언어를 더 유창하게 이해하고 생성할 수 있게 되었습니다. (S V ~, V-ing의 구조 활용)

(recently / breakthroughs / have / made / AI researchers / natural language processing / in / significant), (greater / understand / human / fluency / enabling / generate / language / with / and / machines / to).

→ ______________________________

____

Exercise 04 각 지문을 읽고, 물음에 답하시오.

1

(a)(Henry Rousseau가 태어난 지 100년이 되었다.), and (b)this man who lived all his life in poverty and (c)received little but ridicule from his contemporaries, (d)is now honored as one of (e)the greatest master (f)of the nineteenth century.

1 괄호 (a) 안에 있는 우리말로 아래 제시어를 사용하여 영작하시오. (단, 추가단어는 없으나 문맥에 맞게 단어의 형태를 변형할 것)

| 보기 |
(was / since / has / born / be / it / a hundred / Henry Rousseau/ years)

→ ______________________________

2 밑줄 친 (b)~(f) 중 어법상 틀린 곳을 찾아 바르게 고치시오.

→ ______________________________

3 다음 본문의 내용을 재진술한 것이다. 본문과 일치하도록 박스 안의 단어를 모두 사용하여 빈칸을 채우시오. (단, 추가단어 있고 필요시 단어의 형태를 변형할 것)

pass	mostly	spend
mock	now	
celebrate	birth	

A century ______ ______ since the ______ of Henry Rousseau, and this individual, who ______ his entire life in poverty and ______ ______ ______ ______ his peers, ______ ______ ______ ______ one of the foremost artists of the nineteenth century.

2

Since the early days of Greek philosophy, men (a) <u>tried</u> to find in art a geometrical law, for if art is harmony, and harmony is the due observance of proportions, it seems reasonable to assume that these proportions (b) <u>are fixed</u>. The geometrical proportion (c) <u>known</u> as the Golden Section (f)(수세기 동안, 예술의 불가사의를 푸는 그러한 열쇠로 간주되어지고 있다) to the mysteries of art, and (d) <u>so is universal</u> its application, not only in art but also in nature, that it (e) <u>has at times been treating</u> with religious veneration.

1 (a)~(e) 중에서 어법상 틀린 것을 <u>세 개</u> 골라 알맞게 고치시오.

→ ____

2 괄호 (f)의 우리말을 참고하여 알맞게 배열하시오.

(been / key / regarded / such / for / as / has / a / centuries)

→ ____

3 다음 본문의 내용을 재진술한 것이다. 본문과 일치하도록 박스 안의 단어를 모두 사용하여 빈칸을 채우시오. (단, 추가단어 있고 필요시 단어의 형태를 변형할 것)

seek	fix	understand	such

Since ancient Greek philosophy, people ________ ______ a geometrical law in art, believing that if art is harmony, and harmony involves proportions, these proportions must ______ ______. The Golden Section, considered a key to ________ art's mysteries for centuries, has ______ universal application in both art and nature ______ it has sometimes been regarded with religious reverence.

4 위 글을 요지문을 작성한 것이다. 빈칸에 알맞은 단어를 쓰시오. (단, 철자가 제시된 경우 해당 철자로 시작하는 단어를 쓸 것)

The geometrical proportion called Golden Section is w________ enough to be applied to nature ___ ____ ___ art.

미리 Voca 

- ☐ **telescope** 망원경
- ☐ **complain** 불평하다
- ☐ **cut one's way through** ~을 뚫고 나아가다, ~을 헤쳐 나가다
- ☐ **settlement** 합의
- ☐ **safeguard** 안전장치, 보호하다
- ☐ **legal fee** 법정비용
- ☐ **bring something to market** 시장에 내놓다
- ☐ **pharmaceutical drug** 의약품
- ☐ **clinical trial** 임상시험

- ☐ **regulatory** 규제의
- ☐ **approval** 승인
- ☐ **department** 부문, 부서
- ☐ **spouse** 배우자
- ☐ **selection** 선택
- ☐ **sees something through to the end** 어떤 일을 끝까지 해내다, 끝까지 완수하다
- ☐ **approximately** 거의
- ☐ **complete** 완성하다, 완료하다

🔑 Key Point

형태	It + takes(costs) + 시간/ 돈 + to V ~하는데 시간(돈)이 ~든다.
해석 방법	It takes half an hour / to find his house. 30분이 걸린다 / 그의 집을 찾는데. (it은 가주어이므로, 해석하지 않는다)
참고	• 의미상의 주어와 함께 쓰여 to V 진주어 앞에 위치한다. It takes half an hour for him to find his house. 그가 그의 집을 찾는데 30분이 걸린다. ⇒ It takes him half an hour to find his house. It takes 사람 + 시간 + to V의 어순으로 쓸 수 있다.

Exercise  **주어진 단어만을 활용하여 우리말을 두 개의 문장으로 영작하시오.**

1 당신이 걸어서 역까지 가는데 한 시간이 걸릴 것이다.

Ⓐ (hour / one / It / will / walk / you / to / the / station / take / to)

➜ ____

Ⓑ (for / will / station / one / hour / take / to / to / you / the / walk / It).

➜ ____

____

2 내가 망원경을 사는데 100달러를 썼다.

Ⓐ (It / to / the / cost / dollars / telescope / 100 / buy / me).

➜ ____

Ⓑ (me / 100 / telescope / dollars / It / buy / cost / the / for / to).

➜ ____

3 내가 이 책을 읽고 끝내는데 3일이 걸렸다.

Ⓐ (read / through / to / days / this / took / for / book / It / three / me).

➜ ____

Ⓑ (to / It / three / took / book / me / through / read / days / this).

➜ ____

4 그녀가 숙제를 하는데 2시간이 걸린다.

Ⓐ (two / to / It / homework / her / her / takes / do / hours).

➜ ____

Ⓑ (takes / hours / to / homework / her / for / two / It / do / her).

➜ ____

5 내가 영문법을 마스터하는데 4달이 걸렸다.

Ⓐ (English / months / to / master / me / took / grammar / four / It).

➜ ____

Ⓑ (for / to / four / took / me / grammar / English / months / master / It).

➜ ____

Exercise 02 각 문제를 우리말에 맞게, 괄호 안의 단어를 알맞게 배열하시오.

1 최근 몇 년 동안, 대학을 가는 소년과 소녀의 수가 계속해서 증가해 오고 있지만, 많은 부모님들은 그들이 그들의 자녀들을 대학을 보내는데 많은 돈이 들어가는 것에 대해 불평을 한다.

In recent years (of / on / college / increasing / go / the / boys and girls / been / to / number / who / has), but many parents complain that (to / send / money / their children / it / to college / costs / a lot of / them).

→ ____

→ ____

2 그는 철봉으로 얼음벽을 깨어 길을 내어야만 했다. 그리고 때때로 그 일은 겨우 짧은 거리를 나아가는데 하루 종일 걸렸다.

(to / had / cut / ice / his / walls / an iron bar / with / through / he / way), and sometimes (cover / it / a full / day / took / to / him) only a short distance.

→ ____

3 오늘날 미국인들은 그들의 선조(조상)들이 여러 달을 들여 나가는데 걸렸던 것을 가족 차를 이용하여 하루 동안 여행을 한다.

Today Americans generally go in the family car and travel in one day what (took / cover / their / forefathers / it / to / months).

→ ____

🚩 도전

4 기업들이 고객 정보를 안전하게 보호하지 못할 때, 법률 비용과 합의금으로 수백만 달러가 듭니다.

(customer information / to / and / when / costs settlements / It / safeguard / companies / legal fees / in / fail / millions / they)

→ ____

5 새로운 의약품을 개발하고 시장에 내놓는 데 수백만 달러가 들며, 필요한 임상 시험과 규제 승인 절차를 완료하는 데 종종 10년 이상이 걸립니다. (S V ~, V-ing의 구문을 활용할 것)

(costs / millions of dollars / and / bring to market / develop / to / It / a new pharmaceutical drug) often (and / clinical trials / regulatory approvals / over a decade / to / the necessary / complete / taking).

→ ____

→ ____

Exercise 03 각 지문을 읽고, 물음에 답하시오.

1

(a) This applies not only to the selection of university departments and jobs but also to the choice of spouses. Needless to say, (c) (자신이 좋아하는 길을 선택하는 데 많은 용기가 필요하다) (d) and sees it through to the end.

1 괄호 (a) 를 〈보기〉처럼 같은 의미의 다른 문장으로 전환하고, 알맞게 해석하시오.

┤ 보기 ├

I like not only reading books but also listening to music.
→ I like listening to music as well as reading books.
→ 나는 독서뿐만 아니라 음악 듣는 것도 좋아한다.

→ ____

2 괄호 (c) 의 우리말을 제시어만을 사용하여 영작하시오.

┤ 보기 ├

(takes / a road / a lot of / it / one / to / likes / choose / courage)

→ ____

3 밑줄 친 (d)에서 어법상 틀린 곳을 찾아 올바르게 고치시오.

→ ____

2

(a) It takes a ship approximately eight hours to complete the trip through the Panama Canal and (b) cost an average of fifteen thousand dollars, (c) (그것은 보통의 배가 케이프 혼을 돌아서 가는 데에 드는 비용의 십분의 일이다).

---

1 〈보기〉처럼 밑줄 친 (a)의 문장을 전환하시오.

┤보기├
It takes me three minutes to find his house.
→ It takes three minutes for me to find this house.

→ ____

2 밑줄 친 (b)의 문장에서 어법상 어색한 곳을 찾아 올바르게 고치시오.

→ ____

✔ 고난도

3 괄호 (c)의 우리말을 제시된 단어만을 사용하여 영작하시오. (단, N of what it takes ~의 동격 구문이 활용됨)

┤보기├
(cost / to / of / round / one-tenth / the Horn / an average / what / it / would / ship)

→ ____

목적어의 소유격을 대신하는 the

미리 Voca 

- **gentle** 부드러운, 온화한
- **affectionate** 애정 어린, 다정한
- **gesture** 몸짓; (의도적인) 행동
- **firmly** 단호히, 확고히
- **convey** 전달하다
- **intention** 의도
- **utter** 말하다, 완전한
- **earnest** 진지한, 진정한
- **collar** 칼라, 깃
- **seize** 잡다, 빼앗다, 포착하다
- **intensity** 강렬함, 집중도

- **catch someone off guard** ~를 불시에 놀라게 하다, 허를 찌르다
- **reassuring** 안심시키는, 위안을 주는
- **pat** 가볍게 두드리다, 가벼운 두드림
- **toad** 두꺼비
- **gaze** 응시하다, 응시
- **fist** 주먹
- **displease** 불쾌하게 하다
- **slap** 찰싹 때리다
- **belly** 배, 복부
- **confused** 혼란스러운, 헷갈리는

🔑 Key Point

형태	the + 명사의 형태를 이루며, 정관사 the는 목적어의 소유격 의미를 더한다.
해석 방법	He pulled me / by the sleeve. ⇒ 그는 나를 잡아당겼다 / 나의 소매로 (신체의 일부를 접촉할 때 쓰인다.)
참고	• 의미상 문장전환도 가능하다. 　He pulled my sleeve. 　= He pulled me by the sleeve.

Exercise 01 괄호 안의 단어를 바르게 배열하여 우리말을 영작하시오.

1 부드럽고 다정한 몸짓으로 그녀는 몸을 기울여 내 볼에 부드럽게 키스를 했다.

With a gentle and affectionate gesture, (me / leaned / softly / on / kissed / cheek / the / she / in / and).

➔ ____

2 Tom은 빠르게 손을 뻗어 친구의 손을 단단히 잡았다.

(the / by / reached / quickly / hand / friend / and / Tom / firmly / caught / his / out).

➔ ____

🚩도전

3 John은 아버지의 눈을 똑바로 바라보며, 한 마디 말도 없이 그의 진심을 전달했다. (S V ~, v-ing의 구문을 활용할 것)

(father / John / eye / in / looked / the / his / directly), (his / word / a / uttering / earnest / without / intentions / conveying).

➔ ____

4 그는 내 옷깃을 움켜잡고 나를 당겼는데, 그 강렬함에 나는 놀랐다. (S V ~, v-ing와 N that V의
구문을 활용할 것)

(the / collar / by / he / me / seized), (with / me / intensity / guard / caught / an
/ me / off / closer / that / pulling).

→ ____

5 그는 안심시키고 부드러운 손길로 내 어깨를 가볍게 두드렸다.

With a reassuring and gentle touch, (he / shoulder / on / patted / the / me).

→ ____

Exercise 02 각 문제를 우리말에 맞게, 괄호 안의 단어를 알맞게 배열하시오.

1 "잘 했다. 너는 한 번 해봐" 어린 우체부의 머리를 쓰다듬으며 그녀의 어머니는 말하고, 그에게 편지
를 주었다.

"Very well, you may try." said the mother, as (little / postman / her / she / on the
head / patted), and gave him the letter.

→ ____

2 그는 따뜻하게 나의 손을 잡으며 우리가 거실에 있는 테이블을 함께 써야 한다고 주장했다.

(grasped / by / he / me / the hand / warmly) and insisted that we should share a
table in the dining room.

→ ____

3 나의 삼촌은 두꺼비의 눈을 똑바로 쳐다봤다. 그 두꺼비도 나의 삼촌의 눈을 곧바로 응시했다.
(in the eye / uncle / looked / my / the toad / straight). (my / the toad / uncle / in the eye / also gazed / straight).

→ ____

→ ____

4 Tim은 그의 아버지의 눈을 똑바로 바라보았고, 아버지에게 조언을 구할 때, 그의 시선에는 존경과 결단력으로 가득 차 있었습니다. (분사구문 활용)
(father / eye / Tim / the / looked / in / his), (mixture / respect / a / with / gaze / and / of / filled / his / determination) as he asked for his father's advice.

→ ____

→ ____

5 톰은 친구의 손을 꼭 잡고 북적거리는 군중 속을 헤쳐 나가고 있었습니다.
(his / the / friend / by / hand / Tom / caught) and held on tightly as (crowd / the / bustling / they / through / their / made / way).

→ ____

→ ____

1

But as long as she sat still and let him hug her, he was completely satisfied; it was when (a) (그녀는 그의 얼굴을 때리고, 그의 배를 쳤다) with her fists that he was wholly displeased.

1 괄호 (a) 안의 우리말을 제시어만을 사용하여 영작하시오.

제시어

slapped / him / him / the belly / she / the face / hit / in / on / and

→ ____

2 다음 〈보기〉를 참고하여 밑줄 친 문장을 강조하는 문장을 만드시오. 이 때, It~that 강조구문을 이용하여 완전한 문장으로 만드시오. (단, that 대신 문맥에 맞는 다른 단어를 사용할 것)

| 보기 |

I met the girl in the park <u>at night</u>.
→ It was at night that (= when) I met the girl in the park.

Susan helped me with my homework <u>in my room</u>.

→ ____

2

I once said to a first date "Should I kiss you goodnight?" She looked confused for a moment and said "Yes". I went to kiss her on the cheek, and there was a moment of (a) c_________ about whether (b) (내가 그녀의 입술에 키스를 할 것인지 볼에 할 것인지를), and (c) (그녀는 머리를 어느 방향으로 틀어야하는지 몰랐다).

1 밑줄 친 (a) 에 들어갈 알맞은 단어를 쓰시오. (단, 본문의 단어를 문맥에 맞게 변형할 것)

→ ____

2 괄호 (b) 의 우리말을 참고하여, 〈보기〉의 단어를 알맞게 배열하시오.

| 보기 |
| (her / the cheek / I / or / was / on / to / her lips / kiss / going) |

→ ____

3 괄호 (c) 의 우리말을 참고하여, 다음 두 문장을 이용하여 괄호 (c) 에 들어갈 문장을 쓰시오. (단, should와 to부정사를 각각 포함한 두 가지 표현으로 영작할 것)

She did not know. + Which way should she turn her head?

(should 포함) → ____

(to 포함) → ____

used to (would) ® 구문

미리 Voca 

☐ **walk along** ~을 따라 걷다	☐ **possession** 소유
☐ **tale** 이야기	☐ **conflict** 충돌
☐ **sea-maid** 인어공주	☐ **adversary** (언쟁·전투에서) 상대방[적수]
☐ **moonlight** 달빛	☐ **mutually** 서로, 상호간에, 공통으로
☐ **wholesome** 건강에 좋은, 건전한, 유익한	☐ **assured** 확실한, 확실시 되는, 보장되는
☐ **curricula** 교육과정	☐ **initiate** 개시되게 하다, 착수시키다
☐ **reproduction** 재생산	☐ **improvement** 향상, 개선
☐ **favor** 선호하다	☐ **resistance** 저항, 반대
☐ **existing** 기존의	☐ **face** 직면하다
☐ **dominant** 지배적인	☐ **recover** 회복하다
☐ **norm** 규범	☐ **therapy** 치료
☐ **pedagogical** 교육학의	☐ **fall back into an old habit** 오래된 습관으로 들어가다(예전의 습관으로 돌아가다)
☐ **deterrence** 제지, 저지, 전쟁 억제(력)	☐ **take advantage of** ~을 이용하다
☐ **heavily** 크게	☐ **slip down** 떨어지다, 쇠퇴하다
☐ **concept** 개념	

🔑 Key Point

형태	used to V / would + V
해석방법	When she was old, she would sit / in the corner. ⇒ 그녀가 나이가 들었을 때, 그녀는 앉아 있곤 했었다 / 코너에 He used to have / long hair when he was young. ⇒ 그는 가지고 있었다 / 긴 머리를 그가 젊었을 때. (그러나 지금은 없다.)
참고	• would + V: 과거의 불규칙 습관을 말할 때(~하곤 했다) 　I would go fishing with my father on Sundays. • used to V: 과거의 규칙적 습관을 말할 때(~하곤 했다) 　There used to be a bakery on the corner.(=There is no more) • be used to + V-ing: ~하는 데 익숙하다 (be accustomed to V-ing)

Exercise 01　다음 우리말을 주어진 단어만을 사용하여 영작하시오.

1 그녀는 매주 일요일마다 해변을 따라 걷곤 했었다. (그러나 이제 하지 않는다.)

(Sunday / used / shore / every / the / to / she / walk / along).

→ ____

2 London의 탑은 옛날에 수용소였다. (그러나 이제는 아니다.)

(be / the / Tower / to / prison / of / a / London / used).

→ ____

3 나는 대학생 때 혼자서 가끔 여행을 가곤 했었다.

(alone / I / travel / college / was / I / a / student / sometimes / would / when).

→ ____

4 나는 일찍 일어나곤 했었다. (그러나 이제는 아니다.)
(I / to / up / used / get / early).

➜ ____

5 나는 일요일마다 낚시를 가곤 했었다. (그러나 이제는 가지 않는다.)
(Sundays / used / I / go / on / fishing / to).

➜ ____

6 나는 매주 금요일마다 그녀를 방문하곤 했었다. (그러나 이제는 방문하지 않는다.)
(her / Friday / used / every / call / I / to / on).

➜ ____

7 그녀는 옛날에 선생님이었다. (그러나 이제는 아니다.)
(a / be / she / teacher / to / used).

➜ ____

8 전쟁 전에 여기에 키가 큰 나무 한 그루가 있었다. (그러나 더 이상 없다.)
(the / used / here / before / be / tree / There / tall / war / a / to).

➜ ____

Exercise 02 각 문제를 우리말에 맞게, 괄호 안의 단어를 알맞게 배열하시오.

1 가끔씩 그는 우리에게 달이 비추는 바위 위에 앉아 큰 배가 항해하는 것을 보곤 했었던 작은 인어공주 이야기를 해주곤 했었다.

Sometimes (would / tales of / he / tell / little / us / the / sea-maid) that (on / to / sit / used / a rock) in the moonlight and see the large ships sail.

→ ____

2 스위스에는 여름에만 문을 열곤 했었던 산장 호텔들이 지금은 겨울에도 열고, 많은 사람들에게 건강에 좋은 겨울 스포츠를 제공한다.

In Switzerland, mountain hotels which (open only / used / to / in / summer / be) are now open in winter as well and provide wholesome winter sports for many people.

→ ____

3 그녀는 배우였었고, 그래서 많은 사람들에 의해 보이고, 무대 위에 서 있는 것이 익숙했다.

(be / an actress / to / she / used), and so was used to being looked at by many people and to standing on a stage.

→ ____

4 역사적으로 학교는 지배적 사회 집단의 지식과 문화 규범을 선호하는 교육 과정과 교수 방법을 통해 기존의 사회 구조 재생산을 강조하곤 했습니다.

Historically, schools (curricula / the reproduction / favored / through / used / emphasize / existing social structures / to / that / of / the knowledge / of / the dominant social groups / and / cultural norms / and / pedagogical practices).

➔ ____

____

5 많은 나라들은 핵 억제력의 개념에 크게 의존하곤 했으며, 이러한 무기의 보유가 상호 확증 파괴의 두려움 때문에 잠재적인 적들이 분쟁을 시작하지 못하게 할 것이라고 믿었습니다.

Many countries (rely / on / deterrence / of / the / nuclear / used / heavily / to / concept), and believed that (the possession / the fear / would / conflicts / from / prevent / potential adversaries / mutually assured destruction / of / such weapons / initiating / due to / of).

➔ ____

____

Exercise 03 각 지문을 읽고, 물음에 답하시오.

 **1**

One of the main problems faced by Dr. Milton H. Erickson, a psychologist in the 1950s, was (b) [what/ that] (a) <u>his patients seemed to recover quickly</u>, but (e) (곧 이전의 상태나 더 좋지 않은 상태로 돌아간다) after making an improvement. (c) [That's why/ That's because] they held a deep resistance to the therapy. They would soon fall back into old habits and (d) [blame/ blamed] the doctor.

1 밑줄 친 괄호 (a)를 〈보기〉처럼 같은 의미의 다른 문장으로 바꾸시오.

───┤ 보기 ├───

They seemed to be happy these day.
→ It seemed that they were happy these day.

→ ____

2 (b)~(d) 중 에서 어법상 알맞은 것을 고르시오.

	(b)	(c)	(d)
①	what	That's because	blamed
②	what	That's why	blamed
③	what	That's because	blame
④	that	That's why	blame
⑤	that	That's because	blame

3 괄호 (e)의 우리말을 참고하여, 〈보기〉의 단어를 알맞게 배열하시오.

───┤ 보기 ├───

(go / back / or / a worse / state / to / a previous / into / condition / would soon)

→ ____

According to the National Opinion Research Center at the University of Chicago, people in the United States are gradually becoming more trusting of each other. In response to the question, "Do you think people would try to take advantage of you if they got a chance, or would they try to be fair?" (a) a healthy majority used to vote for "fair," but (b) (this trusting view slipped down. + It is steadily slipping down).

1 문맥상 어색한 단어를 하나 찾고 바르게 고치시오.

어색한 표현: ____

수정한 표현: ____

2 괄호 (a) 의 문장과 같은 의미의 다른 문장을 만들려고 한다. 아래 제시어를 반드시 활용하여 빈칸을 채우시오.

제시어

anymore

A healthy majority ______ for "fair" before, but they ______ ______ ______.

3 괄호 (b) 에 있는 두 문장을 <u>현재완료 진행표현</u>을 활용하여 한 문장으로 표현하시오.

➜ ____

조동사 + have p.p 구문

미리 Voca 

- **slight** 약간의, 가냘픈, 무시하다
- **earthquake** 지진
- **rise above** ~을 넘어서다
- **natural law** 자연법(인간의 이성에 의해 발견될 수 있는 보편적이고 불변하는 도덕적 원칙)
- **parallel** 유사성
- **establish** 설립[설정]하다, 수립하다
- **voluntary** 자발적인
- **legitimate** 정당성, 합법적인
- **authority** 권위
- **cruel** 잔인한, 비참한
- **swampy** 습지의
- **fern** 양치식물
- **flourish** 번성하다, 건강하다
- **deposit** 예금, 보증금, 예금하다, 두다
- **notion** 개념, 생각

- **phenomenon** 현상
- **counter-factual** 사실과 반대되는
- **outcome** 결과
- **affect** 영향을 미치다
- **refer** 언급하다, 참고하다
- **drawback** 결점, 장애
- **occasion** 경우, 기회
- **accustom** 익숙하게 하다
- **stuff** 물건
- **vulnerable** 상처받기 쉬운, 취약한
- **inscribe** 쓰다, 새기다
- **smudge** 오점, 얼룩
- **prevail** 우세하다, 이기다
- **transition** 변화, 전환
- **inevitable** 불가피한

| 형태 | 조동사 have p.p는 과거의 추측이나 유감을 나타낸다. |

해석방법

• 과거의 추측을 나타내는 표현
She may(might) have seen the movie.
　그녀는 (과거에) 그 영화를 봤었을 지도 모른다.
She must have seen the movie.
　그녀는 (과거에) 그 영화를 봤었음에 틀림없다.
She cannot have seen the movie.
　그녀는 (과거에) 그 영화를 봤을 리가 없다.

참고

• 과거의 유감을 나타내는 표현
You should have come earlier. 당신은 좀 더 일찍 왔었어야 했는데.
I would rather have stayed at home. 나는 집에 머무르는 게 나았을 텐데.
I need not have worried about it. 나는 그것에 관해 걱정할 필요가 없었는데.

Exercise 01　조동사 과거표현에 주의하며, 괄호 안의 단어만을 사용하여 영작하시오.

1 그는 그 문제를 풀기 위해 최선을 다했었음에 틀림없다.
(solve / must / his / to / he / have / the problem / done / best).

→ ____

2 그녀는 그 이야기를 알기 위해 그 책을 읽었을지도 모른다.
(to / the story / may / read / she / the book / have / know).

→ ____

★3 그녀가 그의 이름을 알지 못하는 것을 보니 그를 만났을 리 없다.
(to / him / know / not / cannot / met / his / name / have / she).

→ ____

4 그 다리는 예전에 수리되었어야 했는데 하지 않았다.
(repaired / a long time ago / should / been / have / the bridge).

→ ____

5 그들은 그들의 오래된 집에서 이사하지 않았을지도 모른다.
(house / from / may / moved / have / old / not / they / their).

→ ____

Exercise 02 각 문제를 우리말에 맞게, 괄호 안의 단어를 알맞게 배열하시오.

1 당신은 어제 지진을 느꼈을 리 없다. 왜냐하면 그것은 너무 경미한 것이었기 때문이다.
(cannot / you / yesterday / have / the earthquake / felt), for it was so slight a one.

→ ____

2 굴은 너무 징그럽게 생겨서 영국의 어떤 작가가, "굴을 처음으로 먹었던 사람이야말로 매우 용감한 사람임에 틀림없다"라고 말했다.

An oyster looks so ugly that a certain writer in England said, "(a very brave / must / it / have / man / been) who first ate it."

→ ____

3 지능이 중요하다는 것은 당연하다. 왜냐하면 인간으로 하여금 침팬지를 능가할 수 있게 했던 것은 바로 인간의 좀 더 나은 지능이었을지도 모른다.

No doubt memory is important ; (may / have / it / in part, / memory / been, / better / man's) that enables him to rise above the chimpanzee.

→ ____

4 아퀴나스는 우주에서 목적과 질서에 대한 그들의 개념 사이의 명백한 유사점을 고려할 때, 자연법 이론을 발전시키는 과정에서 아리스토텔레스의 철학에 영향을 받았음에 틀림없다.

(of / developing / been / by / natural law / his theory / Aquinas / Aristotle's philosophy / influenced / when / have / must), given (the clear parallels / between / in the universe / of / their concepts / purpose and order).

→ ____

→ ____

고난도

5 로크는 피통치자의 동의를 기반으로 한 정부를 세우는 것이 더 나았을 텐데, 왜냐하면 그는 정당한 정치 권위가 사람들의 자발적인 합의에서 비롯된다고 믿었기 때문이다.

Locke (on / consent / rather / a / established / governed / the / government / the / have / would / of / based), as (from / voluntary / agreement / believed / of / the / political / that / he / arises / strongly / the / authority / legitimate / people).

→ ____

→ ____

Exercise 03 각 지문을 읽고, 물음에 답하시오.

1

(a) The frozen southland was not always so cruel. Ages and ages ago, before the coming of the ice, (a) (날씨는 햇볕도 많이 있었고, 따뜻한 습한 기후였음에 틀림이 없었다). Forests and swampy fern jungles flourished. (c) We know this from fossils and coal deposits that have discovered.

---

1 밑줄 친 (a) 문장을 부분부정 표현에 유의하여 우리말로 옮기시오.

→ ____

2 괄호 (a)의 우리말을 참고하여, 〈보기〉의 단어를 알맞게 배열하시오.

| 보기 |

and / climate / had / it / a warm, humid / have / must / sunshine / plenty of

→ ____

3 밑줄 친 (c)의 문장에서 어법 상 어색한 부분을 찾아 바르게 고치시오.

어색한 표현: ____
올바른 표현: ____

2

I know (a)(그 소녀는 그녀의 정당한 수입으로 이 물건들을 샀을 리가 없다.) I believe she's a really bad person. I don't like to think it, but (b)it must be so. (c)He cannot be so stupid after I said to him.

---

1 괄호 (a)의 우리말을 참고하여, 〈보기〉의 단어를 알맞게 배열하시오.

| 보기 |

have / earnings / the girl / bought / her / proper / cannot / out of / things / these

→ ____

2 다음은 밑줄 친 문장 (b)의 so가 지칭하는 구체적 내용을 포함해서 다시 작성한 것이다. 빈칸을 채우시오.

she must indeed _______ _______ _______ _______ _______.

3 밑줄 친 (c)의 문장에서 어법 상 어색한 부분을 찾아 바르게 고치시오.

어색한 표현: ____

올바른 표현: ____

Exercise 04 각 지문을 읽고, 물음에 답하시오.

1

Most of us think that athletes would feel happier after winning a silver medal than a bronze in Olympic Games. But research suggests that those who win bronze medals are actually happier than those who win silver medals. The reason for this (a)_____ _____ _____ _____(관련이 있다) the way in which the athletes think about their performance. The silver medalists focus on the notion that if they (b)(perform) slightly better, then they (c)(perhaps, win) a gold medal. In contrast, the bronze medalists focus on the thought that if they had performed slightly worse, then they wouldn't have won anything at all. Psychologists refer to our ability to imagine what (d)_____ _____ _____, rather than what actually did happen, as 'counter-factual thinking'.

1 괄호 안의 우리말에 해당하는 표현을 아래 제시어를 포함하여 빈칸 (a)에 채워 넣으시오.

제시어

do, with

(a) _____ _____ _____ _____

2 문맥 상 괄호 (b)와 (c)의 바른 형태를 쓰시오.

(b) _____ _____   (c) _____ _____ _____ _____

3 빈칸 (d)에 들어갈 표현을 쓰시오.

(d) _______ _______ _______

✔ 고난도

4 다음은 본문의 내용을 재진술 한 것이다. 박스 안의 단어만을 사용하여 빈칸을 채우시오. (단, 중복 활용되는 단어 있고, 필요시 단어의 형태를 변형할 것)

alternative	close	emotional
relieve	regret	win
bronze	happy	bronze

Contrary to the common belief that winning a silver medal would make athletes happier than winning a bronze medal, research shows that _______ medalists are actually happier. This difference in _______ is related to how athletes think about their performance. Silver medalists often focus on the idea that if they had performed slightly better, they could have won a gold medal, leading to feelings of _______. On the other hand, _______ medalists think about how _______ they were to not _______ a medal at all, which makes them feel more satisfied and _______. This phenomenon is explained by the concept of 'counter-factual thinking,' where people imagine _______ scenarios and their outcomes, affecting their current _______ state.

Given all the drawbacks and disadvantages of electronic documents, why not just stick with paper? The best way of answering that question is to look back on the one other occasion in human history when a writing medium was replaced. ⒶTo societies accustomed to writing on stone or clay, paper should have seemed terribly short-lived stuff, vulnerable to fire and water, with inscribed marks that all too easily smudged or faded away. And yet paper prevailed. Moses' tablets were stone, but the story of Moses was told on _____. Ⓑ With paper, information became far cheaper to record, to store and to transport. Exactly the same considerations argue that a transition to paperless, electronic writing is now inevitable.

✱ smudge 번지다

1 본문의 내용 전개 상 밑줄 친 Ⓐ 부분에서 어색한 표현을 찾고 해당 부분을 바르게 고치시오.

어색한 표현: ______________________________

올바른 표현: ______________________________

2 본문의 빈칸에 들어갈 단어는?

3 본문의 밑줄 친 Ⓑ의 내용을 참고하여 아래 빈칸에 들어갈 표현을 넣으시오.

The ________ incentives of paper compared to "stone" paper were just too powerful to be ignored.

13 should have p.p

미리
Voca

- **undertake** 착수하다, 맡다
- **take into account** ~을 고려하다
- **delay** 지연시키다, 지연
- **seasick** 뱃멀미
- **feel seasick** 뱃멀미하다
- **calm** 고요한
- **devastating** 대단히 파괴적인, 엄청난 손상을 가하는, 굉장한
- **mitigate** 완화[경감]시키다 (=alleviate)
- **accuracy** 정확성
- **dismiss** (고려할 가치가 없다고) 묵살[일축]하다 (=wave aside), (생각·느낌을) 떨쳐 버리다, 해고하다
- **ethical** 윤리적인

- **utilitarian** 공리주의적인
- **implication** 함의
- **autobiography** 자서전
- **daydream** 몽상하다, 백일몽을 꾸다
- **ultimately** 궁극적으로, 근본적으로
- **enhance** 향상하다
- **concur** 동의하다, 의견일치를 보다
- **insanity** 정신 이상
- **estimated** 형용사 견적의, 추측의
- **be inclined to** ~의 경향이 있다
- **to the point of** ~라고 할 (수 있을)정도로

형태	should have p.p (과거에)~했어만 했는데 (하지 않았다) 과거 사실에 대한 후회.
해석 방법	You should have come / earlier. ⇒ 당신은 왔어야한 했다 / 좀 더 일찍
참고	• I need not have worried about it. 　⇒ 나는 그것에 관해 걱정할 필요가 없었다. • I ought to have tried the Italian food. 　⇒ 나는 그 이탈리아 음식을 먹어봤어야 했다.

Exercise 01 다음 밑줄 친 추측과 후회를 나타내는 조동사 표현에 유의하여 알맞게 해석하시오.

1 You <u>should have presented</u> me to the boss.

→ ______________________________

2 You <u>ought to have read</u> the letter she wrote you.

→ ______________________________

3 You <u>need not have met</u> the man I told you.

→ ______________________________

4 You <u>should have said</u> it earlier than I thought.

→ ______________________________

5   He <u>should not have gone</u> to Saudi Arabia then.

→ ____

6   She <u>need not have taken</u> an umbrella.

→ ____

7   I <u>ought to have seen</u> her before Jane left.

→ ____

Exercise **02**   우리말에 맞게 괄호 안의 단어를 알맞게 배열하시오.

1   과학과 기술 분야에서 좀 더 많은 학생들을 교육하려는 계획은 분명히 매우 좋다. 그것은 좀 더 일찍 착수되었어야 했다.

(plan / more / and / to / educate / the / technology / science / in / students) is of course very good. (undertaken / been / it / have / should / earlier).

→ ____

→ ____

2   당신은 그 편지를 특별 화물로 그녀에게 보냈어야 했다. 당신은 최근에 발생한 메일 배달의 지연을 고려했어야만 했다.

(You / have / sent / ought / to / the letter / her) by special delivery. (you / account / recent delay / have / mail delivery / in / taken / into / should).

→ ____

→ ____

3 그는 뱃멀미에 대해 걱정할 필요가 없었는데, 왜냐하면 바다가 호수처럼 잔잔했기 때문이다.

(being / seasick / worried / he / have / about / needn't), (as / lake / ocean / a / as / calm / the / was / for).

→ ____

→ ____

4 경제학자들은 2008년 금융 위기를 더 정확하게 예측하여 세계 경제에 대한 그것의 치명적인 영향을 완화했어야 했다.

Economists (predicted / more / effects / devastating / with / its / on / mitigate / should / the 2008 financial crisis / accuracy / have / the global economy / to)

→ ____

5 문학 비평가들은 공리주의 철학의 깊은 함의를 고려했다면 '오멜로스를 떠나는 사람들'에서 제기된 윤리적 딜레마를 긴과할 필요가 없었을 것이다.

Literary critics (have / dismissed / ethical / not / need / the / dilemmas) in 'The Ones Who Walk Away from Omelas' (of / the / utilitarian / implications / philosophy / if / deeper / had / they / considered).

→ ____

→ ____

Exercise 03 각 지문을 읽고, 물음에 답하시오.

1

The boy Schweitzer (a) <u>sent</u> to the village school when he was (b) <u>enough old</u>. He says in his autobiography that he (c) <u>found</u> difficult to read and write and (d) <u>that</u> he often sat (e) <u>daydreaming</u> when he (f) <u>must have been studying</u>.

1 (a)~(f) 중에서 어법상 틀린 것 네 개를 찾고 해당 표현을 알맞게 고치시오.

번호	틀린 표현	바른 표현
:		
:		
:		
:		

2

After (a) <u>making</u> a choice, the decision ultimately changes our (b) <u>estimated</u> pleasure, (c) <u>enhances</u> the expected pleasure from the selected option and decreasing the expected pleasure from (f) __________. If we were not inclined to update the value of our options rapidly so that they concur with our choices, we (d) <u>will likely second-guess</u> ourselves to the point of insanity. We would ask (e) <u>ourselves</u> again and again (g)(우리가 태국보다 그리스를 선택해야만 했었는지), the toaster over the coffee maker, and Jenny over Michele.

1 (a)~(e) 중에서 어법상 어색한 것을 두 개 고르시오.

① making
② estimated
③ enhances
④ will likely second-guess
⑤ ourselves

2 문맥상, 괄호 (f)에 들어갈 알맞은 말은?

① the profound choice   ② the absurd option

③ the accepted choice   ④ the rejected option

⑤ the conceivable selection

3 〈보기〉의 단어만을 활용하여 괄호 (g)안의 우리말을 영작하시오.

┤보기├

(we / whether / chosen / Thailand / should / have / over / Greece)

➜ ____

have to 구문

미리 Voca

❏ **conserve** 보존하다, 보호하다	❏ **osmosis** 삼투, 침투
❏ **lighthouse** 등대지기	❏ **solution** 용액
❏ **desperately** 절망적으로, 필사적으로	❏ **concentration** 농도, 집중
❏ **starve** 굶주리다, 갈망하다	❏ **seep** 스며들다
❏ **affection** 애착, 애정	❏ **membrane** 얇은 막
❏ **extraterrestrial** 외계인, 외계의	❏ **draw** 그리다, 끌어당기다(draw-drew-drawn)
❏ **emit** ~을 내뿜다	❏ **liquid** 액체
❏ **elimination** 제거, 탈락, 배설	❏ **internal** 내부의, 체내의
❏ **obtain** 획득하다	❏ **necessity** 필요, 불가피한 일
❏ **primary** 주된	❏ **freshwater** 민물에 사는, 민물의

형태	have to V / has to V ~해야 한다.
해석 방법	You have to read through / the book. ⇒ 당신은 완전히 읽어야한다 / 그 책을
참고	• <u>have to (has to)의 부정</u> = <u>don't have to V / doesn't have to V</u> ⇒ ~해야 한다.　　　　　　　⇒ ~할 필요가 없다 (=need not, don't need to)

Exercise 01 　괄호 안의 제시어만을 활용하여 우리말을 영작하시오.

1 당신은 물건을 사기 전에 두 번 생각해야한다.

(think / buy / anything / twice / you / to / have / you / before).

→ ____

2 당신은 너무 크게 말할 필요가 없다. 나는 당신의 얘기가 매우 잘 들린다.

(have / loud / don't / so / you / to / speak). I hear you very well.

→ ____

3 당신은 그것을 요청해야한다. 그러면 당신은 얻을 수 있을 것이다.

(it, / you / will / and / you / for / to / given / be / have / it / to / only / ask).

→ ____

4 나는 오후에 숙제를 해야 한다. 나는 슈퍼마켓에서 사야할 것이 있다.

(homework / afternoon / in / I / to / have / do / my / the). (have / the / I / at / to / something / supermarket / buy).

→ ____

→ ____

5 우리는 거리에 쓰레기 버리는 것을 멈추어야한다. 왜냐하면 우리는 자연을 보호해야 하기 때문이다.
(to / stop / the / we / street / have / throwing / on / trash), (to / for / have / conserve / nature / we).

→ ____

Exercise 02 괄호 안의 단어를 이용하여 다음 우리말을 알맞게 영작하시오.

1 오늘 밤 파티에 꼭 참석할 필요는 없어요. (don't, the party)

→ ____

2 한국에서는 군복무를 해야 한다. (serve in the army)

→ ____

3 그녀는 기말고사를 위해 열심히 공부해야한다. (the finals)

→ ____

Exercise 03 다음 문장의 해석을 참고하여, 괄호 안의 단어를 알맞게 배열하시오.

1 어떠한 이유 때문에 손님이 식사 중에 테이블을 떠나야 한다면, 그는 항상 그의 호스티스에게 물어본다. "잠깐 실례해도 될까요?"

If for any reason (leave / a guest / during / table / a meal / the / has / to), he always asks his hostess, "(minute / will / please / a / for / me / excuse / you)?"

→ ____

→ ____

2 선상에서 그들은 등대에 관한 모든 것을 그들에게 알려주는 책 한권을 가지고 있고 그들은 그것이 어디에 있는지 알기 위하여 그것을 펼치기만 하면 된다.

On the ship (which / book / they / lighthouses / the / informs / have / about / them / a / all), and (to / but / they / have / it / is / where / out / find / to / open / it).

* have but to ~하기만 하면 되다

→ ____

→ ____

3 모든 운전자들은 백마일마다 연료를 공급받을 필요 없는 차에 대해 꿈을 꾼다.

(not / be / refueled / does / of / motorist / every / dreams / that / a car / to / have) every hundred miles.

→ ____

Exercise **04** 각 지문을 읽고, 물음에 답하시오.

1

"Love," says one writer, "is necessary food for the young; one has only to watch (a) (사랑에 굶주린 아이들의 노력들) (b) to gain attention somehow by any method, to realize how desperately is their need, for starved affections are as much a tragedy as starved bodies."

1 밑줄 친 (a)의 우리말을 참고하여, 〈보기〉의 단어를 알맞게 배열하시오.

── 보기 ──

(of / the / of / efforts / starved / are / who / love / children)

2 What do the writer say about the reason "Love" is necessary for the young?
(1번 문제의 답과 본문에 언급된 표현을 활용할 것.)

Because the young who ________ ________ ________ affection is the same ________
________ ________ .

3 밑줄 친 (b)의 문장에서 어법상 틀린 곳을 찾아 바르게 고치시오.

틀린 표현   바른 표현

_______________ → _______________

2

If a distant civilization were searching for signs of life on Earth, the easiest way to find us would be from (a) (우리가 지난 80년 동안 우주로 누출해 온 전파). If an extraterrestrial culture were similar to ours, it might be emitting radio waves as well. And those are what we're looking for. As we do not find them, they may be evidence of a distant life form's technology. (b) _________, (c) (우리는 이러한 신호들이 어떠한 형태를 취하고 있는지를 모른다.), so we have to search by process of elimination.

---

1 괄호 (a) 안의 우리말을 아래 조건에 맞게 영작하시오.

> **● 조건 ●**
> • 다음과 같은 목적격 관계대명사의 구조로 영작할 것: N (that) S V
> • 아래 제시어만을 사용하여 영작할 것.
>   제시어 space / leaking / we've / the / past / the / for / radio / into / been / waves / years / 80

→ ____

2 문맥상, (b)에 들어갈 알맞은 연결어를 고르시오.

① Therefore   ② On the other hand   ③ Similarly

④ However   ⑤ That is

3 괄호 (c) 안의 우리말을 다음 두 문장을 이용하여 영작하시오.

> We have no idea. + What form might these signals take?

→ ____

Although a fish does drink water, its primary method of obtaining water is through osmosis. The water seeps into its body through tiny holes in its skin. Osmosis is simply the movement of a solution such as salt and water through a membrane such as a fish's skin until the concentration of the solution becomes (가)e_______ on both sides of the membrane. When a fish lives in salt water, the ocean water contains more salt than does the liquid in the fish. Thus, osmosis draws water out of the fish and (a) the fish needs continually to drink water to refill the liquid. (b) And it is being drawn out of its body. When a fish lives in fresh water, the water has less salt than does the liquid in the fish and water is drawn through the fish's skin into its body. Therefore, a freshwater fish does not need to drink water.

* membrane: 세포막

1 문맥 상 빈칸 (가)에 들어갈 단어를 쓰고, 해당 단어를 이용해 문맥에 맞게 제시된 문장의 빈칸을 채워 본문과 일치하는 문장을 만드시오. (단, e로 시작하는 단어를 쓸 것)

(가) e_______

• Osmosis is the movement of solutions through a membrane to e______ concentration on both sides.

2 (a)와 (b)의 두 문장을 하나의 문장으로 만들려고 한다. 빈칸을 채우시오.

(a) the fish needs continually to drink water to refill the liquid. (b) And it is being drawn out of its body.

→ the fish needs continually to drink water to refill the liquid ______ ______ ______ ______ out of its body.

= the fish needs continually to drink water to refill the liquid ______ ______ out of its body.

3 본문의 내용과 일치하도록 박스 안의 단어를 활용하여 빈칸을 채우시오. (단, 필요시 문맥에 맞게 단어의 형태를 변형할 것)

hydrate	concentrate	face
lower	draw	
higher	internal	

- In saltwater environments, fish lose water due to osmosis and must drink water to stay ______.
- In contrast, freshwater fish absorb water osmotically due to the ______ external salt concentration and do not need to drink water.

4 위 본문의 내용을 한 문장으로 요약하려고 한다. (단, 철자가 제시된 경우 제시된 철자로 시작하는 단어를 쓰되, 해당 단어는 본문에 언급된 단어가 아님. 나머지는 빈칸의 경우 본문에서 찾아 쓸 것)

A fish in salt water drinks water to b______ the solution in and out of itself through ______, but there is no necessity for a freshwater fish to (c)______ ______.

15 without ~ing, 유사보어

미리 Voca 

- **scream for help** 살려달라고 외치다
- **unnoticed** 눈치 채지 못한
- **slip out of ~** 밖으로 빠져나가다
- **depressed** 우울한
- **reveal** 밝히다
- **content** 내용물
- **villager** 마을사람
- **undetected** 발견되지 않은
- **commonplace** 평범한
- **proceeding** 과정, 절차
- **suit** ~에 맞다, 어울리다
- **disposition** 기질, 성향

- **pass** 통과시키다
- **be preoccupied by** ~에 사로잡히다, ~로 바쁘다
- **issue** 문제
- **the majority of** 대부분의
- **previously** 이전에, 미리
- **meditate upon** ~에 관해서 명상하다
- **rush into** 급하게(무모하게) ~하다
- **dominant** 지배적인
- **assumption** 추정, 상정
- **unobserved** 관찰되지 않은, 지켜지지 않는
- **prominent** 두드러진
- **hypothesis** 가설, 가정

🔑 Key Point

형태	without V-ing / 유사보어

해석 방법	• 유사보어: 완전자동사 뒤에서 형용사가 주격보어 역할을 하며 쓰이는 보충어 A puppy died / happy. ⇒ 강아지 한 마리가 죽었다 / 행복하게 • 전치사(without) + V-ing:~하지 않고 He left here without saying good bye. 그는 이곳을 떠났다 / 작별인사를 하지 않고

참고	• 유사보어는 분사구문의 형태에서 온 것이기 때문에 문장 전환이 가능하다. She came as she was running into the room. ⇒ She came as was running into the room. ⇒ She came as running into the room. ⇒ She came running into the room. (그녀는 방으로 뛰어서 들어왔다.)

Exercise 01 다음 보기처럼 자연스러운 문장이 되도록 전환하시오.

> She came as she was running into the room.
> ⇒ She came <u>running</u> into the room.

1 He died, when he was young.

→ ________________________________

2 She died, when she was a beggar.

→ ________________________________

3 They ran out of the building as they were screaming for help.

→ ________________________________

1 그 편지가 Tom이 그것 안에 무엇이 있었는지 알지도 못한 채 그녀의 수중에 들어갔다

(it / Tom / without / her hands / what / was / into / knowing / the letter / in / fell)

➜ ____

2 그녀는 아무도 눈치 채지 못한 채 방에서 빠져나갔다.

(unnoticed / out / slipped / the room / by / anyone / of / she)

➜ ____

3 그는 매우 우울한 채로 집에 왔다.

(came / he / home / depressed / very).

➜ ____

4 그 노인은 그의 손자들에 둘러싸여 앉아있었다.

(old / sat / the / grandchildren / his / by / surrounded / man)

➜ ____

5 병은 열리지 않은 채, 내용물을 볼 수 있다.

(without / bottles / their / reveal / can / contents / being / opened).

➜ ____

Exercise 03 각 문제를 우리말에 맞게, 괄호 안의 단어를 알맞게 배열하시오.

1 나는 모든 마을 사람들이 그녀가 내 집에 오는 것을 보지 않고 그녀를 만나고 싶다.

I would like to see her (all / the villagers / house / to / my / coming / her / without / seeing).

→ ____

2 그 다른 종류의 뉴스는 "핫"한 소식이다. 다시 말해 사람들이 그것들을 기대하지 않고 그런 일들이 곧 일어날 것에 대해 모르는 채 생겨나는 모든 일들에 대한 소식.

The other kind of news is 'hot' news, that is, news of all the things that happen (knowing / expecting / people / going / that / they / are / to / happen / or / them / without).

→ ____

3 나는 아무에게도 발견되지 않고, 계단 아래와 앞 문 밖에서 (물건을) 훔쳤을지도 모르지만, 그러한 평범한 과정은 나의 모험이 넘치는 기질과는 맞지 않는다.

I might have stolen (door / out / at / the stairs / and / the front / down / undetected); but such a commonplace proceeding did not suit my adventurous disposition.

→ ____

도전

4 새로운 인플레이션 정책은 대부분의 시민들이 다른 문제들로 바쁘던 와중에 정부에 의해 조용히 통과되었다.

The new inflation policy was quietly passed by the government, (were / the / preoccupied / with / by / other issues / of / citizens / who / unnoticed / the majority).

→ ____

Exercise 04 각 지문에 읽고, 물음에 답하시오.

1

Ⓐ(행동하도록 요청받는 사람은) is more likely to act fortunately if he has previously meditated upon actions of similar kind. If we wish to play an effective part as members of a community, Ⓑ(우리는 자신이 하고 있는 일에 대해 생각하지 않고 성급하게 행동하는 위험을 피해야 합니다.).

1 〈보기〉의 단어만을 활용하여, 괄호 Ⓐ안의 우리말을 영작하시오. (단, 필요시 단어의 형태를 변형할 것)

| 보기 |

(upon / call / act / is / to / who / a person)

→ ____

2 아래 조건에 맞게 괄호 Ⓑ안의 우리말을 영작하시오.

• 조건 •
• without v ing과 관계대명사 what을 활용할 것.
• 아래 제시어만을 활용하되, 필요시 단어의 형태를 변형할 것.
제시어 action / doing / thinking / we / without / about / what / are / must / avoid / danger / into / we / of / the / rushing

→ ____

3 위 글의 내용을 요약할 때, 빈칸에 알맞은 단어를 쓰시오. (단, 글에 언급된 단어만을 변형할 것)

We need to m________ u______ p______ actions so that we can avoid doing something d________ carelessly.

2

The dominant assumptions of an age color the thoughts, beliefs, expectations and imaginings of the men and women who live within it. ⒶBeing always with us, these assumptions usually pass unnoticed – Ⓑlike the pair of glasses which, because they are so often on wearer's nose, simply exist unobserved.

1 〈보기〉처럼 괄호 Ⓐ의 구를 접속사와 함께 부사절로 변환 하시오.

┤ 보기 ├

Having much money, he can buy a car.
→ As he has much money, he can buy a car.

→ ______________________________________

2 밑줄 친 Ⓑ의 문장을 아래 제시된 표현을 주어로 하는 so ~ that 구문으로 바꾸시오.

The wearer has ______________________________________.

3 위 글의 내용을 요약할 때, 빈칸을 채우시오. (단, 첫 번째 빈칸의 경우 제시된 철자로 시작하는 단어를 쓰고, 두 번째의 경우 본문에서 찾아 변형 없이 채워 넣을 것)

The prominent hypothesis is likely to have an e________ on the thoughts, beliefs, expectations and imaginings of the men and women of an age, which commonly exist __________.

→ ______________________________________

미리 Voca 

- **fray** (천이[을]) 해어지다[해어지게 하다]
- **carelessness** 부주의
- **revolutionize** 혁신시키다
- **prestigious** 권위 있는
- **award** 수여하다
- **compete** 경쟁하다
- **inferior** 열등한, 질 낮은
- **adopt** 입양하다, 채택하다
- **interior** 내부, 내부의
- **superior** 뛰어난, 눈에 띄는
- **industrial** 산업의

- **paralyze** 마비시키다
- **organism** 생물
- **exhaust** 기진맥진하게 만들다, 다 써버리다, 배기 가스
- **miserable** 비참한
- **particularly** 특히
- **emphatic** 강조한, 뚜렷한
- **briefly** 잠시, 간결하게
- **miserable** 비참한
- **achievement** 업적, 성취
- **well-being** 행복
- **a sense of well-being** 행복감

🔑 Key Point

형태	선행사 + whose + 명사

해석 방법	I / have a sister / whose job is a nurse. ⇒ 나는 / 여동생 하나 있다 / 그녀의 직업은 간호사이다.

참고	• whose = of which로 바꿀 수 있다. I have a house whose roof is blue. ⇒ I have a house of which roof is blue. ⇒ I have a house the roof of which is blue.

Exercise 01 아래 우리말에 맞게 제시된 단어만을 사용하여 영작하시오.

1 자신의 개를 잃은 사람들은 개를 찾기 위해 온갖 노력을 다합니다.

(effort / every / people / dogs / get / make / lost / find / to / whose / them).

➜ ____

2 표지가 해진 책을 나에게 건네주세요.

(me / the / of / is / cover / hand / the / frayed / which / book)

➜ ____

3 나는 꼭대기가 눈으로 덮힌 산을 보았습니다.

(with / covered / mountain / was / I / snow / saw / whose / top / a).

➜ ____

4 나는 이름도 모르는 꽃을 골랐어요.

(whose / didn't / know / I / flower / I / a / name / picked).

➜ ____

5 나는 아버지가 의사인 소년의 도움을 받았습니다.

(helped / whose / father / was / by / boy / a / the / doctor / is / I).

→ ____

Exercise 02 제시된 우리말에 맞게 괄호 안의 단어만을 활용하여 영작하시오.

1 그럼에도 불구하고, 자전거 사고는 주로 자전거를 타는 사람의 부주의함 때문에 생긴다. 예를 들어 사고는 멈춤 표지판에서 멈추지 않는 자전거 이용자에 의해 생기고, 바지를 입은 다리가 자전거 체인에 걸린 자전거 이용자에 의해 생기기도 한다.

Nonetheless, (bike / are / mainly / accidents / biker's / by / caused / carelessness). For example, accidents can be produced (a / sign / stop / not / does / by / at / stop / a / biker / who) and (get / pants' legs / whose / biker / by / a / in the bike chain / caught).

→ ____

→ ____

→ ____

2 운동장 주변에 나무들이 많이 있다. 가지들이 거의 벗겨진 나무는 이제 매우 오래된 것이다.

We have many trees around the playground. That tree (almost / which / are / bare / the branches / of) now is a very old one.

→ ____

도전

3 분야를 혁신시킨 이론을 가진 연구자가 권위 있는 상을 수상했다.

The researcher (field / the / whom / of / have / revolutionized / theories / the) (prize / a / prestigious / awarded / was)

→ ____

Exercise 03 각 지문을 읽고, 물음에 답하시오.

 1

No nation lives entirely isolated from others and contact between nations always results in affecting their languages. When two languages compete, the victory does not always fall to the most perfect language. (가)(아니면, 항상 문화가 우월한 나라가 아니다) that makes the nation of inferior culture adopt its language.

1 Fill out the blanks with appropriate words.

> When two languages ________, it is not always the nation of interior culture
> that ________ the other language.

➜ ____

2 ★ 괄호 (가)의 우리말을 〈보기〉의 단어만을 활용하여 영작하시오.

| 보기 |
(culture / the / always / is / whose / superior / it / nor / nation / is)

➜ ____

3 〈보기〉 우리말을 주어진 두 문장을 결합하여 한 문장으로 영작하시오.
(단, "전치사 + 관계대명사"의 구조를 이용할 것)

| 보기 |
인간의 몸처럼, 산업 사회는 중요한 기관을 가지고 있어서, 그 기관의 파괴는 전체적인 조직을 마비시킨다.

An industrial society has its vital organs. + Their destruction paralyzes the whole organism.

➜ ____

4 〈보기〉를 참고하여, 주어진 문장을 부정어를 문두로 하는 도치문으로 전환하시오.

> ─────── 보기 ───────
> I like <u>not only</u> reading books but also taking a walk.
> → Not only do I like reading books but also taking a walk.

I could <u>not</u> see her <u>until</u> she called me.

→ ____

2

ⓐ(우리가 말을 할 때 잠깐 멈추는 것은) are not due to the existence of any necessity for shutting off <u>each word</u> as an independent thing by itself, but to quite other causes, (그 이유들 중에서 가장 일반적인 것은 폐로부터의 공기의 공급량이 고갈되기 때문이다), and we pause to take breath. Again, we may pause because we are ⓑ(어떠한 말을 해야 할지 당황한), or because we wish <u>to be</u> particularly emphatic.

1 괄호 ⓐ와 ⓑ의 우리말을 아래 제시어만을 사용하여 영작하시오.

ⓐ speaking / pauses / in / the / make / we / which

⇒ ____

ⓑ word / at / loss / a / for

⇒ ____

★
2 괄호 (가)의 우리말을 아래 조건에 맞게 영작하시오.

> ● 조건 ●
> • [of which N + V ~]의 소유격 관계대명사를 활용할 것.
> • 필요시 제시된 단어의 형태를 변형할 것.
> • 아래 제시어만을 사용할 것.
>   제시어 air / that / which / exhaust / of / is / becomes / the lungs / the commonest / the supply / of / from

→ ____

3 본문의 내용을 한 문장으로 요약할 때 빈칸에 들어갈 단어를 박스 안에서만 찾아 완성하시오. (단, 각 단어는 한 번만 사용하고, 중복 사용 없음)

> we / run / breath / what / unsure / say / separate / of / to / of / out

> We pause, when speaking, not to ______ each word, but mainly because ______ ______ ______ ______ ______, or because we are ______ ______ ______ ______ ______ or want to emphasize something.

Exercise **04**   아래 지문을 읽고, 물음에 답하시오.

> Most people believe that if they had ten percent more income, they would be much more satisfied with their lives. But Ⓐthose are not more satisfied with their lives. ⒷTheir income are now at that higher level. Changes in income do briefly influence our sense of well-being. Decreases make us more miserable than increases make us happy. But even the happiness that comes with an increase in income does not last long. Very soon, (가)(왜냐하면 새로운 수입의 수준이 우리의 성과를 평가하는 표준이 되어 버리기 때문이다).

1 밑줄 친 (a)와 (b)의 두 문장을 관계대명사를 사용하여 하나의 문장으로 쓰시오.

> Ⓐ those are not more satisfied with their lives.
> Ⓑ Their income are now at that higher level.

➜ _______________________________________

2 아래 조건에 맞게 괄호 (가)의 우리말을 영작하시오.

> • 조건 •
> • [전치사 + 관계대명사 + S V]의 구조를 활용할 것.
> • 아래 제시된 단어만을 사용하여 영작하시오.
> [제시어] the new level / becomes / that's / against / the standard / because / our achievements / income / measure / we / which / of

➜ ____

3 괄호 안의 단어를 바르게 배열하여 본문과 일치하는 우리말 영작이 되게 하시오. (단, 어형변화 있음)

> "소득은 변화는 증가로 인한 행복이 오래가지 않기에 일시적으로만 웰빙에 영향을 미친다."

Changes in income only briefly affect well-being, (an / from / happiness / short-lived / increase / be / with / the).

➜ ____

4 위 지문의 내용을 한 문장으로 요약하려고 한다. 아래 빈칸에 들어갈 표현을 쓰시오. (본문에 나온 단어를 쓰되, 필요시 단어의 형태를 변형할 것)

> An increase in income is not always _________, because happiness does not _______ according to the increase in income.

as (유사관계대명사) 구문

미리 Voca 

❑ **barely** 간신히, 좀처럼 ~ 않은	❑ **pursue** 추구하다
❑ **muddy** 진창인, 진흙투성이인	❑ **charity** 자선 단체
❑ **narrow** 좁은	❑ **bachelor** 미혼남, 학사학위 소지자
❑ **content** 만족하는, 내용	❑ **modest** 겸손한, 미천한
❑ **cultivate** 재배하다, 배양하다	❑ **hospitality** 환대
❑ **contribute to** ~에 공헌하다, 기여하다	❑ **stubborn** 완고한, 고집 센
❑ **impact** 영향	

형태	such, as 다음에 오는 관계대명사는 as이다
해석 방법	Read <u>such</u> books / as will be helpful. ⇒ 그런 책들을 읽어라 / 도움이 되는
참고	• 앞 문장, 또는 뒤에 있는 문장이 선행사이며, which나 that로 바꿔 쓸 수 없다. This is the same watch <u>as</u> I lost. ⇒ 이것은 내가 잃어버렸던 것과 똑같은 시계이다. I have as much money <u>as</u> is needed. ⇒ 나는 필요한 만큼 많은 돈을 가지고 있다.

Exercise 01 다음 유사관계대명사 as의 용례에 주의하여 우리말을 제시된 단어만을 사용하여 영작하시오.

1 조용히 너의 말을 들어줄 수 있는 그런 친구들을 선택해라.

(quietly / listen / choose / friends / as / will / you / to / such)

→ ____

★
2 우리들은 간신히 먹고 살 만큼의 음식들을 받는다.

(as / we / as / can / barely / live / much / food / given / are / on / we)

→ ____

3 이것은 내가 런던에서 샀었던 것과 똑같은 지갑이다.

(in / bought / is / this / as / London / wallet / same / I / the)

→ ____

4 런던의 거리는 그 당시에 종종 그러했듯이 비좁고, 진흙이 많았다.

(The / of / muddy / narrow / were / and / streets / London), (the / time / was / that / often / case / as / at).

→ ____

→ ____

5 그는 이제껏 고용된 적 있는 누구 못지않게 열심히 일하는 근로자이다.

(employed / has / as / a / been / as / worker / is / hard / ever / He)

→ ____

Exercise **02** 각 문제를 우리말에 맞게, 괄호 안의 단어를 알맞게 배열하시오.

1 옛날에 어디서나 인간은 그들 자신의 집 근처에서 경작되거나 발견 되어질 수 있는 그러한 식량에 만족해야만 했다.

Long ago men everywhere had to (cultivated / be / contented / with / such / foods / found / as / could / or / be) near their own homes.

→ ____

2 모든 인간들은 태어난 순간부터 동등한 권리를 갖는다. 그래서 다른 나라 사람들은 우리가 가지고 있는 것과 똑같은 권리를 갖고 있다.

(equal / they / are / born / have / the / rights / human / from / time / all / beings). So (rights / the same / of / other / countries / have / the / people / we / as / have).

→ ____

3 시장으로 가져가지는 많은 야채들은 대략 두시간만에 팔렸습니다.

(the / brought / market / many / as / vegetables / as / to / were) (out / a / hours / two / in / sold / matter / were / of).

→ ____

→ ____

4 내가 말했었던 그런 세상은 인간이 그것을 선택한다면 존재할 수 있다.

(a world / exist / I / speaking of / can / such / as / was) if men choose it.

→ ____

5 기후 변화와 그 세계적 영향을 이해하는 데 크게 기여할 학문적 연구를 추구해라.

Pursue (to / contribute / and / academic research / climate change / will / its / such / global impact / the understanding / of / as / significantly).

→ ____

Exercise 03 각 지문을 읽고, 물음에 답하시오.

1

I had almost no interest in trying to Ⓐ(필요한 것보다 더 많은 돈을 벌다) to keep myself clothed, fed, warm, and clean, to perform such small acts of charity or present-giving and make Ⓑ(가난한 독신 남자에게 가능할지 모르는 후대에 적당한 그런 보답)

＊ hospitality 후대

1 more ~ than의 유사관계대명사를 활용하여 괄호 Ⓐ의 우리말을 아래 제시어만을 사용하여 영작하시오.

제시어

make / money / needed / than / more / was

➜ ____

2 such ~ as의 유사관계대명사를 활용하여 괄호 Ⓑ의 우리말을 아래 제시어만을 사용하여 영작하시오.

제시어

bachelor / might / modest / of / poor / be / hospitality / for / returns / as / possible / a / such

➜ ____

1 밑줄 친 (a) 에서 어법상 어색한 곳을 골라 바르게 고치시오.

틀린 표현   바른 표현

_______________ ⇨ _______________

2 괄호 (b) 안의 우리말을 제시된 단어만을 사용하여 영작하시오.

제시어

very / people / as / clever / the / case / with / is / young / often

→ _______________________________________

3 부정사의 부사적 용법의 결과를 나타내는 〈보기〉를 참고하여, 밑줄 친 (c) 를 알맞게 해석하시오.

┤ 보기 ├

She woke up to be a famous singer.
: 그녀가 눈을 떠보니 유명한 가수가 되어 있었다.

→ _______________________________________

but, than (유사관계대명사) 구문

미리 Voca 

☐ **accept** 받다, 받아들이다	☐ **awful** 끔찍한
☐ **expense** 비용	☐ **utter** 말하다, 완전한
☐ **unconditionally** 무조건적으로	☐ **inefficient** 비효율적인
☐ **unavoidable** 불가피한	☐ **sophisticated** 세련된, 정교한
☐ **circumstance** 상황	☐ **conclude** 결론을 내리다, 끝내다
☐ **consequence** 결과	☐ **a great deal** 다량, 상당량, 많이
☐ **dull** 따분한, 흐릿해지다	☐ **approach** (어떤 문제에) 접근하다
☐ **scrape** 긁어내다, 긁기	☐ **rather** 다소
☐ **stock crash** 주식 붕괴	☐ **a variety of** 다양한
☐ **solemn** 진지한, 엄숙한	☐ **a point of view** (특정) 관점

형태	than + 명사 or 절

해석 방법	• 유사관계대명사 but There is no rule / but has exceptions. ⇒ 규칙은 없다 예외 없는 • 유사관계대명사 than You / have more books / than I have. ⇒ 당신은 / 좀 더 많은 책들이 있다 / 내가 가지고 있는 것 보다

참고	• but, than은 해석만 다를 뿐 유사관계대명사 as와 쓰임이 같다. but = that~not~ 〈~하지 않는〉

Exercise 01   유사관계대명사에 유의하면 괄호 안의 단어만을 활용하여 우리말을 영작하시오.

1   약간의 오타가 없는 책들은 없다. (N but V 구문 활용)

(few / books / are / misprints / there / have / some / but).

→ ____

✔ 고난도

2   그는 실제로 그의 비용을 위해 필요한 더 많은 돈을 받을 수 없었습니다. (bring oneself to와 more ~ than 구문 활용)

(couldn't / more / bring / he / to / he / for / money / than / actually / accept / his / needed / himself / expenses).

→ ____

3   자식을 무조건 사랑하지 않는 어머니는 없습니다. (no N but V 구문 활용)

(no / mother / children / is / loves / her / but / there / unconditionally)

→ ____

4 그 작업은 원래 예상했던 것보다 훨씬 더 어렵다는 것이 밝혀졌습니다. (more ~ than 구문 활용)
(expected / to / much / than / been / difficult / had / the work / out / more / turned / be).

➜ ____

5 나는 불가피한 사정으로 인해 외국에 가는 것 외에는 선택권이 없다.
(abroad / no / to / I / due / circumstances / unavoidable / to / go / have / choice / but).

➜ ____

✔ 고난도

6 모두가 떠난 후 나 외에는 방에 남은 사람은 아무도 없었습니다. (no N but N 구문 활용)
(had / there / no / me / everyone / gone / was / but / in / the / after / room / one / left)

➜ ____

✔ 고난도

7 어느 누구도 지적으로 계속 배울 수 없는 만큼 그렇게 나이가 많이 든 사람은 없습니다.
(and / but / to / old / may / so / he / is / man / intellectually / no / learn / grow / continue).

➜ ____

☑ 고난도

1 인간이 행한 일중에 결과와 책임이라는 꼬리표를 달고 오지 않는 일이 없다.

There is not (done / carries / an act / with it / but / a train of / by / a human being / consequences).

→ ____

🚩 도전

2 나는 교과과정의 첫 2년은 매우 지루하다는 것을 알았으며 나는 시험을 통과하기에 필요한 정도이상의 관심을 공부에 보이지 않았다.

(of / two years / I / dull / found / the first / the curriculum / very) and didn't give my work (necessary / attention / than / the / to / examinations / scrape through / more / was).

* scrape through 겨우 통과하다

→ ____

→ ____

🚩 도전

3 1929년 주식 시장 붕괴의 영향을 받지 않은 금융 역사상의 사건은 없습니다.

There is (been / influenced / financial / the 1929 market stock crash / in / has / by / event / no / but / history).

→ ____

Exercise 03   각 지문을 읽고, 물음에 답하시오.

1

(a) <u>There is</u> (b) <u>something solemn</u> and awful in the thought (c) <u>which</u> there is not an act done or a word (d) <u>uttered</u> by a human being but (e) <u>carries</u> with it a train of consequences, (f)(우리가 결코 쫓을 수 없는 일련의 결과의 끝).

1   (a)~(e) 중에서 어법상 어색한 것을 골라 바르게 고치시오.

번호	틀린 표현	바른 표현
____ :	________________	________________

도전

2   괄호 (f)의 우리말을 아래 조건에 맞게 영작하시오.

조건
- S V ~ , (N of which S V ~)에서 괄호 안의 구조를 활용할 것.
- 아래 제시된 단어만을 변형 없이 사용하여 영작할 것.
  제시어   the / we / may / never / which / of / trace / end

→ ____

(가)Human memory, formerly believed to be rather inefficient, is really (a)<u>much more</u> sophisticated than (나)<u>that</u> of a computer. Researchers (b)<u>approached</u> the problem from a variety of points of view (c)<u>have</u> all concluded that there is a great deal more (d)<u>storing</u> in our minds than (e)<u>have been</u> generally supposed.

1 〈보기〉를 참고하여, 밑줄 친 (가)에서 생략된 표현을 문맥에 맞게 쓰시오.

─┤ 보기 ├─

The man, (who is) an Englishman lives in Africa, is doing research and develop in the center.

(가) <u>Human memory, formerly believed to be rather inefficient</u>

→ ______________________________________

2 (a)~(e) 중에서 어법상 어색한 것을 세 개 골라 바르게 고치시오.

번호		틀린 표현	바른 표현
______	:	______________	______________
______	:	______________	______________
______	:	______________	______________

3 밑줄 친 (나)가 지칭하는 것을 쓰시오.

(나) that = ____________

미리 Voca

- **deserve** ~을 받을 가치가 있다
- **heroism** 영웅적 자질
- **be worth v-ing** ~할 가치다 있다
- **receive** 받다
- **sting** 일침
- **soul** 영혼
- **Romanticism** 낭만주의
- **intensely** 강렬하게
- **capture** 사로잡다
- **embrace** 포용하다
- **sublime** 숭고한
- **rebel** 반항하다

- **mongrel** 잡종, 혼혈아
- **concerning** ~와 관련된
- **subjective** 주관적인
- **reveal** 폭로하다, 드러내다
- **indicate** 나타내다, 가리키다
- **intimation** 암시, 통지
- **entity** 독립체, 실체
- **unfamiliar** 익숙하지 않은
- **incompatible** 양립할 수 없는, 공존할 수 없는
- **conversely** 정반대로, 역으로
- **acquire** 습득하다
- **physical optics** 물리광학

| 형태 | 연속적인 관계대명사 두 개가 위치한다. |

| 해석
방법 | There is no one / that I know of / who deserves to love her
⇒ 아무도 없다 / 내가 아는 / 그녀를 사랑할 만한.
⇒ 내가 아는 사람 중에는 그녀를 사랑할 만한 사람이 아무도 없다. |

| 참고 | • 동일한 선행사에 관계대명사절이 두 개가 나와야한다.
Is there anything that you want which you don't have?
⇒ 네가 원하는 것 중, 가지지 않은 것이 있느냐? |

Exercise 01   다음 이중관계대명사 구문에 유의하여 알맞게 해석하시오.

1 This is the thing which I had begged for the longest time that I needed the least.

→ ____

2 This is the only guide book that I was recommended to read and which is really useful.

→ ____

3 Is there anything you bought that you shouldn't have?

→ ____

4 There are a lot of things you can do that are worth doing.

→ ____

5 There are many items, which are necessary to live on, which we have long hope to buy.

→ ____

Exercise 02 다음 우리말을 이중관계대명사를 활용하여 영작하려고 한다. 제시된 단어만을 사용하여 문장을 완성하시오.

🚩도전

1 당신이 아는 사람 중에 그러한 행동을 할 만한 사람은 없다.
(know / can / no / is / that / a thing / such / do / one / there / you / who).

→ ____

🚩도전

2 서울에 사는 사람 중에 그의 이름을 모르는 이는 없다.
(is / in / there / Seoul / not / know / who / lives / does / his name / not / a man / who).

→ ____

🚩도전

3 영웅주의가 전혀 아닌데 영웅주의로 치부되는 것이 있다.
(at all / passes / for / is / is / which / heroism / not / that / something / heroism / there).

→ ____

  각 문제를 우리말에 맞게, 괄호 안의 단어를 알맞게 배열하시오.

1 자신의 영혼에 일침을 받아들이지 않는 사람에게 죄를 묻는 사람은 없다.

(carries / that / there / no / man / is) guilt about (receive / does / his soul / a sting / into / who / not / him).

→ ____

→ ____

2 때때로 사람들은 영화 속 등장인물만큼이나 힘이 세거나 영리할 수 있다고 생각한다. 그러나 매우 흥미로운 것 중에 영화 속에서 James Bond가 했었던 것들을 실제 생활에서 하려고 노력했을 때 매우 나쁜 사고들이 발생하기도 한다.

Sometimes people think (as / as / can / strong / they / a character / in / be / film / or / clever / as). But when they try to do the things in real life (does / which / in / a film / James Bond) (that / very / exciting / are), very bad accidents can happen.

→ ____

→ ____

→ ____

✔ 고난도

3 낭만주의처럼 세대의 상상력을 강렬하게 사로잡은 운동이 또 있을까, 이 운동은 이성과 반항하며 숭고함을 포용한다.

Is there any movement (generations / the imagination / that / Romanticism / of / captured / as / intensely / has / as), (reason / and / embraces / against / the sublime / rebels / which)?

→ ____

→ ____

Exercise  04 각 지문을 읽고, 물음에 답하시오.

 1

Suppose we had called an animal a mongrel, we have used a word (가)(객관적으로는 '잡종 개'와 같은 뜻은 의미이지만, 이는 또한 그 특정한 개에 대해 우리가 가지고 있는 부정적인 감정을 드러내는). A word, accordingly therefore, can not only indicate an object, but also suggest concerning that object an emotional attitude.

✔ 고난도

1 괄호 (가)의 우리말을 아래 조건에 맞게 영작하시오.

• 조건 •

- [N which V ~ , which V ~]의 이중관계대명사 구조와 목적격관계대명사의 생략 구조인 [N S V]를 활용할 것.
- 아래 제시된 단어만을 사용할 것.

  제시어 the same / have / means / objectively / 'a dog of mixed breed' / as / which / also / about / a negative feeling / which / but / reveals / we / that particular dog

→ ____

2 위의 글을 요약했을 때, 빈칸에 알맞은 단어를 쓰시오. (단, 본문에 언급된 단어만을 사용할 것)

In summary, a term gives an intimation of both an _______ and psychological _______ when it comes to entity.

* intimation 넌지시 알림, 시사

That pattern is not unfamiliar in a number of creative fields today, (a) (or it is <u>not</u> incompatible) with significant discovery and invention. It is not, conversely, (b) (물리광학이 이룬 발전 방식이며, 다른 자연과학들이 오늘날 익숙한 발전방식도).

1 〈보기〉를 참고하여 괄호 (a) 안에 들어있는 밑줄 친 부정어 not을 강조하는 도치구문을 만드시오.

| 보기 |

I have never been to Korea.
→ Never have I been to Korea.

(a) (or it is <u>not</u> incompatible)

→ ___________________________

✅ 고난도

2 괄호 (b)의 우리말을 아래 조건에 맞게 영작하시오.

• 조건 •

• [N that S V ~ and that S V]의 이중관계대명사의 수식을 받는 구조를 활용할 것.
• that은 둘 다 목적격관계대명사이며, that절 내 3형식과 5형식 구조를 가짐.
• 아래 제시어만을 사용하여 영작할 것.
  제시어 today / that / after Newton / make / familiar / and / that / acquired / physical optics / of / other natural sciences / development / the pattern

→ ___________________________

who[m]ever (복합관계대명사) 구문

미리 Voca 

- **master** 숙달하다
- **win the election** 당선하다
- **party** 정당
- **deal with** 다루다, 대처하다
- **sympathy** 연민, 동의
- **resolve** 해결하다, 결심하다, 녹이다
- **humbly** 겸손하게, 볼품없이
- **criticism** 비판
- **seek to** ~하려고 애쓰다
- **highlight** 강조하다
- **voice** 목소리, 발언권

- **literary canon** 문학정전(특정 시대나 문화에서 가장 중요하고 영향력 있는 문학 작품들)
- **marginalize** 소외시키다
- **pension** 연금
- **christen** 세례를 주다, 이름을 붙이다
- **disorder** 무질서
- **restrict** 제한하다
- **stand out** 두드러지다
- **come up with** ~을 떠올리다, 생각해 내다
- **competitor** 경쟁자
- **collapse** 붕괴하다
- **disorder** 무질서, 질병

형태	who + ever , whom + ever

해석 방법	• 명사절을 이끄는 복합관계대명사 Whoever comes will be welcome.(주어역할) (=anyone who) ⇒ 오는 사람은 누구든지 모두 환영이다. • 부사절을 이끄는 복합관계대명사 Whoever may come, he will be welcome. (=no matter who) ⇒ 오는 사람이 누구일지라도, 그는 환영받을 것이다

참고	복합관계대명사의 명사절 역할(문장에서 주어, 목적어의 역할)과 부사절 역할은 주로 , (comma)의 유무에 따라 결정된다.

복합관계대명사	명사절	부사절
who(m)ever	anyone who (누구든지)	no matter who(m) (누구일지라도)
whichever	anything that (어느 것이든지)	no matter which (어떤 것일지라도)
whatever	anything that (무엇이든지)	no matter what (무엇일지라도)

복합관계부사	시간장소 부사절	양보부사절
wherever	at any place where (어디서든지)	no matter where (어디서 ~할지라도)
whenever	at any time when (~할 때마다)	no matter when (언제 ~할지라도)
however		no matter how (may)(아무리 ~해도)

Exercise  보기처럼 밑줄 친 복합관계대명사 whoever, whomever가 이끄는 절의 활용에 유의하여 해석하고, 명사절인지 또는 부사절인지 구분하시오.

─── 보기 ───

He told the story to whoever would listen.
⇒ 그는 들어줄 누구나에게 그 이야기를 말했다. (명사절)

1 Whoever leaves the office last should switch off the office. (   )

➔ ____

2 Whomever you ask, you will not be able to get the answer. (   )

➔ ____

3 I would like to see him, <u>whom you love</u>. (   )

→ ____

4 <u>Whoever masters Formula English</u> can speak English very well. (   )

→ ____

5 The columnist feels sure <u>that whoever wins the election</u> will have the support of the parties. (   )

→ ____

Exercise 02 각 문제를 우리말에 맞게, 괄호 안의 단어를 알맞게 배열하시오.

1 아이들을 상대해야만 하는 누구든지 너무 많은 동정심은 실수가 된다는 것을 곧 알게 된다. 그렇다고 너무 적은 동정심은 물론 더 나쁜 실수가 된다.

(has / deal / with / whoever / to / children) soon learns that too much sympathy is a mistake. Too little sympathy is, of course, a worse mistake.

→ ____

2 나는 어떤 사회로 나를 이끌 수 있는 나의 관심사들을 개발하고 그것들을 철저히 추구함으로써 내가 어디에 속했는지를 발견하기로 결심했다.

(belonged / I / resolved / where / out / I / to / find) by developing my interests and by following them through into (society / me / would / they / whichever / bring).

→ ____

→ ____

3 나는 최고의 군인이 되려고 결심을 해왔다. 나는 내 앞에 무엇이 있는지 모르겠지만, 그것이 무엇이 됐든 나는 것을 겸손하게 준비한다.

I have made up my mind to be the best soldier. I have no idea what is ahead, but (is / whatever / it), I am humbly ready for it.

→ ____

4 우리가 아름다움을 파괴할 때마다, 아니면 우리는 땅의 자연적 특징을 인공적인 무언가로 대체할 때마다 우리는 인간 영혼의 성장의 속도 또한 줄여왔다.

(destroy / we / beauty / whenever), or (artificial / whenever / we / something / for / a natural feature / of / the earth / substitute), we have slowed down man's spiritual growth.

→ ____

→ ____

5 버지니아 울프가 어떤 비평을 쓰더라도, 그녀는 문학 정전에 소외된 여성의 목소리를 강조하고자 했다.

(criticism / whatever / wrote / she), Virginia Woolf sought to highlight the voices of women, (whose / stories / in / been / the literary canon / had / marginalized).

→ ____

→ ____

Exercise 03 각 지문을 읽고, 물음에 답하시오.

1

(a) (이 아이디어를 생각해낸 사람이 누구이든 그에게는 큰 장려금이 지급되어야 한다), because it helps Fortune Brands(FO)-owned Maker's (b) ________ (stand out) from its competitors in (c) (유럽인들이 "이너투어리즘"이라고 명명해 온 것에 대한 위스키 버전)," or wine tourism, a large and growing business.

1 괄호 (a) 안의 우리말을 제시어만을 사용하여 영작하시오.

제시어

idea / a large / be / this / given / whoever / came up with / pension / should

→ ____

2 주어진 두 문장을 재진술할 때 빈칸에 들어갈 단어를 채워 넣으시오.

• Whatever she tries, it is not possible for her to make it.

= (   ) (   ) (   ) she tries, it is not possible for to make it.

• I can do whatever you want.

= I can do (   ) (   ) you want.

3 주어진 단어를 변형하여 괄호 (b) 안에 알맞은 단어를 쓰시오

→ ____

4 괄호 (c) 의 우리말을 제시어만을 사용하여 영작하시오.

제시어

what / have / the whiskey / of / oenotourism / Europeans / christened / version

* christen 이름[명칭]을 붙이다

→ ____

When people live in a community they cannot do exactly as they please. Motorists, (a)
(　　　　　), cannot drive (b) (　　　　　) they like without creating disorder; (c) (kill /
can / men / neither) nor rob (d) (　　　　　) they please without causing society (e)
＿＿＿＿＿ (collapse). If men were not thus restricted, if they had, in name, the *liberty* to
do what they liked, they would, in fact, have very much *liberty*.

1   괄호 (a)에 들어갈 알맞은 연결어를 고르시오.

① that is to say   ② in particular   ③ in the first place

④ otherwise   ⑤ for instance

2   〈보기〉에서 괄호 (b)와 (d)에 들어갈 알맞은 복합관계사를 고르시오.

―| 보기 |―

who(m)ever/ whichever / whatever/ wherever/ whenever/ however

(b): ＿＿＿＿＿＿

(d): ＿＿＿＿＿＿

3   괄호 (c) 안의 단어를 바르게 배열하여 자연스러운 글의 흐름이 만드시오.

→ ＿＿＿＿＿＿＿＿＿＿＿＿＿＿＿＿＿＿＿＿

4   주어진 단어를 변형하여 괄호 안의 단어의 바른 형태를 빈칸 (e)에 넣으시오.

→ ＿＿＿＿＿＿＿＿＿＿＿＿＿＿＿＿＿＿＿＿

5   글의 흐름상, 어색한 단어를 찾아 바르게 고치시오.

어색한 표현: ＿＿＿＿＿＿＿＿＿＿＿＿＿＿＿＿

바른 표현: ＿＿＿＿＿＿＿＿＿＿＿＿＿＿＿＿

미리

Voca 

- **skyrocket** 급격히 상승하다
- **receive** 받다
- **lower** 낮추다
- **drop by** 들리다 (= swing by)
- **vibrate** 진동하다
- **victim** 피해자
- **eminent** 저명한, 탁월한
- **observe** 관측하다
- **adapt** (상황에) 적응하다, 각색하다
- **surrounding** 주변 환경
- **species** 종
- **variety** 다양성 (=diversity), (식물·언어 등의) 품종[종류]
- **compensation** 보상금, 보상
- **conventional** 관습적인, 틀에 박힌

- **exceptionally** 예외적으로
- **parenthood** 부모임
- **characteristic** 특유의, 특징
- **proclaim** 선언하다
- **impose** 부과하다, 강요하다
- **qualify** 자격[자격증]을 얻다[취득하다], (…할) 자격[권리]이 있다, 자격[권리]을 주다
- **beneath** 밑에, 아래쪽에
- **run the risk of** ~의 위험을 무릅쓰다
- **eliminate** 제거하다
- **assurance** 확언, 장담, 자신감, (보장성) 보험
- **attribute** ~의 덕분으로 여기다, 속성, 특질
- **attribute A to B** A는 B 덕분이다, A(결과)는 B(원인) 때문이다
- **refuse** 거절하다

형태	when + ever, where + ever

해석 방법	• 부사절을 이끄는 복합관계사 Sales skyrocketed / <u>whenever</u> we lowered our prices.(시간부사절) ⇒ 판매가 급격히 상승했다 / 우리가 우리의 가격을 낮출 때마다. • 양보부사절을 이끄는 복합관계사(with comma) The newly elected president was warmly received, <u>wherever</u> he went. ⇒ 새롭게 뽑힌 대통령은 따뜻하게 환대를 받았다 / 그가 어디를 갈지라도.

참고	복합관계대명사의 명사절 역할(문장에서 주어, 목적어의 역할)과 부사절 역할은 주로 , (comma)의 유무에 따라 결정된다.

복합관계대명사	명사절	부사절
who(m)ever	anyone who (누구든지)	no matter who(m) (누구일지라도)
whichever	anything that (어느 것이든지)	no matter which (어떤 것일지라도)
whatever	anything that (무엇이든지)	no matter what (무엇일지라도)

복합관계부사	시간장소 부사절	양보부사절
wherever	at any place where (어디서든지)	no matter where (어디서 ~할지라도)
whenever	at any time when (~할 때마다)	no matter when (언제 ~할지라도)
however		no matter how (may)(아무리 ~해도)

Exercise  01 보기처럼 다음 복합관계대명사 whenever, wherever의 용례에 유의하여 괄호 안을
채우고, 알맞게 해석하시오.

You can visit me whenever you like.
⇒ You can visit me <u>at any time</u> you like.
당신은 당신이 좋아하는 언제든지 나를 방문해도 좋다.

1 Wherever you are, remember that we will be thinking of you.

⇒ (   ), remember that we will be thinking of you.

[해석] ____

2 Come whenever it is convenient for you.

⇒ Come (   ) it is convenient for you.

[해석] ____

3 However much he eats, he never gets fat.

⇒ (   ) much he eats, he never gets fat.

[해석] ____

4 However much money is spent for TV commercials, a poor product will not sell.

⇒ (   ) much money is spent for TV commercials, a poor product will not sell.

[해석] ____

5 Please drop by whenever you happen to come to this neighborhood.

⇒ Please drop by (   ) you happen to come to this neighborhood.

[해석] ____

Exercise 02   각 문제를 우리말에 맞게, 괄호 안의 단어를 알맞게 배열하시오.

1 내가 시간당 55마일의 속도를 넘어 내 오래된 차를 운전할 때 마다, 그것은 심하게 진동했다. 그래서 나는 그것을 팔기로 결심했다.

(my / car / drove / old / hour / over / 55 / miles / per / whenever / I), it vibrated terribly, so I decided to sell it.

➜ ____

2 당신이 무엇을 해도, 당신이 어디에 살지라도, 당신이 그것을 좋아하든 아니든, 당신이 그것을 알든, 모르던지 범죄의 희생자가 된다.

(do / you / whatever), (live / you / wherever), you are a victim of crime (not / like / or / you / whether / it), (it / you / know / not / whether / or).

→ ____

→ ____

→ ____

→ ____

3 판사가 아무리 현명하거나 저명하다해도, 인간이고 실수를 할 수 있다.

Judges, (eminent / wise / or / however), (and / are / can / mistakes / make / human).

→ ____

→ ____

4 아무리 우리의 기술이 훨씬 발달했어도, 우리는 여전히 생각하고 읽는 방법을 알아야한다.

(advance / however / technology / our / we / far), (still / to / think / to / we / will / know / read / need / and / how).

→ ____

→ ____

🚩도전

5 다윈이 자연을 관찰할 때마다, 그는 주변 환경에 적응하는 종들의 끝없는 다양성을 알아차렸다.

(nature / observed / Darwin / Whenever), (adapting / endless / variety / of / species / surroundings / their / noticed / the / to / he).

→ ____

→ ____

Exercise 03 — 각 지문을 읽고, 물음에 답하시오.

1

(a) <u>Whenever</u> society demands a mother's sacrifice to her child (b) <u>who</u> goes beyond reason, the mother, if she is not unusually (c) <u>saintly</u>, will expect from her child compensations exceeding (가) <u>those</u> she has a right (d) <u>expecting</u>. The mother who is conventionally called self-sacrificing is, in a great majority of cases, exceptionally selfish towards her children, for, although parenthood is as important as an element in life, it is not (e) <u>satisfied</u> if it is treated as the whole life.

1 (a) ~ (e) 중에서 어법상 어색한 것을 세 개 골라 바르게 고치시오.

번호	틀린 표현	바른 표현
______ :	____________	____________
______ :	____________	____________
______ :	____________	____________

2 밑줄 친 (가)의 those가 지칭하는 단어 또는 내용을 쓰시오.

→ ____

★3 위의 글을 요약할 때, 아래 조건에 맞게 빈칸에 알맞은 단어를 채워 넣으시오.

> **• 조건 •**
> • 제시된 철자로 시작하는 단어를 쓰되, 본문에 언급된 단어를 그대로 또는 변형할 것.

When society demands un________ sacrifices from a mother, she often expects e________ c________ from her child, leading to s______, as p________ alone cannot s______ the entirety of her life.

The characteristic of the hour is (a)<u>that</u> the commonplace mind, (b)<u>known</u> itself (c)<u>to be</u> commonplace, has the assurance to proclaim the rights of the commonplace and (d)<u>imposes</u> (f)<u>them</u> wherever (g)<u>it</u> will. The mass crushes beneath it everything that is different, everything that (e)<u>qualifies</u>. (h)<u>Anybody who is not like everybody</u>, who does not think like everybody, (i)(being / runs / of / eliminated / the risk). Nowadays, "everybody" is the mass alone.

1 (a)~(e) 중에서 어법상 틀린 곳을 <u>세 개</u> 골라 알맞게 고치시오.

번호	틀린 표현	바른 표현
______ :	______________	______________
______ :	______________	______________
______ :	______________	______________

🚩도전

2 괄호 (f)와 (g)가 지칭하는 것을 각각 쓰시오.

(f): ______________________

(g): ______________________

3 괄호 (h)를 재진술할 때 빈칸에 들어갈 단어를 쓰시오.

Anybody who is not like everybody = (　　　　　) is not like everybody

4 글의 흐름에 맞게 괄호 (i)의 단어를 바르게 배열하시오.

➜ ____

🚩도전

5 본문의 요약한 내용이다. 빈칸을 채우시오. (단, 제시된 철자로 시작하는 단어를 쓸 것)

One of the attributes of the time is that o________ people assume that they are c______ and declare it as their r______. The problem with it is that they refuse to a________ different thoughts and q________ behaviors.

whatever, whichever, however (복합관계대명사) 구문

미리 Voca 

- **excuse** 변명, 이유, 구실, 용서하다
- **nothing but** 단지 (= only)
- **means** 수단
- **costly** 비싼 (= pricey)
- **vast** 광범위한
- **worthwhile** 가치 있는
- **organization** 조직, 기관
- **perform** 이행하다, 실행하다, 수행하다, 연기하다
- **strength** 힘, 기운, 용기
- **geopolitical** 지정학적인
- **emerge** 발생하다
- **hedge** (특히 금전 손실을 막기 위한) 대비책, 산울터리
- **reputation** 명성
- **stability** 안정성
- **persuade** 설득하다

- **characteristic** 특유의, 특징
- **merit** 장점, 훌륭함 (=worth), 가치, (칭찬·관심 등을) 받을 만하다[자격/가치가 있다] (=deserve)
- **comparatively** 비교적, 상당히
- **trivial** 사소한
- **proportionately** 비례적으로
- **provisional** 임시의, 잠정적인
- **hypothesis** 가설, 가정
- **contradict** 모순되다, 반박하다
- **philosopher** 철학자
- **emphasize** 강조하다
- **a number of** 많은 (= many)
- **prediction** 예측
- **experiment** 실험
- **disprove** 틀렸음을 입증하다
- **falsify** 위조하다, 왜곡하다

형태	what + ever, which + ever

해석방법	Whatever they say to you, / never mind. ⇒ 그들이 너에게 무슨 말을 할지라도,/ 신경쓰지마라 Take whichever you want. ⇒ 가져가라 / 네가 원하는 어떤 것이라도.

참고	복합관계대명사의 명사절 역할(문장에서 주어, 목적어의 역할)과 부사절 역할은 주로 , (comma)의 유무에 따라 결정된다.

복합관계대명사	명사절	부사절
who(m)ever	anyone who (누구든지)	no matter who(m) (누구일지라도)
whichever	anything that (어느 것이든지)	no matter which (어떤 것일지라도)
whatever	anything that (무엇이든지)	no matter what (무엇일지라도)

복합관계부사	시간장소 부사절	양보부사절
wherever	at any place where (어디서든지)	no matter where (어디서 ~할지라도)
whenever	at any time when (~할 때마다)	no matter when (언제 ~할지라도)
however		no matter how (may)(아무리 ~해도)

Exercise 01 밑줄 친 복합관계대명사의 표현을 바꾸어 쓰려고 한다. 빈칸을 채우고, 각 문장을 해석하시오.

1 Whatever excuse he makes will not be believed.

⇒ _______ excuse he makes will not be believed.

[해석] ____

2 Whatever problems you have, you can always come to me for help.

⇒ _______ _______ _______ _______ you have, you can always come to me for help.

[해석] ____

3 I think you will enjoy whichever one you choose.

⇒ I think you will enjoy _______ one you choose.

[해석] ____

4 Whichever TV channel he turned on, he saw nothing but pictures.

⇒ _______ _______ _______ TV channel he turned on, he saw nothing but pictures.

[해석] ____

5 Whichever you choose, you don't have to pay for it.

⇒ _______ _______ _______ you choose, you don't have to pay for it.

[해석] ____

Exercise 02 각 문제를 우리말에 맞게, 괄호 안의 단어를 알맞게 배열하시오.

✓ 고난도

1 광고주들은 그들이 생각하기에 그들에게 최고로 효과적인 수단이나 미디어 어떤 것이라도 사용한다. 예를 들어 라디오와 텔레비전 광고는 비싸지만, 그것들은 광범위한 청중에게 미치고, 이것은 그것들을 가치 있게 해준다. (단, "복합관계사 N + S V + V"의 삽입구조를 활용할 것)
(means, / use / they / whichever / will / for / work / best / them / advertisers / think / or media,). For example, radio and television ads are costly, but they reach a vast audience and this makes them worthwhile.

➜ ____

2 오늘날 조직이 인간을 평범하게 만들고, 그것의 일원들이 있는 곳에 어떤 힘이든지 가져오게 해서 그들이 할 수 있는 것보다 더 잘 이행하게 한다는 것은 중요하다.

Today it is very important to the organization to make ordinary human beings perform better than they can, (there / bring / out / to / strength / whatever / its / is / in / members).

→ ____

3 어떤 지정학적 위기가 발생하더라도, 비트코인은 전통적인 금융 시스템에 대한 대비책으로서의 명성을 유지하며, 불확실한 시기에 안정성을 추구하는 투자자들을 끌어들인다.

(geopolitical / crises / may / whatever / emerge), (traditional / financial systems / remains / a hedge / as / Bitcoin's reputation / against / strong), attracting investors who seek stability in uncertain times.

→ ____

→ ____

Exercise **03** 각 지문을 읽고, 물음에 답하시오.

1

Every morning, (가)<u>whatever the weather</u>, he would leave the house and set off on foot toward the edge of the town. (나) (　　　　　), the houses thinned out, and (다)(즐거운 산책의 마지막부분은 그를 탁 트인 시골을 가로질러 넓은 초지에 덩그러니 혼자 떨어져 있는 한 큰 건물로 데려다 주었다).

1 괄호 (가)와 의미가 같은 다른 문장을 만들기 위해 빈칸에 들어갈 알맞은 단어를 쓰시오.

___________________________ the weather,

2 괄호 (나)에 들어갈 알맞은 연결사를 고르시오.
① Unfortunately   ② Similarly   ③ Conversely
④ Gradually   ⑤ Incidentally

3 괄호 (다)의 아래 조건에 맞게 영작하시오.

> **• 조건 •**
> • 괄호 안의 밑줄 친 표현은 [N + V-ed ~] 과거분사가 명사를 후치하는 구조임.
> • 아래 제시된 단어만을 사용하여 영작할 것.
> [제시어] took / to / him / of / the last part / set off / a large building / quite / the
> pleasant walk / by itself / open country / a in broad meadow / across

➜ ____

4 3번 문제의 영작문을 아래와 같이 재진술할 때 빈칸에 들어갈 단어를 채워 넣으시오. (단, 제시된
철자로 시작하는 단어를 쓸 것)

> The pleasant walk led him through open fields to a large building s_______ a_______
> in a wide meadow.

2

We are all, (가)(세상의 어떤 지역 출신이든 간에), (a) <u>persuading</u> that our own nation is superior
(b) <u>than</u> all others. Seeing that each (c) <u>nation</u> has its characteristic merits and demerits, we
adjust our standard of values so as to make out that the merits (d) <u>possessed</u> by our nation
are the really important (e) <u>one</u>, while its demerits are comparatively trivial.

1 (a)~(e) 중에서 어법상 틀린 것을 <u>세 개</u>를 골라 알맞게 고치시오.

번호	틀린 표현	바른 표현
_____ :	______________	______________
_____ :	______________	______________
_____ :	______________	______________

2 괄호 (가)의 우리말을 아래 제시된 단어만을 사용하여 영작하시오.

→ ____

3 위 글을 읽고, 본문과 일치하도록 빈칸에 들어갈 단어를 본문에서 찾아 쓰시오. (단, 필요시 문맥에 맞게 단어의 형태를 변형할 것)

The reason that we ________ our standard of values is for the sake of ________ that the ________ are proportionately ________.

Exercise 04  아래 지문 읽고, 물음에 답하시오.

Any physical theory is always provisional, in the sense that it is only a hypothesis: you can never prove it. (가)(실험의 결과들이 아무리 여러 번 어떤 이론에 부합한다 해도), you can never be sure that the next time the result will not contradict the theory. On the other hand, (나)(당신은 어떤 이론이 예측하는 것과 부합하지 않는 단 하나의 관찰사실을 찾아내어도 그 이론이 틀렸음을 입증할 수 있다). As philosopher of science Karl Popper has emphasized, a good theory is characterized by the fact that it makes a number of predictions that could in principle be disproved or falsified by observation.

✔ 고난도

1 괄호 (가)의 우리말을 아래 제시된 단어를 포함하여 영작하시오. (단, 추가 단어 있음)

→ ____

2 괄호 (나)의 우리말을 아래 조건에 맞게 영작하시오.

> **• 조건 •**
>
> • [N that V ~]의 주격관계대명사의 구조를 활용할 것.
> • 아래 제시어만을 사용하여 영작하되, 필요시 동사의 형태를 변형할 것.
>   제시어 the theory / with / you / of / can / disagree / that / disprove / the predictions / by / even a single observation / a theory / find

→ ____

3 다음은 본문의 요약이다. 괄호 안의 단어를 바르게 배열하여 자연스러운 흐름이 되도록 하시오. (단, 추가단어는 없지만, 필요시 단어의 형태를 변형할 것)

> Ⓐ(are / to / agree / each time / new / experiments / observed / with / the predictions), the theory survives, and our confidence in it is increased; but Ⓑ(new / is / if ever / disagree / observation / a / found / to), we have to abandon or modify the theory.

Ⓐ(are / to / agree / each time / new / experiments / observed / with / the predictions)

→ ____

Ⓑ(new / is / if ever / disagree / observation / a / found / to)

→ ____

미리 Voca

❑ **property** 재산	❑ **tectonic** 지각의, (지질) 구조상의
❑ **set off** 청산하다	❑ **be associated with** ~와 관련이 있다
❑ **accumulate** 모으다, 축적하다	❑ **make the most of** ~을 최대한 활용하다
❑ **endeavor** 노력하다, 노력	❑ **affectionate** 애정 깊은, 다정한
❑ **ancestor** 조상	❑ **heartily** 진심으로
❑ **develop** 개발하다	❑ **sigh** 한숨 쉬다
❑ **utilize** 활용하다	❑ **sense** 지각
❑ ***subduction zone** 섭입대	❑ **direct** 지도하다
❑ **geologist** 지질학자	❑ **good sense** 분별력
❑ **underwater** 해저의	❑ **profit** 이득, 이익
❑ **seismic activity** 지진활동	❑ **of profit** 이득이 되는

* subduction zone 판구조론에서 판과 판이 수렴하는 경계에서 상대적으로 밀도가 높은 판이 밀도가 낮은 판 아래로 밀려 들어가는 곳을 지칭한다.

🔑 Key Point

| 형태 | 관계대명사 what + 명사/ 관계대명사 which + 명사 |

| 해석
방법 | We traveled as far as Cairo, / at which place we parted.
⇒ 우리는 카이로까지 여행을 했고 / 거기서 우리는 헤어졌다.
I gave him / what money I had with me. (= all the money)
⇒ 나는 그에게 주었다 / (적지만) 내가 가지고 있던 돈 모두를. |

| 참고 | • 관계 형용사로 쓰이는 단어는 which, what 두 종류뿐이다.
He came at noon, and I am usually in the garden at that time.
⇒ He came at noon, at which time, I am usually in the garden.
I have read what books I have. (= all the books)
• what에는 "모든"의 의미가 있으므로, what + 복수명사를 써 준다. |

Exercise **01** 다음 우리말을 제시된 단어만을 사용하여 영작하시오.

1 그는 그가 가지고 있었던 어떤 적은 양의 돈이라도 소비했다. (썼다)

(what / he / little / had / money / he / spent).

→ ____

2 그는 그가 가지고 있었던 어떠한 적은 재산이라도 모두 써서 배를 사고, 떠났다. ("V ~, V ~ and V ~l의 서술부병치를 활용)

(what / and / he / property / a / boat / he / bought / had, / sold / little / set off).

→ ____

🚩 도전

3 그는 때때로 스페인어로 말하지만, 그 언어를 나는 이해할 수 없다. (계속적 용법의 관계형용사를 활용할 것)

(Spanish, / he / I / sometimes / can't / language / speaks / understand / which).

→ ____

4 그는 나에게 휴식을 취하라고 말했다. 그리고 그 충고를 나는 따랐다. (계속적 용법의 관계형용사를 활용할 것)

(rest, / followed / take / me / which / advice / told / to / I / a / he).

→ ____

5 나는 너에게 그가 가지고 있는 책 모두를 너에게 줄 것이다.

(he / I / what / has / few / will / give / you / books).

→ ____

Exercise 02 각 문제를 우리말에 맞게, 괄호 안의 단어를 알맞게 배열하시오.

1 당신이 위험에 처해있을 때 마다 나에게 오세요. 그러면 나는 당신에게 내가 할 수 있는 어떠한 작은 도움이라도 줄게요.

Come to me (in / whenever / you / are / trouble); (help / I'll / you / what / give / can / I / little).

→ ____

→ ____

2 우리가 아는 어떠한 작은 것이라도, 우리가 가지고 있는 어떠한 적은 힘이라도, 우리는 조상들의 축적되어온 노력에 빚을 지고 있다.

(know / we / little / what), (possess / little / we / power / what), (owe / we / to / endeavors / our / accumulated / ancestors / the / of).

→ ____

→ ____

3 "나는 의사입니다."라고 그가 정중하게 고개를 숙이며 말했다. "당신의 이웃은 나에게 당신의 병에 대해 알려왔습니다. 그리고 나는 내가 할 수 있는 어떠한 작은 도움이라도 드리려고 합니다."

"I am a physician, madam," he said bowing respectfully ; "(your / me / informed / your / illness / neighbors / have / of), and (service / I / little / what / can / I / come / have / offer / to)."

→ ____

→ ____

🚩 도전

4 과학자들은 바이러스에 대해 가지고 있는 모든 지식을 활용하여 효과적인 치료제를 개발하고 있다.

(they / what / virus / about / utilizing / have / develop / the / knowledge / treatments / scientists / effective / are / to).

→ ____

✅ 고난도

5 지질학자들은 서브덕션 존(subduction zones)에 관한 모든 정보를 연구했는데, 여기에는 역사적인 지진 활동과 해저 지형 등이 포함되며, 이러한 지각 활동과 관련된 잠재적인 쓰나미 위험을 더 잘 이해하고 예측하기 위해서이다.

(what / information / subduction zones / had / studied / geologists / they / about), including historical seismic activity and underwater topography, (predict / to / risks / processes / the potential / better / understand / tectonic / these / and / associated / with / tsunami).

→ ____

→ ____

6 헬렌 켈러는 장애인의 능력에 대해 사회가 가지고 있던 적은 믿음조차 최대한 활용했다.

(of / made / people / society / what / faith / had / with / of / in / Helen Keller / the abilities / the / little / disabilities / most).

→ ____

Exercise 03   각 지문을 읽고, 물음에 답하시오.

1

(a) (그 효자는 얼마 안 되는 모든 힘을 사용했다) to tie (b) (그가 의사로부터 받았던 약) around the dog's neck, and sent him home with (c) it.

1 괄호 (a) 의 우리말을 아래 제시어만을 활용하여 영작하시오.

> **제시어**
>
> what / used / son / he / strength / had / the affectionate / little

→ ____

2 괄호 (b) 의 우리말을 아래 제시어만을 활용하여 영작하시오.

> **제시어**
>
> from / he / received / the medicine / had / the doctor / that

→ ____

3 위 글의 (c) 가 지칭하는 단어 또는 내용을 쓰시오.

→ ____

2

(a) I heartily wish that in my youth I had had someone of good sense to direct my reading. I sigh when I reflect on the amount of time wasted on book that were of no great profit to me. (b) (그나마 내가 받았던 독서에 대한 방법) I owe to a young man who came to live with (c) (내가 Heidelberg에서 함께 살았었던 바로 그 가족).

---

1 〈보기〉를 참고하여 밑줄 친 (a) 와 같은 의미의 다른 문장을 만들고자 한다. 빈칸에 알맞은 단어를 쓰시오.

---| 보기 |---

You wish that you had known his name.
→ You are sorry that you did not know his name.

I wish that I had had someone of good sense to direct my reading.
= ________________________ someone of good sense to direct my reading.

2 괄호 (b) 안의 단어를 알맞게 배열하시오.

제시어

I / little / what / guidance / had

3 괄호 (c) 의 우리말을 아래 조건에 맞게 영작하시오.

• 조건 •

• the same ~ as의 <u>유사관계대명사</u> 구문을 활용할 것.
• 아래 제시어만을 사용할 것.
제시어 I / family / with / was / the same / as / in Heidelberg / living

→ ________________________

To one's 감정명사 (독립부사구) 구문

미리 Voca 

- **surprise** 놀람, 놀라게 하다
- **accept** 받아들다, 인정하다, 수락하다
- **hesitation** 주저함
- **sorrow** 슬픔
- **battle** 싸우다
- **void** 빈 공간, 공동; 공허감, 무효의, 법적 효력이 없는
- **fill** 채우다
- **relief** 안도, 안심, 경감, 구호품, 구호물자
- **regret** 후회, 유감
- **unfortunate** 불행한
- **outcome** 결과
- **delight** 기쁨
- **marketplace** 시장
- **produce** 농산물, 생산하다
- **a wide variety of** 아주 다양한
- **pass away** 사망하다[돌아가시다]
- **intense** 극심한, 치열한

- **remorse** 회한, 후회
- **pull down** 철거하다
- **add to** ~에 더하다
- **be informed** (~에 대해서) 통보를 받다, (~에 대해) 알게 되다
- **be informed of N** N에 대해서 통보를 받다
- **be informed that S V** S V에 대해서 통보를 받다
- **permit** 허락하다
- **embarrassment** 어색함, 쑥스러움
- **infant** 유아
- **apt** 적절한, 곧잘 ~하는
- **apply** 지원하다, 적용되다
- **occasion** 경우, 기회
- **pretend** ~인 척하다
- **It will be a long time before S V** ~하려면 오랜 시간이 걸리다
- **win back** 다시 얻어 내다
- **confidence** 신뢰, 자신감, 확신

🔑 Key Point

| 형태 | To one's + 감정명사 |

| 해석 방법 | To my gladness, / my son passed the exam.
⇒ 기쁘게도, / 내 아들이 시험에 합격했다. |

| 참고 | • To his sorrow, he could not see her any more.
슬프게도 그는 더 이상 그녀를 볼 수 없었다. |

감정명사	astonishment	surprise	wonder	amazement	frustration
	gladness	happiness	displeasure	amusement	cheerfulness
	sadness	grief	bitterness	relief	eagerness(열망)
	worry	agony	distress	shame	shock
	fear	anger	satisfaction	jealousy	

Exercise 01 — 아래 우리말을 제시된 단어만을 사용하여 영작하시오.

1 놀랍게도 그녀는 망설임 없이 내 청혼을 받아들였고, 나는 세상에서 가장 행복한 사람이 되었다.
(surprise / my / to), (accepted / any / hesitation / my / she / marriage / proposal / without).

→ ____

2 그가 큰 슬픔에 잠긴 것은, 그의 아버지가 오랜 병마와 싸운 끝에 화요일에 돌아가셨고, 결코 메울 수 없는 빈자리를 남겼기 때문이었다.
(great / sorrow / his / to), his father died on Tuesday after battling a long illness, (void / that / be / leaving / filled / could / a / never).

→ ____

3 다행히도 그녀의 차는 심한 폭풍으로 인해 주변 차량들이 심각한 피해를 입었음에도 불구하고 손상되지 않았다.

(her / to / relief), the car was not damaged (to / intense / the / despite / other / storm / had / the / vehicles / area / that / in / caused / damage / significant).

→ ____

4 유감스럽게도 그것은 모두 사실이며, 나는 그 불행한 결과를 바꿀 수 있는 아무런 방법도 없다.

(regret / my / to), it is all true and (unfortunate / to / outcome / change / do / I / can / there's / the / nothing).

→ ____

5 그들은 기쁘게도 식료품을 파는 시장을 발견했고, 그곳에는 다른 곳에서는 찾을 수 없었던 다양한 신선한 농산물이 있었다. (~ N, which V의 구조 활용)

(delight / their / to), they found a marketplace, (which / and / been / sold / find / anywhere else / had / that / able / they / hadn't / a wide variety of / to / fresh produce / groceries).

→ ____

6 충격적이게도 할아버지는 사고 후 며칠 만에 돌아가셨고, 의사들은 처음에는 회복 중이라고 생각했었다.

(shock / my / to), grandfather passed away a few days after the accident (was / the road / initially / he / had / recovery / the doctors / thought / to / on / even though).

→ ____

Exercise 02 각 문제를 우리말에 맞게, 괄호 안의 단어를 알맞게 배열하시오.

1 나는 놀랍게도 내가 태어나고 자라온 집이 철거당하고 그 자리에 현대식 건물이 있었다는 것을 발견했다.

(to / I / found / my / surprise) that (the house / brought / pulled / up / been / born / down / had / and / had / been / I / where), and that in its place there was a modern building.

➔ ________________________, ____________________________________

2 대단히 슬프게도 나의 아버지가 화요일에 돌아가셨다. 그는 나를 강렬하게 사랑해 주셨고, 그것은 여러 해 동안, 그를 보기 위해 Dublin에 가지 않았다는 나의 슬픔과 후회를 더했다(슬픔을 더하고, 후회스러웠다).

(great / my / sorrow / my / father / to / died) on Tuesday. He had an intense love for me and it adds now to (not / years / so / to / my grief / see / remorse / that / to / and / did / him / I / many / go / Dublin / for).

➔ ____

➔ ____

3 어느 날 아침식사에 우리 어린이들은 우리가 더 이상 야생에서 뛰어 놀 수 없을 거라는 것에 완전히 실망한 채로 연락을 받았다.

One morning at breakfast we children were informed (to / our / utter / dismay) that (run / be / we / would / no / to / wild / permitted / longer).

➔ ____

➔ ____

1

As most mothers know, (a) (to / embarrassment), an infant able to use the word "Daddy" (b) (아기가 보는 어떤 남성에게도 가끔 사용할지도 모른다.). (c) On learning to use "Kitty" for a cat, it is apt to apply it to a dog.

1 문맥상 괄호 (a)의 단어를 바르게 배열하여 자연스러운 글의 흐름이 되도록 하시오. (단, 추가 단어 한 개 있음)

(a) (to / embarrassment)

➜ ______________________________

2 괄호 (b) 의 우리말을 아래 제시어만을 사용하여 영작하시오.

제시어

to / it / occasion / on / sees / may / apply / male / any / it

➜ ______________________________

3 〈보기〉를 참고하여, (c) 의 문장을 알맞게 부사절로 바꾸시오.

─┤ 보기 ├─

On arriving at home, I started to do my homework.
→ As soon as I arrived at home, I started to do my homework.

On learning to use "Kitty" for a cat, the baby is apt to apply it to a dog.

➜ ______________________________

4 위의 글을 요약하고자 할 때, 박스 안의 단어를 활용하여 빈칸을 채우시오. (단, 필요시 단어의 형태를 변형할 것)

extend	encourage	reject
physical	disguise	mental
perplex	lexical	similar

When a child learns a new word, he or she tends to _______ the term by using it as a label for _______ _______ objects.

2

The surest way Ⓐto lose child's trust is Ⓑto pretend that you know when you really don't. It may work once, and it may work twice, but in the end you Ⓒwill find out and Ⓓit will be a long time Ⓔbefore you win back the child's confidence. I don't mean that (a) (아이가 물어보는 모든 질문을 아이가 완벽히 만족하도록 대답해주어야 한다).

1 밑줄 친 Ⓐ~Ⓔ 중 어법 상 어색한 것을 한 개 찾고, 해당 표현을 문맥에 맞게 바르게 고치시오.

번호   틀린 표현   바른 표현

_______ : _________________   _________________

2 본문의 내용과 일치하도록 빈칸에 들어갈 적절한 표현을 넣으시오. (단, 철자가 제시된 경우 해당 철자로 시작하는 단어를 문맥에 맞게 쓸 것)

Once you lose your child's trust, it t______ a long time to _______ _______.

→ ____

3 괄호 ⓐ의 우리말을 아래 제시어만을 사용하여 영작하시오.

→ ____

when, before (시간의 부사절) 구문

미리 Voca 

❑ **drop by** 들리다	❑ **condition** 상태
❑ **give someone a call** ~에게 전화를 걸다	❑ **stability** 안정(성)
❑ **immigrant** 이주민, 이민자	❑ **force** 힘
❑ **come upon** ~을 우연히 만나다	❑ **readjust** 다시 조정하다
❑ **pant** (숨을) 헐떡이다	❑ **preserve** 보존하다, 보호하다
❑ **scene** 장면	❑ **a variety of** 다양한
❑ **come across** 우연히 만나다	❑ **disturb** 방해하다
❑ **oak** 떡갈나무	❑ **appear** 나타나다, ~인 것 같다
❑ **vanish** 사라지다	❑ **excess** 초과
❑ **replace** 대신[대체]하다, 바꾸다[교체하다]	❑ **primarily** 주로
❑ **fundamental** 근본적인	❑ **substance** 물질, 본질, 요지
❑ **art** 기술, 예술	❑ **equilibrium** 평형 (상태)
❑ **seek to** ~을 추구하다	❑ **ascendancy** 지배력을 행사할 수 있는 위치
❑ **maintain** 유지하다	

형태	접속사 before/ when + 주어 동사

해석 방법	When I saw her last, / she lived in L.A. ⇒ 내가 그녀를 지난번에 만났을 때, 그녀는 L.A에 살았다. You must finish the work before I come back. ⇒ 당신은 끝마쳐야 한다. / 내가 돌아오기 전에

참고	• 시간, 조건의 부사절에서 현재 시제가 미래 시제를 대신한다. I will go on a picnic when he will come back.(x) I will go on a picnic when he comes back home.(o) cf) I don't know when she will come. ⇒ 타동사 know의 목적어로 의문사절이 쓰여 여기서의 when은 의문사이므로, "언제"라고 해석한다.

Exercise 01 우리말에 맞게 괄호 안의 단어를 바르게 배열하시오.

1 내가 소나기를 만났을 때, 나는 매우 멀리까지 가지는 못했다.

(gone / far / not / in / was / had / shower / a / I / very / when / I / caught).

→ ____

2 내가 그를 다시 만나기 전까지 5년이 흘렀다.

(met / him / before / was / five / I / again / years / It).

→ ____

3 그녀가 내일 여기에 오게 되면, 나는 그녀에게 저녁식사를 살 것이다.

(buy / will / when / comes / her / dinner / tomorrow / she / here / I).

→ _______________________, _______________________.

4 그들이 집에 도착하기 전에, 그들은 Jane의 집에 들를 것이다.

(by / house / before / they / Jane's / are / get / drop / they / going / to / home).

→ ________________________ , ________________________ .

5 Joe는 그가 그의 일을 끝마치기 전에 너에게 전화할거라고 말했다.

(his / finishes / Joe / to / before / will / said / you / he / he / call / work / give / a).

→ ________________________

6 당신이 당신의 일이 끝날 때 우리에게 알려주세요.

(us / work / please / you / let / when / know / with / are / done / your).

→ ________________________

7 최초의 이주민들이 캐나다에 도착했을 때 아무도 살고 있지 않았다.

(no / one / arrived / when / first / living / in / the / there / Canada / immigrants / was).

→ ________________________

Exercise 02 각 문제를 우리말에 맞게, 괄호 안의 단어를 알맞게 배열하시오.

1 그가 나이 먹은 개를 우연히 만났을 때, 멀리까지 가지 못했다. 그 나이 먹은 개는 마치 먼 길을 달려온 것처럼 숨을 헐떡거렸다.

(far / not / had / gone / he / came / when / an old dog / upon / he). The dog was panting, (a / it / been / long / had / if / way / as / running).

→ ________________________

→ ________________________

2 30분도 안 되어 안개가 걷히기 시작하고, 이상한 장면이 나타났다.

(hour / an / half / was / it / began / clear / to / up / before / the fog) and (presented / strange / itself / scene / a).

→ ____

→ ____

3 그는 길옆에 큰 떡갈나무의 그늘 아래서 쉬고 있는 네 명의 낯선 사람들을 만나기 전 1마일도 가지 않았다.

(a mile / had / not / he / / gone / came / across / before / four strangers, / he) (shade / a / the side / oak / by / in / the road / big / of / resting / the / of).

→ ____

Exercise 03 각 지문을 읽고, 물음에 답하시오.

1

(a) (고양이가 나에게 그의 근처로 오라고 허락한 것이 여러 날이 지났다) without bounding away and vanishing, and (b) (he would <u>not</u> allow me to put a hand on him <u>for two or three weeks</u>).

1 괄호 (a) 의 우리말을 참고하여, 〈보기〉의 단어를 바르게 고치시오.

┤보기├

(days / come / to / was / the cat / It / me / near / when / allowed / many / him)

→ ____

2 〈보기〉를 참고하여 괄호 (b) 의 문장을 부정어 강조 문장으로 바꾸시오.

┤보기├

Jane did <u>not</u> come back <u>until</u> Tom went to see her.
→ Not until Tom went to see her did Jane come back.

→ ____

2

Although paper was used all over China, and had replaced other materials by the fifth century, it was three hundred years (a)(멀리 있는 Baghdad의 도시까지 퍼지게 되었다). (b) The invention was <u>not</u> introduced into Europe <u>until the twelfth century</u>.

1 괄호 (a)의 우리말을 아래 제시어만을 사용하여 영작하시오.

> **제시어**
>
> even / as / the city / Baghdad / before / it / of / as / far / reached

2 〈보기〉를 참고하여 밑줄 친 (b)의 문장을 부정어 강조하는 문장으로 바꾸시오.
(단, 접속사 until + S + V, 전치사 until + 명사는 부정어와 함께 It was not until [강조어] that 강조구문을 이용하여 도치할 것.)

> ────┤ 보기 ├────
>
> I could <u>not</u> see her <u>until the fall</u>. → <u>It was not until</u> the fall <u>that</u> I could see her.

The invention was <u>not</u> introduced into Europe <u>until the twelfth century</u>.

→ ____

Exercise 04 아래 지문을 읽고, 물음에 답하시오.

To the Hippocratic physician, the fundamental principle of his art was the concept that nature seeks to maintain a condition of stability; its forces are constantly adjusting and readjusting the normal parts of the body to preserve a balance among them. When this balance exists, we are healthy. Under any of a variety of influences, the equilibrium may be disturbed, (가)(한 부분이 과도하게 보이는 결과를 가져온다). When this happens, sickness appears, (특정 질병은 주로 어느 물질이 우세하게 되었느냐에 따라 달라진다).

＊ equilibrium 평형 (상태) ascendancy 지배력을 행사할 수 있는 위치

1 괄호 (가)의 우리말을 아래 조건에 맞게 영작하시오.

─● 조건 ●─
- [S V ~ , V-ing ~]에서 분사구문에 해당하는 부분을 영작할 것.
- 동명사의 의미상의 주어 표현이 포함되어 있음.
- 아래 제시된 단어를 모두 포함하되 동사의 형태를 문맥에 맞게 적절하게 변형할 것.
  제시어 in / in / part's / excess / appear / result / one

→ ____

✔️ 고난도

2 괄호 (나)의 우리말을 아래 조건에 맞게 영작하시오.

─● 조건 ●─
- 아래의 예시와 같은 독립분사구문이 되게 할 것.
  예시: The sun set, birds singing in the trees.
- 의문형용사가 이끄는 명사절을 포함할 것.
- 아래 제시된 단어만을 사용할 것.
  제시어 the ascendancy / depending / the particular disease / primarily / upon / substance / has gained / which

→ ____

3 본문의 내용과 일치하도록 조건에 맞게 제시된 문장의 빈칸을 채우시오.

─● 조건 ●─
- ⑧의 경우 아래에 정의되는 r로 시작하는 총 7개의 철자로 된 단어임.
  정의: to return something or someone to an earlier good condition or position
- Ⓐ와 Ⓒ의 경우 본문에서 찾아 넣을 것.

It is the function of the physician to help the patient's Ⓐ_______ body to ⑧_______ the state of Ⓒ_______.

Ⓐ_______ ⑧ r_______ Ⓒ_______

until, since (결과, 시간의 부사절) 구문

미리 Voca 

- **faint** (빛·소리·냄새 등이) 희미한[약한], (가능성 등이) 아주 적은 (=slight)
- **part** 갈라지다, 헤어지다
- **hear from** ~의 소식을 듣다
- **nibble** 조금씩 물어뜯다
- **take** (~로) 데리고 가다
- **distant** 먼 적개심
- **have an opinion of** ~에 대해 견해를 가지다
- **reflect** 반영하다
- **attitude** 태도
- **homely** (자기 집처럼) 아늑한[편안한], 가정적인, 따뜻한

- **torture** 고문, 고문하다
- **resentment** 분개
- **smolder** 연기나다, 밖으로 나타나다
- **flare** 확 타오르다, 불길
- **hostility** 적대감
- **poverty** 빈곤
- **in poverty** 가난한, 가난하게
- **but** ~이외에는
- **ridicule** 조롱
- **contemporary** 동시대의, 당대의, (어떤 사람과) 동년배[동시대인]

형태	until/since + 주어 동사

해석 방법	I will <u>wait</u> here / until you come back. ⇒ 여기서 기다릴 것이다 / 나는 당신이 돌아올 때까지 Cath has not phoned since she went to NewYork. ⇒ 전화를 한 적이 없다 / Cath는 뉴욕에 간 이후로

참고	• since가 현재완료 구문과 함께 쓰일 때 since와 함께 하는 종속절의 시제는 『과거부터 지금까지 쭉』 의 의미이므로, 과거형을 써준다. I <u>have lived</u> in Anyang <u>since</u> I <u>got married</u> in 2011.

Exercise 01 다음의 밑줄 친 접속사의 의미에 주의하여, 알맞게 해석하시오.

1 The sound became fainter and fainter, <u>until</u> it disappeared.

→ ____

2 Ten years have passed <u>since</u> we parted.

→ ____

3 It was the first time I'd had visitors <u>since</u> I'd moved to London.

→ ____

4 They moved here in 2002, <u>until</u> then they'd always been in the London area.

→ ____

5 <u>Until</u> she spoke, I had not realized she wasn't English.

→ ____

6 He left home two weeks ago <u>and</u> we haven't heard from him since.

→ ____

Exercise 02 각 문제를 우리말에 맞게, 괄호 안의 단어를 알맞게 배열하시오.

1 Dick의 고양이는 대양으로 이동해서 건너갔다. 그 배는 항해하고 또 항해했다. 마침내 그 배가 멀리 떨어저 있는 나라에 도착할 때까지.

Dick's cat was taken across the ocean. The ship sailed and sailed, (until / came / at last / to / a distant country / it).

→ ____

2 그 쥐는 야금야금 먹어서 그녀의 날카로운 치아로 밧줄로 이어진 그물을 자르기 시작했다. 그 쥐는 차례로 밧줄을 빠르게 씹어 먹었다. 그물에 큰 구멍이 생겨 사자가 풀려날 때 까지.

(cutting / of / the net / and / her / sharp / nibbling / the ropes / the mouse / with / teeth / began). One rope after another she bit through quickly, (hole / the / until / in / there / was / net / a large) and the lion was free.

→ ____

→ ____

3 우리의 세상은 당신이 성장한 이후로 크게 변해왔다. 그러나 우리 학교는 (당신만큼이나) 아주 빠르게 변하지 않는다. 오늘날의 교육은 대단하지 않다.

(you / changed / our / grew / has / a / world / up / since / lot). But our schools aren't changing fast enough. Education today is not great.

→ ____

1

You cannot love others, if you do not honestly love yourself. Having a poor opinion of yourself – (a)(그것에 대한 이유가 있든지 없든지)–will be reflected in your attitude toward the people around you. If (b)<u>you are tortured by being too short or too homely or too unsuccessful</u>, your resentment will smolder, (c)(마침내 세상에 대한 적개심으로 타오르게 된다).

1 괄호 (a)의 우리말을 아래 제시어를 사용하여 영작하시오.

> **제시어**
>
> not / or / for / is / whether / there / it / reason

🏁 도전

2 밑줄 친 (b)의 문장을 다음 단어로 시작하는 3형식 능동문이 되도록 재진술하시오.

If being ____

3 괄호 (c)의 우리말을 아래 제시어만을 사용하여 영작하시오.

> **제시어**
>
> toward / flares / until / it / into / hostility / the / world

4 다음은 본문을 요약한 것이다. 박스 안의 단어를 활용하여 빈칸을 채우시오. (단, 필요시 본문의 단어를 변형시킬 것)

inferior	honest	hostility
stance	attractive	superiority
negative	reflection	encouraging

Having a(n) __________ opinion of yourself will have an effect on your ________ on people around you. In other words, if you have ________ point of view toward the world, you will be __________ to everything around you.

2

It (a) __________ (be) hundred years since Henry Rousseau was born, and this man who (b) __________ (live) all his life in poverty and (c) __________ (receive) little but ridicule from his contemporaries, (d) __________ (now, honor) as one of the greatest masters of the nineteenth century.

1 괄호 안의 단어를 활용하여 밑줄 친 (a), (b), (c), (d) 안에 들어갈 동사의 바른 형태를 쓰시오. (단, (d)의 경우 부사의 위치에 주의할 것)

(a) _________________

(b) _________________

(c) _________________

(d) _________________

2 다음은 위 글을 요약한 것이다. 다음 빈칸을 채우시오. (단, 본문의 단어를 그대로 또는 변형하여 활용하되, 마지막 빈칸은 본문에 언급되지 않은 c로 시작하는 단어임)

This passage is about a biography of master Henry Rousseau, where he had hard time ______ in poverty and ______ ______ by contemporaries, nonetheless, he is ______ to be a great maestro in time.

27 when (관계부사) 구문

미리 Voca 

- **By the time S V,** S V ~할 때 쯤
- **the majority of** 대부분의
- **glorious** 영광스러운
- **pass away** 지나가다, 사라지다
- **be worth v-ing** ~할 가치가 있다
- **reach** 다다르다
- **ominous** 불길한 (=foreboding)
- **mist** 안개
- **existence** 존재
- **essence** 본질, 정수
- **existentialism** 실존주의

- **content** 만족한
- **loaf** 한 덩이, 빵 한 덩어리
- **diversity** 다양성
- **adversity** 역경
- **progress** 진전, (목표 달성·완성을 향한) 진척[진행]
- **choked** 숨이 막히는
- **stale** 신선하지 않은, 진부한
- **ventilate** (방 등을) 환기하다
- **unventilated** 환기되지 않은
- **chill** 아주 춥게 만들다, 냉기, 한기, 오한

Key Point

형태	명사(선행사) + 관계부사(when) + 주어 + 동사

해석 방법	That was the day / when we met for the first time. ⇒ 이 날은 그 날이었다 / 우리가 처음으로 만났었던.

참고	• by the time A, B~: ~할 때쯤 A시점에서 B가 완료되었음을 나타낸다. 그리고 A는 미래 사건일지라도 현재형을 사용한다. It'll be almost dark / by the time we refuel. ⇒ 우리가 다시 주유를 할 때쯤이면, 거의 어두워질 것이야.

Exercise 01 아래 우리말을 제시된 단어만을 활용하여 영작하시오.

1 당신이 나의 도움을 필요하게 될 날이 올 것이다.

(you / will / my / come / when / will / need / the time / help).

→ ____

2 그 회의는 당신이 거기에 도착할 때쯤이면, 끝날 것이다.

(over / by the time / be / there / will / you / get / when / the meeting).

→ ____

3 제발 내일 다시 와주세요, 그러면 그 때 그가 집에 도착할 것이다.

Please come again tomorrow, (at / home / be / when / he / will).

→ ____

4 그는 이번 휴가로부터 돌아올 때쯤에 모든 일이 완성되어 있기를 원한다.

(everything / he / from / wants / this vacation / back / done / comes / by the time / he).

→ ____

5 크리스마스 시즌은 많은 사람들이 다른 날들 보다 좀 더 행복해하는 시기이다.

Christmas season is (time / when / people / happier / than / a / other days / feel / many).

→ ____

6 그가 졸업할 때쯤이면, 그는 대학에서 4년을 보낼 것이다.

(time / he / graduates / the / by), (spent / he / in / will / four / have / years / college).

→ ____

Exercise 02 각 문제를 우리말에 맞게, 괄호 안의 단어를 알맞게 배열하시오.

1 다행히도, 대부분의 사람들은 전쟁을 영광스러운 것이라고 생각하는 시절은 지나갔다.

Fortunately, (the days / away / passed / have) (the majority of/ when / people / thought) of war as something glorious.

→ ____

→ ____

2 그가 내년 봄에 집으로 돌아갈 때쯤이 되면 London에서 볼만한 가치가 있는 모든 연극을 다 보는 것이다.

(will / He / seen / have) every play in London that is worth seeing (time / the / returns / next / by / spring / home / he).

→ ____

→ ____

3 우리가 산 정상에 도착했을 때쯤 이미 해가 떠 있었다.

The sun was already up (by the time / of / we / the mountain / reached / the top).

→ ____

도전

4 영웅이 어두운 하늘을 배경으로 불길하게 서 있는 성에 도착할 때쯤, 그 용은 이미 안개 속으로 사라졌었다.

(time / castle / the / the / hero / by / the / reached), (stood / which / sky / ominously / dark / the / against), (the / had / mist / the / into / vanished / dragon / already).

→ ____

→ ____

→ ____

고난도

5 그 시대가 바로 인간 존재의 본질을 의문시하는 철학인 실존주의가 새로운 삶의 의미를 찾으려는 사상가들 사이에서 인기를 얻었던 때였다. (관계부사절 내 동격의 코마 활용)

That was (who / gained / among / questioned / sought / life / when / new meaning / of / thinkers / human existence, / the very essence / a philosophy / in / existentialism, / popularity / that / the era).

→ ____

____

____

1

Civilization is a product of (a) ___________ . (b) <u>The great civilizations of all time seem to have arisen</u> where nature made production possible only a part of the year, and thus (c) (man / it / for / to / work / necessary / made) and (d) (그가 농사지을 수 없는 때를 대비하여 저축하다). Man does not naturally like to work steadily, and if nature enables him (e) _________ (avoid) (f) <u>it</u>, he usually seems content to loaf rather than labor and progress.

1 위 글을 읽고, 밑줄 친 (a) 에 들어갈 알맞은 단어를 고르시오.

① diversity ② university ③ varsity ④ nature ⑤ adversity

2 〈보기〉를 참고하여, 밑줄 친 (b) 의 문장과 같은 의미의 문장으로 바꾸시오.

───── 보기 ─────

The production of the company seems to have decreased recently.
→ It seems that the production of the company decreased recently.

The great civilizations of all time seem to have arisen.

→ ____

3 괄호 (c) 의 단어를 "가목적어/진목적어" 구문에 맞게 배열하시오.

→ ____

4 괄호 (d) 안의 우리말을 아래 제시어만을 활용하여 영작하시오.

제시어

save / he / when / not / for / up / the / time / produce / could

→ ____

5 괄호 안의 단어를 활용하여 밑줄 친 (e)의 바른 형태를 쓰시오.

6 밑줄 친 (f)의 it이 지칭하는 단어나 문장을 우리말로 쓰시오.

➜ ____

2

When do you get into the telephone box, you feel half choked by stale, unventilated air; and (a)(by / begun / your / you / conversation / have / the time), your back is chilled by the cold looks of (b)(조급한 마음으로 자기 순서를 기다리는 누군가).

1 괄호 (a)의 단어를 문맥에 맞게 바르게 배열하시오.

➜ ____

2 괄호 (b)의 우리말을 아래 제시어만을 사용하여 영작하시오. (단, 필요시 단어의 형태를 변형할 것)

제시어

take / who / place / is / impatience / somebody / to / your

미리 Voca 

- **philosophical** 철학적
- **accept** 받아들이다
- **explore** 탐구하다
- **universally** 보편적으로
- **lead to** ~로 이끌다
- **masterpiece** 명작
- **compose** 작곡하다
- **timeless** 시간을 초월한, 영원한
- **phenomena** 현상
- **long-term** 장기적인
- **gain** 이득
- **intend** 의도하다
- **efficiency** 효율성
- **operate** 작동되다, 가동[조작]하다, 수술하다, 운영하다
- **have one's nose in a book** 책에 몰두하다, 책벌레이다

- **poetry** 시 cf. **poet** 시인
- **advancement** 진보, 발전
- **accessible** 접근 가능한
- **absolute** 절대적인
- **given** 특정한, 정해진
- **fittest** 적임자, 가장 잘 적응한
- **superior** 뛰어난, 눈에 띄는
- **inferior** 열등한, 질 낮은
- **relate** (말·글로) …에 대하여 이야기하다[들려주다], 관련시키다
- **firsthand** 직접적으로, 직접 체험으로
- **inventive** 발명의
- **appropriate** 적절한, 알맞은
- **liven up** 활기를 띠다, 활기를 띠게 만들다
- **eliminate** 제거하다
- **dull** 따분한, 흐릿해지다

🔑 Key Point

형태	부정어 + all, both, always, every, necessarily

해석방법	Bottled water / is not necessarily safer / than tap water. ⇒ 생수가 / 반드시 좀 더 안전한 것만은 아니다 / 수돗물 보다

참고	• Tap water is not always less healthy than bottled water.
	  ⇒ 수돗물은 생수보다 항상 덜 건강한 것은 아니다.
	• All that glitters is not always gold.
	  ⇒ 빛난다고 해서 항상 모두 금은 아니다.

Exercise 01 다음 우리말을 제시된 단어만을 활용하여 영작하시오. (단, 각 문장의 동사 한 개의 형태를 변형할 것)

1 현실의 본질을 탐구하기 위해 고안된 모든 철학적 사상들이 보편적으로 받아들여지는 진리를 이끄는 것은 아니다.

(truths / design / to / philosophical ideas / accepted / all / explore / to / reality / not / the nature / universally / of / lead).

→ ____

2 뛰어난 기술로 작곡된 모든 음악 작품이 영원한 명작이 되는 것은 아니다.

(masterpiece / compose / musical piece / skill / a / every / becomes / with / not / timeless / great).

→ ____

3 자연 현상을 설명하려는 모든 과학적 이론이 시간이 지나면서 입증되는 것은 아니다.

(time / every / correct / proven / natural phenomena / aim/ explain / to / is / scientific theory / not / over).

→ ____

4 권력을 얻기 위해 만들어진 모든 정치적 전략이 장기적인 성공으로 이어지는 것은 아니다.

(in / power / all / result / not / long-term / gain / political strategies / to / create / success).

→ ____

5 행동을 지침하기 위해 고안된 모든 사회적 규범이 사회 구성원들 모두에게 받아들여지는 것은 아니다.

(accepted / is / society / to / all members / not / guide / of / by / every / behavior / intend / social norm).

→ ____

6 효율성을 향상시키기 위해 설계된 모든 AI 시스템이 오류 없이 작동하는 것은 아니다.

(every / improve / efficiency / operates / to / AI system / not / without / errors / design).

→ ____

Exercise 02 각 문제를 우리말에 맞게, 괄호 안의 단어를 알맞게 배열하시오.

1 우리들은 모든 소년과 소녀들이 독서하는 것은 좋아하는 것은 아니다 라는 것을 안다. 이것은 항상 책만 들여다보는 아이들보다 덜 똑똑하다는 것을 의미하지 않는다.

We know that (like / read / to / not all / girls / boys / and). This doesn't mean that these children are less "bright" than ("their noses in a book." / have / always / who / those).

➜ ____

➜ ____

2 대부분의 시인들은 행복하지 않기에 시를 쓴다고 여겨진다. 그러나 비록 그것 안에 약간의 진실이 있을지라도 이것은 완전히 사실은 아니다. 그러나 Poe의 경우, 그것은 사실이었다.

(unhappy / write / they / to / poetry / said / because / most poets / are / are) ; (this / not / is / altogether / true), though there is some truth in it. But in Poe's case it was true.

➜ ____

➜ ____

🚩 도전

3 생명을 구하기 위해 개발된 모든 의학적 진보가 모든 환자에게 접근 가능한 것은 아니다.

(all / is / every / not / advancement / to / patients / lives / accessible / developed / medical / to / save).

➜ ____

____

1

It must be clearly understanding that the 'fittest' which survive are not necessarily best or highest on any absolute standard, but simply fittest for the given conditions.

1 본문과 일치하도록 괄호 안의 단어를 바르게 배열하시오.

In brief, we must keep in mind that (fittest / means / condition / fittest / something / for / the / given / merely)

➜ ____

2 위의 문장 전체에서 어법상 <u>어색한</u> 부분을 찾아 바르게 고치시오.

틀린 표현		바른 표현
_______________	⇨	_______________

2

(a) (어떤 나라나 타국들로부터 전적으로 고립되어서는 살 수 없다) and contact between nations always results in affecting their languages. When two languages compete, (b) (승리가 반드시 가장 완전한 언어에 돌아가는 것은 아니다.) (c) <u>Nor is it always the nation whom culture is superior that makes the nation of inferior culture to adopt its language.</u>

1 괄호 (a) 의 우리말을 제시어만을 사용하여 영작하시오.

제시어

lives / entirely / others / no / nation / isolated / from

2 괄호 ⓑ 의 우리말을 제시어만을 사용하여 영작하시오.

> **제시어**
>
> perfect / fall / to / always / not / does / language / the victory / the most

3 밑줄 친ⓒ 의 문장에서 어법상 어색한 부분을 <u>두 곳</u> 찾아 바르게 고치시오.

틀린 표현		바른 표현
_______________	⇨	_______________
_______________	⇨	_______________

Exercise  **04** 아래 지문을 읽고, 물음에 답하시오.

> People tell about their own experiences all the time, but ⒜<u>they do not necessarily tell about the same experience in the same way every time</u>. The telling process, even in the relating of a firsthand experience, can be a highly inventive process. That is, (b)(이야기하는 기술이란 자신의 경험을 청중에게 적절하게 표현할 수 있는 좋은 방법을 찾는 것을 의미한다). A fine line exists, therefore, between invented stories and the relation of firsthand experiences. The entertainment factor exists in relating firsthand experiences just as it does in inventing stories. (c) <u>Nobody wants to listen to what happened to you today unless you cannot make what happened appear interesting</u>. The process of livening up an experience can involve simply telling that experience in such a way as to eliminate the dullest parts, or it also can involve 'improving' the dull parts by playing with the facts.

1 밑줄 친 ⒜ 의 표현을 같은 의미의 다른 문장으로 표현하려고 한다. 빈칸에 들어갈 말을 채워 넣으시오. (단, 반드시 way를 사용할 것)

> People tell about the same experience _____ _____ _____ when they tell about their own experiences.

2 괄호 (b)의 우리말을 아래 제시어만을 사용하여 영작하시오. (단, 필요시 단어의 형태를 변형할 것)

제시어

express / one's / ways / find / in / to / a / to / involves / the art / storytelling
/ appropriate / of / way / the listener / experiences / good

3 밑줄 친 (c)에서 틀린 부분을 찾아 바르게 고치시오.

틀린 표현		바른 표현
	⇨	

4 본문의 내용을 한 문장으로 요약하려고 한다. 빈칸에 들어갈 단어를 본문에서 찾아 문맥에 맞게 쓰시오.

When we narrate our (a) _______ experiences, we tend to (b) _______ what happened
in order to make our story (c) _______ for the listeners.

이중부정 구문

미리 Voca 

- **misunderstanding** 오해
- **be done with** ~을 끝내다
- **think of** ~을 떠올리다
- **perfume** 향수
- **semiconductor** 반도체
- **complete** 완전한, 완료하다, 끝마치다
- **perspective** 관점
- **uneasy** 불안한
- **attendant** 수반되는
- **evil** 악, 사악한
- **fairy** 요정

- **midst** 한가운데
- **silver lining** 희망의 빛줄기
- **saying** 속담
- **Every dog has his day.** 쥐구멍에도 볕 들 날이 있다.
- **permanence** 영성속, 불편, 내구성
- **inspire** 고무[격려]하다, 영감을 주다
- **lasting** 지속하는
- **universal** 보편적인
- **occupy** 차지하다, 사로잡다
- **calling** 소명 (의식) (=vocation), 천직

| 형태 | 한 문장에 부정표현이 두 개가 있어 긍정의 의미를 나타낸다. |

| 해석
방법 | I never see this picture / without thinking of her.
⇒ 나는 이 그림을 본 적이 없다 / 그녀를 생각하지 않고서는.
= Whenever I see this picture, I think of her.
　　나는 이 그림을 볼 때 마다, 그녀를 생각한다.
There is nothing in history but teaches us a good lesson.
= There is nothing in history that doesn't teach us a good lesson.
　　우리에게 훌륭한 교훈을 가르쳐주지 않는 것은 역사에 아무 것도 없다. |

| 참고 | • but은 that ~ not과 같이 절의 형태로 바꿀 수도 있지만, except 또는 except for와 같은 전치사(구)로 바꿀 수 있다.
Nobody sets the rules but you. = Nobody sets the rules except for you.
　　당신을 제외하고는 어느 누구도 규칙을 정하지 못한다. |

Exercise 01 　 **다음 우리말을 주어진 단어만을 활용하여 영작하시오.**

1 나는 너의 어머니를 생각하지 않고서는 너를 본 적이 없다.

(never / your / I / see / think / but / I / of / mother / you).

→ ____

2 그가 너무 영리해서 그가 그 쉬운 문제를 풀지 못할 어떠한 이유도 거의 없었다. (so ~ that구문 활용)

(any / there / solve / was / the / problem / hardly / why / he / clever / was / that / he / reason / couldn't / so / easy).

→ ____

3 아무도 내일 무슨 일이 일어나는지에 대해 모른다.
(happen / tomorrow / what / no / will / knows / one).

→ ____

4 이러한 종류의 오해는 흔치 않은 것은 아니다.
(misunderstanding / of / is / this / uncommon / kind / not).

→ ____

5 그녀는 그 일을 끝내지 않는다면, 너를 만날 수 없다.
(see / done / you / with / she / she / it / unless / cannot / is).

→ ____

6 쏟아지지 않으면 비는 오지 않는다. (= 비만 오면 쏟아진다.)
(it / pours / but / never / rains / it).

→ ____

7 나는 그의 이름을 모르는 어떠한 누구도 찾을 수 없다. (= 그의 이름만 알면 찾을 수 있다.)
(cannot / know / find / his / who / I / any / one / not / does / name).

→ ____

1 삼촌 John은 나의 돌아가신 아빠랑 너무 많이 닮아서 삼촌을 보면 나의 아버지가 생각난다.

Uncle John resembles my dead father so much that (never / but / father / I / him / look at / my / I / think of).

→ ____

2 행복은 향기와 같아서 먼저 자기 자신에게 몇 방울 뿌리지 않고서는 다른 사람에게도 냄새를 낼 수 없다.

Happiness is perfume (others / on / you / cannot / put) (without / getting / a few drops / yourself / on).

→ ____

→ ____

3 당신은 물감으로 그 안에 있는 즐거움을 즉시 깨우지 않고서는 다른 사람에게 그림을 그리라고 시킬 수는 없다.

(paint / man / have / a / pictures / you / cannot) (in him / without / waking / instantly / a pleasure) in the paints.

→ ____

🚩 도전

4 반도체 산업의 잠재력을 제외하고는 세계 경제 성장에 대한 어떠한 논의도 결코 완전하지 않다.

(is / economic / but for / global / about / the potential / complete / discussion / no / of / growth / the semiconductor industry).

→ ____

5 나는 19세기 여류 작가의 소설을 읽을 때마다, 새로운 사회적 관점을 발견한다.

(a / by / a new perspective / read / on / a novel / 19th-century / I / society / never / without / discovering / female author).

→ ____

Exercise 03 각 지문을 읽고, 물음에 답하시오.

1

Men seem always to have had an uneasy feeling that unusual good luck must have an attendant evil. That is, good fairies never arrive _________ a bad one in their midst. However, every silver lining had a cloud.

1 위의 글과 일치하도록 빈칸에 알맞은 단어를 쓰시오. (단, 해당 철자로 시작하는 단어를 쓸 것)

Most people tend to f________ u________ when they meet odd good luck with a_______ evil, yet it is important to remember that there is a saying, "Every dog had his day".

2 문맥 상 빈칸에 들어갈 전치사는?

→ _______________________

As a form of literature a newspaper (a) lack, it is true, the element of permanence; but the ideas (b) with that it seeks (c) to inspire its readers produce an effect that is lasting. It is the only kind of a reading that is universal. No one is so (d) occupied with the business of his calling but he finds time (e) reading the newspaper.

1 위 글의 내용과 일치하도록 괄호 안의 단어를 바르게 배열하시오. (단, 추가 단어는 없지만, 필요시 어형변화 할 것)

Although a newspaper lacks permanence, the ideas it seeks to inspire in its readers have a lasting effect, ⓐ(of / the / form / most / universal / make / it / reading), as ⓑ(time / busy / schedules / their / finds / everyone / despite / it / to / read).

ⓐ of / the / form / most / universal / make / it / reading

➜ ____

ⓑ time / busy / schedules / their / find / everyone / despite / it / to / read

➜ ____

2 (a)~(e) 중에서 어법상 틀린 것을 <u>세 개</u> 골라 알맞게 고치시오.

번호	틀린 표현		바른 표현
______ :	______________	⇨	______________
______ :	______________	⇨	______________
______ :	______________	⇨	______________

미리 Voca 

☐ **curious** 호기심 많은	☐ **weigh down** ~을 (마음·기분을) 짓누르다
☐ **performance** 성능	☐ **jettison** 버리다, 폐기하다
☐ **sleek** 세련된, 윤이 나는, (모양이) 매끈한[날렵한]	☐ **get rid of** 제거하다
☐ **issue** 문제	☐ **conceivable** 상상할 수 있는, 가능한
☐ **exhibit** 전시하다	☐ **cooperate** 협력하다
☐ **artifact** (특히 역사적·문화적 의미가 있는) 인공물[가공품]	☐ **accompany** 동행하다
☐ **fitness** 건강	☐ **insane** 정신 이상의, 미친
☐ **reduce** 줄이다	☐ **complacent** 자기만족의
☐ **greenhouse gas emissions** 온실가스배출	☐ **needless** 불필요한
☐ **carbon capture** 탄소포집(대기 중의 이산화탄소를 분리하는 기술)	☐ **acceptance** 받아들임[수락], 동의, 승인
☐ **combat** 막다, 퇴치하다	☐ **commonplace** 아주 흔한
☐ **revolutionize** 대변혁[혁신]을 일으키다	☐ **progressively** 계속해서
☐ **conduct** 수행하다, 행하다	☐ **vibe** 분위기, 느낌
☐ **decentralize** 탈중앙화하다	☐ **retail** 소매, 소매하다
☐ **transaction** 거래	☐ **virtuous** 덕이 있는, 고결한
☐ **oblige** 강요하다, ~하게 하다	☐ **reciprocate** 주고받다, 보답하다
☐ **obey** 따르다	☐ **jollity** 명랑, 즐거움
☐ **fulfil** 실현하다	☐ **suffer from** ~을 앓다
☐ **ambition** 야망	☐ **depression** 우울증
☐ **be aware that S V** ~인 것을 인식하다	☐ **at risk of** ~의 위험에 처한
☐ **talent** 재능	☐ **in kind** 동일한 것으로, 현물로
☐ **status** 지위	☐ **transmit** 전송하다, 전염시키다, 전도하다

| 형태 | not only A but also B 구문 (B as well as A) |

| 해석
방법 | I like to eat / not only apples / but also bananas.
⇒ 나는 먹는 것을 좋아한다 / 사과뿐만 아니라 / 바나나도.
It goes without saying that/ healthy men / are happier / than sick men.
⇒ ~라고 말할 필요도 없다 / 건강한 사람이 / 더 행복하다 / 아픈 사람보다 |

| 참고 | • I like to eat not only apples but also bananas.
= I like to eat bananas as well as apples.
(사과뿐만 아니라 바나나 먹는 것도 좋아한다.)
• It goes without saying that healthy men are happier than sick men.
= It is needless to say that healthy men are happier than sick men.
(건강한 사람이 아픈 사람보다 더 행복하다는 것은 말할 필요도 없다.) |

Exercise 01 다음 우리말을 제시된 단어만을 활용하여 영작하시오.

1 이 책은 역사뿐만 아니라 과학도 다뤄서 호기심 많은 독자들에게 좋다.

(but / science / not / only / covers / this / also / book / history), making it a great choice for curious readers.

→ ____

2 새 스마트폰은 세련된 디자인뿐만 아니라 강력한 성능으로도 찬사를 받고 있다.

The new smartphone is (performance / powerful / design / but also / praised / for / its / its / sleek / not only).

→ ____

3 그녀의 연설은 환경 문제뿐만 아니라 사회 정의에도 초점을 맞춰 청중들에게 영감을 주었다.

Her speech inspired the audience (environmental / also / on / but / not / justice / only / issues / social / focusing / by).

→ ____

4 그 박물관은 현대 미술뿐만 아니라 고대 유물도 전시하는 것으로 유명하다.

The museum is (exhibiting / also / only / ancient / but / not / famous / for / modern / art / artifacts).

→ ____

5 클럽에 가입하면 당신의 신체 건강뿐만 아니라 당신의 정신 건강도 개선하는 데 도움이 된다.

Joining the club will (physical / fitness / also / help / your / your / not / mental / only / but / improve / health / you).

→ ____

🚩 도전

6 탄소 포집은 온실가스 배출을 줄일 뿐만 아니라 기후 변화를 효과적으로 막는 데도 도움을 준다. (단, not only를 문두로 하는 도치문이 되도록 할 것)

(reduce / emissions / gas / carbon capture / does / greenhouse / not only), (change / combat / it / helps / but / effectively / climate / also).

→ ____

→ ____

🚩 도전

7 비트코인은 금융 시장에 혁명을 일으켰을 뿐만 아니라, 거래를 탈중앙화된 방식으로 수행하는 방법을 도입했다.

(Bitcoin / market / revolutionized / has / financial / not / only / the), (conducting / a / has / introduced / of / but / also / way / decentralized / it / transactions).

→ ____

→ ____

1 시민으로서 우리는 단순히 법을 제정하는 것에서만 책임을 지는 것이 아니라 그 법을 따르는 것에도 책임을 진다.

We, as citizens, are responsible (merely / not / for / laws / making) (also / them / for / but / obeying).

→ ____

2 나는 그가 그의 문학적인 야심을 실현할 수 있을지 없을지 의심스럽다, 왜냐하면 나는 그것이 능력과 노력뿐만 아니라 행운이 뒷받침되어야한다는 것을 알기 때문이다.

(able / to / will / whether / am / be / fulfil / I / doubtful / he / his literary ambitions), for I am aware that (effort / as / well / it / good / and / talent / as / requires / luck).

→ ____

→ ____

3 나는 그들이 비합리적인 요구를 할 것 같아 유감스럽다. 그러나 당신이 지불해야하는 것 이상으로 지불할 필요 없다는 것은 말할 나위 없다.

I am afraid that they will make an unreasonable demand. But (goes / saying / that / not / pay / you / need / you / obliged / are / than / to / more / it / without).

→ ____

🚩도전

4 사람들은 자신의 절대적인 지위뿐만 아니라 다른 사람의 지위와 관련된 자신의 지위에도 관심을 갖는다.

People (relative / about / care / only / other / also / status / status / but / to / absolute / not / status / about / people's / their / their).

→ ____

📌 **도전**

5 우리를 짓누르는 쓰레기를 버려야 할 뿐만 아니라, 필수적이지 않은 것은 무엇이든 제거해야 합니다.
(단, not only를 문두로 하는 도치문이 되도록 할 것)

(weighs / us / not only / jettison / we / that / the junk / should / down), but (that / we / not / need / get rid of / is / anything / essential / also / to).

* jettison 버리다

→ ____

→ ____

✔ **고난도**

6 기후 변화를 해결하는 시급성은 알려진 위험을 이해하는 것뿐만 아니라 앞으로 닥칠 수 있는 예측 불가능하고 잠재적으로 치명적인 미지의 위험에 대비하는 것에도 있다.

The urgency to address climate change (for / and / not only / the / potentially / risks / lethal / known / preparing / in / that / ahead / unpredictable / in / the / lies / understanding / unknowns / may / but also / lie).

→ ____

Exercise 03 각 지문을 읽고, 물음에 답하시오.

1

In any (a) <u>conceivable</u> kind of culture, man needs to cooperate with others if he wants to survive, (b) (적 또는 자연의 위험에 대해 자신을 방어하기 위한 목적이든), or (c) (그가 일을 하여 생산할 수 있도록). Even Robinson Crusoe was accompanied by his man Friday; (d) <u>without him, he would probably not only have become insane but would actually have died.</u>

1 밑줄 친 (a)와 바꿔 쓸 수 있는 것을 고르시오.

① applicable   ② imaginable   ③ available

④ derivable   ⑤ intangible

2 괄호 ⓑ의 우리말을 제시어만을 사용하여 영작하시오.

┤ 보기 ├

(enemies / defending / of / himself / or / nature / the purpose / of / for / whether / against / dangers)

➜ ____

3 괄호 (c)의 우리말을 제시어만을 사용하여 영작하시오.

┤ 보기 ├

(may / in order that / be / he / to / produce / able / and / work)

➜ ____

4 아래 〈보기〉를 참고하여, 밑줄 친 (d)의 문장을 전환하시오.

┤ 보기 ├

<u>Without</u> a car, we could have had time moving a remote distance.
→ <u>But for</u> a car, we could have had time moving a remote distance.
→ <u>If it had not been for</u> a car, we could have had time moving a remote distance.
→ <u>Had it not been for</u> a car, we could have had time moving a remote distance. (if 생략도치)

Without him, he would not only have become insane but would actually have died.

➜ ____

➜ ____

➜ ____

2

It began to seem that one would have to hold in the mind forever (a) (상반되는 것처럼 보이는 두 개의 생각). The first idea was acceptance of life as it is, and men as they are: in the light of this idea, (b) it goes without saying that injustice is a commonplace. Nevertheless this did not mean that one could be complacent, for the second idea was of equal power: in other words one must never accept this injustice as commonplace but must fight them with all one's strength.

1 괄호 (a)의 우리말을 제시어만을 사용하여 영작하시오.

> **제시어**
>
> ideas / seemed / two / in / opposition / which / to / be

➜ ____

2 아래 〈보기〉를 참고하여, 밑줄 친 (b) 의 문장을 전환하시오.

> ─────────────| 보기 |─────────────
>
> It goes without saying that good health is more important than wealth.
> → It is needless to say that good health is more important than wealth.

It goes without saying that injustice is a commonplace.

➜ ____

3 본문의 내용과 일치하도록 빈칸을 채우시오. (단, 본문의 언급된 단어만을 활용하되 필요시 문맥에 맞게 단어의 형태를 변형할 것)

> Even if ________ is prevalent, man should not ________ it as ________ and instead ________ it with all his force.

➜ ____

If you're sharing a living space with someone suffering from mild depression, you're at risk of becoming <u>progressively</u> more depressed the longer you live with them – <u>you pick up their negative vibes</u>. Likewise, (가)<u>bank tellers and retail staff really can lift the mood of customers by smiling at them and asking them how they are</u>. When <u>customers respond in kind</u>, which they usually do, <u>that rubs off on the staff</u>. It leads to a virtuous circle of reciprocated jollity and, more to the point if you're a bank or shop manager, increased sales. <u>Some retailers have taken this to heart</u>; one high-end fast-food chain has shown that (나)<u>such feelings can transmit not just from one person to another</u>, but across entire social worlds of friends and work colleagues.

＊ vibe (보통 pl.) 분위기, 모양, 기분, 느낌

1 본문의 <u>문맥적</u> 정의로 옳지 <u>않은</u> 것은?

① <u>progressively</u>: gradually or step by step

② <u>pick up negative vibes</u>: to absorb or sense negative feelings or emotions

③ <u>respond in kind</u>: to react in the same way or manner

④ <u>rub off on</u>: to influence or have an effect on someone in a good way

⑤ <u>take something to heart</u>: to be deeply affected by or take something very seriously

✔ 고난도

2 밑줄 친 (가)의 문장을 아래 조건에 맞게 영작하시오.

• 조건 •
• Not only로 시작하는 도치문이 되게 할 것.
• do so를 포함하여 영작할 것.

(가) bank tellers and retail staff really can lift the mood of customers by smiling at them and asking them how they are.

➡ ____

3 본문의 밑줄 친 (나)의 내용에 비추어 아래 빈칸에 들어가기에 적절한 표현을 쓰시오. (힌트. c로 시작하는 10개의 철자로 구성된 단어임)

According to the passage, feelings are __________.

미리 Voca 

☐ **groundbreaking** 획기적인	☐ **layer** 층
☐ **relativity** 상대성	☐ **layers of** 여러 층의
☐ **dominant** 지배적인	☐ **hostile** 적대적인
☐ **urgent** 긴급한	☐ **deprive** 빼앗다
☐ **invention** 발명(품)	☐ **noble** 숭고한, 귀족의
☐ **impact** 영향	☐ **temple** 사원
☐ **intention** 의도	☐ **intolerance** 참을 수 없음
☐ **atmospheric** 대기의, 분위기 있는	☐ **impose** 부과하다, 강요하다
☐ **superstition** 미신	☐ **vivid** 생생한, 선명한
☐ **weave** 엮다	☐ **considerably** 많이, 상당히
☐ **existential** (인간의) 존재에 관한[관련된], 실존주의적인	☐ **snail** 달팽이
☐ **surrealism** 초현실주의	☐ **stuck** 움직일 수 없는
☐ **complexity** 복잡성	☐ **rage** 격노, 격노하다
☐ **thorough** 철저한	☐ **passage** 통로, 구절
☐ **struggle** 갈등	

🔑 Key Point

| 형태 | No/ Nothing + as 원급 as or No/ Nothing + 비교급 than |

| 해석방법 | Nobody / in the world / is as brave / as he.
이 세상에서 / 아무도 용감하지 않다 / 그만큼. |

| 참고 | • He is the bravest in the world. (최상급)
　= No one is as brave as he in the world. (원급)
　= No one is more brave than he in the world. (비교급)
　= He is more brave than any other person in the world. (비교급)
• Health is the most important thing in the world.
　= Nothing is as important as health in the world. (원급)
　= Nothing is more important than health in the world. (비교급)
　= Health is more important than any other thing in the world. (비교급) |

Exercise 01　다음의 우리말을 괄호 안의 단어만을 바르게 배열하여 영작하시오.

1　역사상 어떤 발견도 상대성 이론만큼 획기적이지 않았다.

(of / the / in / been / history / theory / relativity / no / groundbreaking / has / than / more / discovery).

→ ____

2　현대 문학에서 어떤 소설도 앵무새 죽이기만큼 영향력 있지는 않았다.

("To Kill a Mockingbird" / modern / more / influential / has / no / in / been / than / novel / literature)

→ ____

3　농구에서 어떤 선수도 마이클 조던만큼 지배적이지 않았다.

(in / has / more / than / player / dominant / Michael Jordan / been / ever / no / basketball).

→ ____

4 어떤 환경 문제도 기후 변화만큼 긴급하지 않다.

(than / is / no / change / climate / more / issue / urgent / environmental).

→ ____

5 어떤 발명품도 스마트폰만큼 통신에 큰 영향을 미치지 않았다.

(had / the smartphone / communication / a / than / on / has / invention / impact / greater / no).

→ ____

Exercise 02 **각 문제를 우리말에 맞게, 괄호 안의 단어를 알맞게 배열하시오.**

1 어떤 것도 너의 말을 들으려는 최소한의 의도가 없는 누군가와 이야기하려고 하는 것보다 우스꽝스러운 일은 없다.

(than / more / absurd / is / nothing) trying to talk to (the / of / someone / hasn't / least / you / to / listening / intention / who).

→ ____

→ ____

2 어떠한 사람들도 영국사람 만큼이나 날씨에 대해 너무 많은 이야기를 하지 않는다. 그 날의 대기 상태로 너의 대화를 시작하고 끝내라 그러면, 당신은 당신의 영국인 친구와의 흥미를 계속해서 이어나가는데 실패하지 않을 것이다.

(British / so much / talk / no people / the / weather / about / the / as). Begin and end your conversation with the atmospheric condition of the day, and (up / interest / never / you / of / your British friends / will / the / keep / to / fail).

→ ____

→ ____

3 아마도 어떠한 주제도 날씨만큼이나 많은 미신을 가지고 있는 것도 없을 것이다. 그것은 날씨가 우리에게 너무나 중요하기 때문이다.

Perhaps (superstitions / so / many / as / no subject / the weather / has). It is probably (weather / so / is / important / because / the / to / us).

→ ____

→ ____

🚩 도전

4 많은 작가들이 하루키 무라카미처럼 초현실주의와 존재론적 질문들을 이야기 속에 효과적으로 엮을 수는 없다.

(many authors / as / a story / of / weave / not / surrealism / effectively / as / Haruki Murakami / into / existential questions / can / elements / and)

→ ____

🚩 도전

5 맥컬러(McCullough)가 자신의 저서에서 한 것처럼, 가장 철저한 역사적 분석도 미국 혁명의 복잡성을 완전히 포착할 수 없다.

(most / the American Revolution / capture / analysis / can / as / the complexity / fully / not even / writings / thorough / does / his / the / in / McCullough / of / historical).

→ ____

✔ 고난도

6 한강(Han Kang)의 글에서 한 번의 제스처도 무시되지 않으며, 모든 작은 움직임이 등장인물들의 심리적 갈등의 깊은 층을 드러낸다.

(goes / unnoticed / in / not / writing / single / Han Kang's / a / gesture), as (struggles / her / layers / reveals / characters' / psychological / deeper / of / every / movement / small).

→ ____

→ ____

2

No loss by flood and lightning, no destruction of cities and temples by the hostile forces of nature, (a) <u>has deprived man of so many noble lives as those which his intolerance has been destroyed</u>.

1　밑줄 친 (a)에서 어법상 어색한 부분을 골라 알맞게 고치시오.

➜ ____

2　다음은 본문의 내용을 재진술 한 것이다. 아래 힌트에 맞게 괄호 안의 단어를 바르게 배열하여 재진술문을 완성하시오.

┤ 힌트 ├

• 비교급을 활용한 최상급 표현임.
• 관계대명사 what의 [what + S + V]의 구조를 포함하고 있음.

The antagonistic forces of nature (it / life / man's / impact / imposes / on / than / less / his / intolerance / on / have / what).

➜ ____

2

(a) They say that nothing is more vivid than a picture. We disagree. (b) (단어에 반응하여 정신세계에 의해 창출되는 이미지보다 더 생생한 시각적 이미지는 없다).

1 They say that구문을 수동태 구문으로 바꾸려고 한다. 〈보기〉를 참고하여 제시된 문장을 전환하시오.

| 보기 |

They say that health is more important than wealth.
  S   V   O

→ That health is more important than wealth is said (by them).
                   S   V

→ It is said that health is more important than wealth. (일반인 주어 생략)
   S V

They say that nothing is more vivid than a picture.

→ ____

2 괄호 (b) 의 우리말을 아래 제시된 단어만을 활용하여 영작하시오.

제시어

in response to / no / so / created / the image / is / words / by / as / visual image / the mind / vivid

→ ____

Exercise 04 아래 지문을 읽고, 물음에 답하시오.

> Nothing is worse than driving on a two-lane road with a speed limit of 40 mph and coming up behind someone going 25. You have to slow down considerably, and (가)(그 운전자가 속도를 내지 않거나 차를 길가에 대지 않을 때에는 짜증이 난다). ⓐ(차선이 더 많은 고속도로에서), slow drivers should move to the right and ⓑ(더 빠른 운전자가 추월하다). When you're stuck behind someone traveling at a snail's pace and ⓒ(그를 돌아 갈 공간이 없다). ⓓ(이것이 도로 분노와 사고의 원인이다).

1 괄호 (가) 안의 우리말을 아래 단어를 사용하여 영작하시오. (추가단어와 어형변화 있음)

that / frustrate / when / neither / pull over / speed up / it

➜ ____

2 괄호 ⓐ~ⓓ의 우리말을 아래 제시된 단어를 활용하여 영작하시오.

ⓐ more / on / where / lanes / are / highways / there

➜ ____

ⓑ faster / them / let / pass / drivers / the

➜ ____

ⓒ no / around / room / there's / him / to / get

➜ ____

ⓓ rage / accidents / what / that's / causes / and / road

➜ ____

3 According to the passage, what is most responsible for highway accidents? (본문에 제시된 단어만을 활용할 것)

someone ________ ________ ________ ________ ________

미리 Voca 

☐ **remarkable** 놀라운	☐ **enormous** 거대한
☐ **achievement** 성취	☐ **figure** 숫자, 인물, 이해하다, 계산하다
☐ **persuasive** 설득력 있는	☐ **solitude** 고독
☐ **argument** 주장	☐ **wander** 돌아다니다, 헤매다
☐ **competitor** 경쟁자	☐ **interval** 간격, 사이
☐ **masterpiece** 걸작	☐ **solitary** 혼자의, 고립된
☐ **detrimental** 해로운	☐ **drawback** 결점, 장애
☐ **destabilizing** 불안한	☐ **frequent** 빈번한
☐ **measure** 조치	☐ **criticism** 비판, 비평
☐ **stabilize** 안정화시키다	☐ **niche** 틈새, 딱 맞는 위치
☐ **conduct** 실행하다	☐ **affluent** 부유한
☐ **comprehensive** 포괄적인	☐ **globe** 지구본, 구체
☐ **besides** 게다가	☐ **judicious** 신중한, 판단력 있는
☐ **respectable** 존경할만한	☐ **premium price** 특정 제품이나 서비스가 유사한 다른 제품이나 서비스에 비해 높은 가격
☐ **lamb** 양	☐ **weed** 잡초
☐ **digest** 소화시키다	☐ **boost** 신장시키다, 북돋우다, 증가시키다
☐ **district** 지역	☐ **face** 직면하다
☐ **be subject to** ~을 당하기 쉽다, 걸리기 쉬운 쉽다, ~의 지배를 받다	

🔑 Key Point

형태	as 원급 as any other + 단수명사 / 비교급 than any other + 단수명사

해석 방법	The book / is as interesting / as any other thing. ⇒ 그 책은 / 재밌다 / 어떠한 다른 것만큼 Tom / is wiser / than any other man / in the world ⇒ Tom은 좀 더 현명하다 / 어떠한 다른 사람보다 / 세상에서

참고	• The book is as interesting as any other thing.
	  : The book이 any other thing과 비교대상이 되어야 하므로, 주어와 일치하는 단수명사를 써 준다.
	• Tom is wiser than any other man in the world.
	  : Tom이 any other man과 비교대상이 되어야 하므로, 주어와 일치하는 단수명사를 써 준다.

Exercise  아래 우리말을 주어진 단어만을 활용하여 영작하시오.

1 이 발명은 현대 과학의 어떠한 다른 업적만큼 놀랍다.

(other / in / science / remarkable / invention / this / as / any / as / achievement / is / modern)

2 제인은 그녀의 반에서 어떠한 다른 학생보다 더 부지런하다.

(than / Jane / more / her / other / in / diligent / is / class / any / student)

3 그의 주장은 우리가 들었던 어떠한 다른 제안만큼 설득력이 있었다.

(persuasive / as / his / heard / as / any / other / was / argument / proposal / we've).

4 그 운동선수는 그 경기에서 어떠한 다른 경쟁자보다 더 빨리 달렸다.

(other / competitor / than / the athlete / in / ran / any / the race / faster).

5 이 그림은 박물관의 어떠한 다른 명작만큼 아름답다.

(as / is / other / beautiful / as / in / masterpiece / this painting / the museum / any).

Exercise 02   아래 우리말을 주어진 단어만을 활용하여 영작하시오.

1 인플레이션은 경제를 불안정하게 만드는 데 어떠한 다른 요인보다 더 해롭다.
(detrimental / factor / than / in / other / is / an economy / inflation / more / destabilizing / any)

2 그 정책은 경제를 안정시키기 위해 도입된 어떠한 다른 방책만큼 효과적이다.
(to / the policy / other / effective / measure / is / introduced / stabilize / any / as / as / the economy)

3 이 연구는 심리학 분야에서 진행된 어떠한 다른 연구보다 더 포괄적이다.
(than / any / the / conducted / more / psychology. / is / other / study / research / field / of / in / this / comprehensive)

Exercise 03   각 문제를 우리말에 맞게, 괄호 안의 단어를 알맞게 배열하시오.

도전

1 그는 매우 잘생기고 부자였다. 그리고 게다가 그는 내가 여태껏 만났던 사람들 중에서 가장 존경할만한 사람이었다.
He was very handsome and rich. And besides (was / a gentleman / I / he / ever met / as / respectable / as).

➔ ____

2 모든 일반적인 고기 중에서, 소고기, 양고기는 확실히 최고의 맛이며, 어떠한 다른 것만큼이나 쉽게 소화가 된다.
Of all the ordinary meats, beef and lamb certainly taste the best, and (easily / other / as / are / any / digested / as).

➔ ____

3 인생에서 행복과 성공은 어떠한 다른 유일한 것 보다 건강에 달려있다. 어떤 사람이 나무가 거의 없고, 신선한 공기와 풀도 거의 없는 지역에서 산다고 했을 때, 그는 많은 질병의 대상이 된다.

(health / than / in / and / upon / life / happiness / depend / success / any / more / good / other / single / thing). When a man lives in a district (there / trees / are / few / where), and (is / little / there / grass / and / where / air / fresh), (is / to / many / subject / he / disease).

→ ____

→ ____

→ ____

Exercise 04   각 지문을 읽고, 물음에 답하시오.

1

(가)(그는 우리 시대의 위대한 소설가들 중의 한 사람이었다). He was an enormous figure. (나)(그의 소설들은 어느 것 못지않게 후세에 남을 가능성이 많다) that have been written in the last hundred years.

1 괄호 (가)의 우리말을 아래 제시어를 활용하여 영작하시오. (단, 필요시 어형변형을 하고 추가 단어 있음)

제시어

of, great, novelist, our day

→ ____

2 괄호 (나)안의 우리말을 제시된 단어만을 활용하여 영작하시오.

제시어

his / good / surviving / a chance / any / as / as / of / have / novels

→ ____

2

(a) <u>My life, more than that of anyone I know, has spent in solitude and wandering.</u> From my fifteenth year–save for a single interval–(b) (나는 현대인이 경험한 아마 가장 고독한 생활을 했다).

1 밑줄 친 (a)에서 어법상 어색한 곳을 찾아 바르게 고치시오.

틀린 표현   ⇨   바른 표현

_________________   _________________

✔ 고난도

2 괄호 (b) 안의 우리말을 참고하여 〈보기〉 안의 단어를 알맞게 배열하시오.

─┤ 보기 ├─

제시어 modern / lived / about / have / as / as / life / any / has / a / solitary / man / experienced / I

→ _______________________________________

Exercise 05

Organic food production is growing by leaps and bounds now. Many consumers are willing to pay premium prices for organic foods. However, organic farming has some drawbacks. One of the most frequent criticisms is that (가)(유기농가의 곡물생산량은 전통적 농가의 그것보다 훨씬 낮다). That's because organic fields suffer more from weeds and insects than traditional fields. Another argument often offered by experts is that (나)<u>organic farming can supply food for niche markets of affluent consumers but cannot feed billions of hungry people around the globe.</u> Only judicious use of chemical inputs, not the costly organic methods, could help boost food production significantly in the countries facing hunger.

1 괄호 (가) 안의 우리말을 영작하려고 한다. 제시어를 모두 사용하여 영작하시오.

➜ ____

2 밑줄 친 (나)를 통해 알 수 있는 organic farming의 특징을 작성하려고 한다. 아래 빈칸에 들어갈 표현으로 가장 적절한 것은?

> Organic farming is not _________, which means it is not for everyone.

① democratic　　② practical　　③ scalable　　④ sustainable　　⑤ efficient

3 아래 빈칸에 들어갈 적절한 표현을 본문에서 찾아 문맥에 맞게 쓰시오.

> The author allows the judicious use of chemical inputs because _________________
> _______________________________.

4 본문의 내용을 한 문장으로 요약하려고 한다. 아래 빈칸에 들어갈 적절한 표현을 쓰시오.

> Organic agriculture is not as p________ as conventional farming and also cannot serve as the solution to world s___________.

미리
Voca 

❏ **advance** 발전	❏ **expose** 노출시키다, 폭로하다
❏ **issue** 문제	❏ **consciously** 의식적으로
❏ **confident** 자신감 있는, 확신하는	❏ **subconscious** 잠재의식적인
❏ **infant** 유아, 젖먹이, 아기	❏ **involve** 관련시키다, 포함하다
❏ **morality rate** 사망률	❏ **withstand** 견디다, 버티다
❏ **evolutionary** 진화의, 점진적인	❏ **adverse** 불리한, 반대의
❏ **instinct** 본능, 직관	❏ **root** 뿌리, 근원
❏ **stir** 유발하다[불러일으키다], 자극하다, 마음을 흔들다[동요시키다]	❏ **subject** 지배를 받는, 받기 쉬운, 주제, 과목
❏ **fade** 서서히 사라지다, 점점 희미해지다	❏ **sturdy** 튼튼한, 견고한
❏ **integrity** 진실, 완전함	❏ **virtually** 사실상, 가상으로
❏ **encounter** 마주치다, 부닥치다, 만남	❏ **vegetation** 초목

형태	The + 비교급 + 주어 + 동사, the + 비교급 + 주어 + 동사
해석 방법	The higher / we go up, the colder / the air becomes. 점점 높이 / 우리가 올라갈수록 / 점점 차가워진다 / 공기가
참고	• The 비교급, the 비교급은 이유의 부사절 As(이유)로 의미전환 할 수 있다. The more we eat, the more we get fat. = As we eat more, we get fat more. • John is the taller of the two boys. ⇒ John은 두 소년 중에서 키가 좀 더 크다 (둘을 비교할 때 정관사 the 사용에 주의한다.)

Exercise 01   괄호 안의 단어만을 사용하여 우리말을 영작하시오.

1 학업에 더 많은 노력을 기울일수록, 성공할 확률은 더 커질 것이다.

(greater / into / will / the / your / success / the / chances / you / of / effort / be / your / studies / put / more)

→ ______________________________, ______________________________

____

2 기술이 빠르게 발전할수록, 우리의 사회적 문제는 더 복잡해진다.

(advances / become / societal / our / the / complex / issues / technology / faster / more / the).

→ ______________________________, ______________________________

____

3 결정을 미룰수록, 올바른 선택을 하는 것이 더 어려워진다.
(the / it / longer / to / wait / make / a / right / the / decision / to / choose / you / the / difficult / becomes / option / more).

→ _________________________ , _________________________

____

4 자신의 능력을 향상시키기 위해 더 열심히 노력할수록, 자신감은 더 커질 것이다.
(harder / confident / the / your / you / more / in / abilities / will / you / skills / the / your / become / to / improve / work).

→ _________________________ , _________________________

____

5 역사에 대해 더 많이 배울수록, 과거의 사건들이 현재 세계를 어떻게 형성하는지 더 명확해진다.
(shape / about / how / you / events / more / becomes / present / learn / past / the / history / it / world / the / our / clearer)

→ _________________________ , _________________________

____

Exercise 02 다음 제시된 문장을 As로 시작하는 문장으로 전환하시오.

1 The more expensive a film is to produce, the more money it is likely to make.

→ _________________________

2 The more devices a hospital had, the more advanced its care was thought to be.

→ ____

3 The higher the infant morality rate, the greater the need for public health services.

→ ____

4 The higher an animal is in the evolutionary chain, the less it depends on instinct.

→ ____

Exercise 03 각 문제를 우리말에 맞게, 괄호 안의 단어를 알맞게 배열하시오.

1 우리가 숨을 쉴 때, 폐안으로 공기가 많이 들어가면 갈수록, 우리의 건강에 좀 더 좋다. 그래서 몇몇 가지의 운동이 너무나 좋은 이유이나.

(can / the more air / take / we / into / the lungs) at a breath, (for / health / is / the better / our / it). This is why some kinds of exercise are so good.

→ ____

2 그가 꽃을 바라보는 동안조차 그것이 사라져가고 있는 것을 알고 있었기 때문에 산사나무의 아름다움은 그를 더욱 깊이 감동시킨다.

The loveliness of May (all the more/ him / stirs / deeply) because he knows that it is fading even as he looks at it.

→ ____

3 Tom은 May랑 Sally와 사이좋게 지낸다. Mary는 부유하고 예쁘지만, Sally는 그렇지 않다. 그럼에도 불구하고, Tom은 둘 중에 Sally를 더 많이 사랑한다.

Tom gets along with Mary and Sally. Mary is rich and pretty, but Sally is not. Nonetheless (loves / Sally / of the two / Tom / the better).

➡ ____

도전

4 사회적 이동성이 민주주의 사회에서 많이 허용될수록, 더 많은 개인이 사회적 구별을 위해 노력한다.
(for / more / societies / democratic / individuals / the / more / strive / mobility / is / social / allowed / in / social / the / distinction).

➡ ______________________________ , ______________________

____

고난도

5 유명인이 소셜 미디어에서 팔로워와 더 많이 상호 작용할수록, 더 많은 팬이 그들에게 개인적인 참여와 책임을 기대합니다.
(more / more / their / on / personal / the / social / expect / and / the / followers / involvement / them / from / interact / fans / celebrities / media, / accountability / with).

➡ ______________________________ , ______________________

____

1

And (a) (그가 나이를 먹을수록, 그가 더 많은 고통을 받을 수 록, 그는 그녀를 좀 더 이해하게 되었다. (b) He understood that she had had a simple and an integrity, (c) (그가 어느 누구에게서도 만나지 못한 그런).

1 괄호 (a)의 우리말을 아래 제시어만을 사용하여 영작하시오.

제시어

suffered / more / older / to / the / more / understand / came / her / he / he / he / the / the / grew

➡ ＿＿＿＿＿＿＿＿＿, ＿＿＿＿＿＿＿＿＿＿＿＿＿, ＿＿＿＿＿＿＿＿＿＿

＿＿＿＿＿＿＿＿＿＿＿＿＿＿＿＿＿＿＿＿＿＿＿＿＿＿＿

2 밑줄 친 (b)에서 어법 상 어색한 것을 찾고, 해당 부분을 바르게 고치시오.

틀린 표현　　　　　　　　　바른 표현

＿＿＿＿＿＿＿＿＿　➪　＿＿＿＿＿＿＿＿＿

✔ 고난도

3 코마의 용례에 주의하여 괄호 (c) 안의 우리말을 아래 제시어만을 사용하여 영작하시오.

제시어

person / had / such / he / as / other / never / in / encountered / any

➡ ＿＿＿＿＿＿＿＿＿＿＿＿＿＿＿＿＿＿＿＿＿＿＿＿＿

2

The urban worker (a) <u>is exposed to noise,</u> (b) <u>most of it he learns</u> (c) <u>not to hear consciously,</u> but (d) <u>which nonetheless wear</u> him out, all the more owing to the subconscious (e) <u>effort involving in</u> not hearing it.

1 (a)~(e) 중에서 어법상 틀린 세 곳을 찾아 바르게 고치시오.

번호	틀린 표현		바른 표현
______	: ______________	⇨	______________
______	: ______________	⇨	______________
______	: ______________	⇨	______________

2 본문의 내용과 일치하도록 빈칸에 들어갈 단어를 본문에서 찾아 문장을 완성하시오.

> After all, all the more __________ wears the urban worker out on account of the
> __________ __________ not to hear it.

Exercise 05 아래 지문을 읽고, 물음에 답하시오.

After a windstorm, only the sturdiest trees remain standing. ①<u>The wind becomes harsh.</u> ②<u>A tree must be strong in order to withstand.</u> Trees that survive the most adverse weather conditions develop deep roots. (폭풍우를 겪은 숲은 보호 구역의 삼림 지대보다 훨씬 더 튼튼하다). The weaker trees have been removed, allowing more room for the stronger trees to thrive. A forest protected from adverse weather becomes overcrowded with thin, weak trees all competing for nutrients and sunlight. When this area is eventually exposed to a storm, virtually all of the vegetation will be leveled.

1 ①과 ②의 문장을 the 비교급, the 비교급을 활용하여 한 문장으로 영작하시오.

→ ____

2 괄호 안의 우리말을 아래 조건에 맞게 영작하시오.

> • 조건 •
> • 관계대명사를 포함한 주어가 포함되어 있음.
> • 아래 제시어만을 사용할 것.
> 제시어 storms / woodlands / areas / a forest / has / that / been / subjected / is / than / sturdier / to / protected / much / in

→ ____

3 본문에서 드러나는 자연의 법칙을 괄호 안의 단어를 포함하여 문맥에 맞게 빈칸 채워 넣으시오.
(survive, fit)

A law of ________ ________ ________ ________

4 본문의 내용을 두 문장으로 요약하려고 한다. 아래 빈칸에 공통으로 들어갈 단어를 본문에서 찾아 쓰시오. (단, 빈칸의 위치에 따른 품사의 변형 있음)

A forest constantly tested by ________ will grow and endure. The protected area, which is seldom exposed to ________ conditions, becomes weak with little longevity.

미리 Voca 

❑ **sense** 지각	❑ **vanquish** 이기다, 극복하다
❑ **be ashamed of** ~을 부끄러워하다	❑ **delicate** 연약한, 섬세한, 미묘한
❑ **employ** 고용하다, 도입해서 사용하다	❑ **amaze** 놀라게 하다
❑ **dull** 따분한	❑ **operation** 수술
❑ **skillful** 능숙한	❑ **surgeon** 외과의사
❑ **treat** 다루다	❑ **slip** 미끄러지다, 실수하다, 미끄러짐, 실수, (종이 등의) 쪽지
❑ **telescope** 망원경	❑ **instant** 즉각적인, 순간
❑ **accuracy** 정확성	❑ **impress** 감명을 주다, 인상을 남기다
❑ **means** 수단	❑ **calmness** 차분함, 평온함
❑ **dispute** 논쟁하다, 논쟁, 분쟁	❑ **hysterical** 지나치게 흥분한, 히스테릭한

| 형태 | 『~한다면』과 같은 조건문으로 해석되는 몇 가지 유형에 유의해서 학습한다. |

| 해석
방법 | Without air,/ we could not live for a long time.
⇒ 공기가 없다면,/ 우리는 오랫동안 살 수 없을 것이다. |

| 참고 | • In my shoes, you would not do such a thing. (shoes=입장)
⇒ 나의 입장이라면, 너는 그렇게 행동하지 못 할 것이다.
• Without air,/ we could not live for a long time.(If 생략문)
= But for air, we could not live for a long time.
⇒ 공기가 없다면,/ 우리는 오랫동안 살 수 없을 것이다. |

Exercise 01   우리말을 제시된 단어만을 사용하여 영작하시오.

1 지각이 있는 사람이 그렇게 행동한다면 부끄러울 것이다.

(do / man / would / be / of / ashamed / sense / so / a / to).

→ ____

2 그가 이야기하는 것을 들었다면, 너는 그녀를 위해 그를 데려갔을 텐데.

(would / for / hear / take / a / him / girl / talk / you / him / to).

→ ___________________, ___________________________

3 너의 입장이라면, 나는 그를 고용하지 않았을 것이다.

(your / I / place / employ / would / him / not / in).

→ ___________, ___________________________

4 음악이 없다면, 세상은 따분한 곳이 되었을 것이다.

(music / would / place / be / dull / the / world / without / a).

→ ___________, ___________________________

5 그가 그녀의 전화번호를 알았더라면, 그는 그녀에게 전화를 했었을 텐데.

(number / phone / had / he / her / known), (would / a / her / he / given / call / to / have).

➜ ________________________, ________________________

6 우산을 가져가라, 그렇지 않으면 너는 완전히 젖을 것이다.

(will / you / umbrella / wet / all / your / take / or / get).

➜ ________________, ________________________

Exercise 02   각 문제를 우리말에 맞게, 괄호 안의 단어를 알맞게 배열하시오.

1 더 능숙한 선생님이라면, 그런 학생을 다르게 다루었을 지도 모른다.

A more skillful teacher (such / treated / have / would / a student) otherwise.

➜ ________________________________

2 캘리포니아 Palomar 산 위에 있는 망원경은 가장 많은 실용성이 있는 망원경이라 믿어지고 있다. 좀 더 큰 망원경은 지구의 공기가 시야를 가리기 때문에 천문학자들로 하여금 좀 더 멀리 보게 하지 못할 것이다.

The telescope on Mount Palomar, California, (the / is / believed / telescope / be / largest / practical / to). A bigger one (allow / astronomers / not / to / see / farther / would), (view / because / air / earth's / the / the / clouds).

➜ ________________________________

➜ ________________________________

➜ ________________________________

3 내가 20살이라면, 나는 지금은 꽤 불가능했을 섬세함으로 내 학창시절에 관한 역사를 쓸 수 있었을 텐데.

At twenty (the history / could / I / have / school / of / days / my / written) (quite / impossible / an / now / accuracy / would / which / with / be).

→ ____

→ ____

Exercise 03 각 지문을 읽고, 물음에 답하시오.

1

(가) The free nations are doing their utmost to find peaceful mean for settling international disputes. (나) They know that another great war could destroy the victor and the vanquished like.

1 다음은 본문의 내용을 재진술한 것이다. 괄호 안의 단어만을 배열하여 문장을 완성하시오.

ⓐ(strive / to / international / free / reason / nations / settle / disputes / the / the) is that they are aware that ⓑ(war / victor / great / more / both / the / could / sweep / and / equally / the / vanquished / one).

2 밑줄 친 (a)와 (b)에서 어법상 어색한 것을 골라 바르게 고치시오.

	틀린 표현		바른 표현
(가)	____________	⇨	____________
(나)	____________	⇨	____________

2

Not long ago, I had a chance (a) <u>watching</u> a surgeon (b) <u>to perform</u> a delicate brain operation. (가)A slight slip of his hand would have meant an instant death for the patient. (c) <u>What</u> impressed me about the doctor (d) <u>was</u> not his skill but his (e) <u>amazed</u> calmness.

1 (a)~(e) 중에서 어법상 어색한 세 개를 골라 바르게 고치시오.

번호	틀린 표현	바른 표현
___ :	___________	___________
___ :	___________	___________
___ :	___________	___________

2 〈보기〉의 가정법 if의 대용 표현을 참고하여, 본문의 밑줄 친 문장 (가)를 제시된 표현으로 시작하는 문장으로 전환하시오.

| 보기 |

A woman of common sense wouldn't dare shout so hysterically.
→ If she were a woman of common sense, she wouldn't shout so hysterically.

(가) A slight slip of his hand would have meant an instant death for the patient.

= If there ___________________________, it would have meant an instant death for the patient.

= If his hand ___________________________, it would have meant an instant death for the patient.

양보(이유)를 나타내는 도치 구문

미리 Voca 

☐ **remarkable** 놀라운	☐ **groundbreaking** 획기적인
☐ **challenging** 힘든, 어려운	☐ **challenging** 어려운
☐ **task** 일, 작업	☐ **crucial** 중요한
☐ **refuse** 거절하다	☐ **subtle** 미묘한, 교묘한, 예민한
☐ **achieve** 성취하다	☐ **delicate** 연약한, 섬세한, 미묘한
☐ **against the odds** 어려운 상황을 무릅쓰고, 희박한 가능성을 이겨내며	☐ **faint** 희미한, 기절하다
☐ **primarily** 주로	☐ **obvious** 분명한, 명백한
☐ **fame** 명성	☐ **fame** 명성
☐ **face** 직면하다	☐ **circumstance** 상황, 형편
☐ **contribution** 공헌, 기여	☐ **publicity** 언론의 관심

🔑 Key Point

형태	(주격보어가 되는 품사) 형용사 or 명사 / as 주어 + 동사, 동사 as 주어 조동사~
해석방법	Happy / as they were,/ there was something missing. ⇒ 행복했을지라도 / 그들이 / 무언가 부족했다.
참고	• Try as he might, he could not open the door. 　그가 노력했을지라도, 그는 그 문을 열수 없었다.

Exercise 01

제시어를 포함하여, 각 우리말을 <u>양보도치구문</u>에 맞게 영작하시오. (단, 필요시 제시어의 형태를 변형할 것)

1 그가 어리긴 하지만, 그는 놀라운 리더십을 가지고 있다.
(young, remarkable)

→ ＿＿＿＿＿＿＿＿＿＿, ＿＿＿＿＿＿＿＿＿＿＿＿＿＿＿＿.

2 그 작업이 힘들긴 했지만, 그녀는 그것을 성공적으로 완료했다.
(challenging, task, complete)

→ ＿＿＿＿＿＿＿＿＿＿, ＿＿＿＿＿＿＿＿＿＿＿＿＿＿＿＿.

3 팀이 피곤하긴 했지만, 그들은 포기하지 않고 목표를 달성했다.
(tire, refuse, achieve)

→ ＿＿＿＿＿＿＿＿＿＿, ＿＿＿＿＿＿＿＿＿＿＿＿＿＿＿＿.

4 그 해결책이 불가능해 보였지만, 그것은 완벽하게 작동했다.
(improbable, solution, work)

→ ＿＿＿＿＿＿＿＿＿＿, ＿＿＿＿＿＿＿＿＿＿＿＿＿＿＿＿.

5 그들이 불리한 상황에 처해 있었지만, 그들은 낙관적인 태도를 유지했다.
(against, the odds, remain)

→ _________________________, ____.

Exercise 02 제시된 우리말에 맞게, 괄호 안의 단어를 알맞게 배열하시오. (단, <u>양보도치구문</u>에 주
의해서 영작할 것)

1 미국에서 비즈니스와 커뮤니티에서의 여성들의 역할이 중요했을 지라도, 대단히 많은 여성들이 그들
자신을 주로 아내의 입장으로 바라보았다.
(important / women's / is / America / life / and / community / in / in / business /
role / as), (primarily / a / many / housewives / themselves / great / as / see / women).

→ ____

→ ____

2 그가 용감한 소년이었기 때문에, 그는 그의 아버지와 함께 눈이 쌓인 산에 올라가라는 말을 들었을
때 두려워하거나, 무서워하지 않았다.
(was / boy / as / brave / he), he was neither afraid nor surprised (to / with / go /
up / he / mountain / his / father / when / snowy / told / the / was).

→ ____

→ ____

3 그는 위대한 발명가였을지라도, 그는 한 인간으로서 훨씬 위대했다. 그는 대단한 명성을 이뤄냈지만,
그는 결코 그것에 자만하지 않았다.
(great / he / as / inventor / was), he was much greater as a man. (achieved / he /
it / never / fame / a / but / great / took / pride / in).

→ ____

→ _________________________, ____.

✔ 고난도

4 그가 개인적인 삶과 경력에서 겪은 어려움이 얼마나 컸든지 간에, 앨런 튜링은 계산 이론과 인공지능 분야에 획기적인 기여를 했다.

(as / the challenges / his personal life and career / significant / faced / were / he / in), Alan Turing (to / and / artificial intelligence / the fields / made / of / contributions / groundbreaking / computation).

→ ____

→ ____

🚩 도전

5 탄소 포집 기술이 대규모로 구현하기 어려운 일이긴 하지만, 그것은 기후 변화에 맞서 싸우는 중요한 도구로 남아 있다.

(to / as / challenging / on a large scale / is / implement / carbon capture technology), (remains / tool / change / in / crucial / a / climate / it / combating).

→ ____

→ ____

Exercise 03 각 지문을 읽고, 물음에 답하시오.

1

(a) (비록 우리가 우리의 좋은 취향에 대해 자부심을 가진다 할지라도,) we are no longer free to choose the things we want, for advertising exerts a (b) <u>subtle</u> influence on us.

1 괄호 (a) 안의 우리말을 제시어만을 활용하여 영작하시오.

제시어

pride / ourselves / may / much / good / as / our / on / we / taste

→ ____

2 밑줄 친 (b)와 의미가 반대되는 단어를 고르시오.

① delicate   ② understated   ③ slight   ④ faint   ⑤ obvious

2

(a) (그는 비록 대단한 물리학자이지만), he is still great as a man. (비록 그가 공적 관심에 무관심하고 명성에 불편해하더라도), he achieved a greater fame than (b) <u>that</u> of any other scientist, Fame or external circumstances can change him very little.

---

1 괄호 (a)의 우리말을 아래 제시어만을 사용하여 영작하시오.

제시어

physicist / is / great / he / as

➡ ____

2 괄호 (c)의 우리말을 참고하여, 〈보기〉의 단어를 알맞게 배열하여, 밑줄 친 부분을 완성하시오.

| 보기 |

제시어 fame / indifferent / uncomfortable / publicity / so / is / with / about / and / he / as

➡ ____

3 밑줄 친 (b)의 that이 지칭하는 단어는?

미리 Voca 

☐ **struggle** 힘겹게 나아가다[하다]	☐ **voice** 목소리, 발언권
☐ **cabbage** 양배추	☐ **ignore** 무시하다
☐ **obstacle** 장애물	☐ **discussion** 논의
☐ **complete** 완료하다	☐ **marginalize** 사회적으로 소외시키다, 하찮게 여기다
☐ **be determined to** ~하기로 결심하다, ~하려고 굳게 마음먹다	☐ **driving force** 추진력, 원동력, 동기부여요인
☐ **be committed to** ~에 전념하다, ~에 책임을 다하다	☐ **order** 질서
☐ **solution** 해결책	☐ **irrespective of** ~와 관계없이
☐ **pull out** (어디에서) 나가다, 빠져나오다	☐ **affinity** 친밀감, 애정, 유사성
☐ **keep diaries** 일기를 쓰다	☐ **allegiance** 충성
☐ **explore** 탐구하다	☐ **mutual** 상호간의
☐ **realize** 깨닫다, 실현하다	☐ **obligation** 의무
☐ **existence** 존재	☐ **promote** 증진시키다
☐ **criticize** 비판하다	☐ **well-being** 행복, 복지

형태	No matter who, No matter which, No matter what, No matter when, No matter where, No matter how
해석 방법	No matter where I go,/ my dog follows me. ⇒ 내가 어디를 갈지라도, 나의 개는 나를 따라온다.
참고	•양보를 나타내는 부사절 구문: 주로, comma의 유무로 결정한다.

No matter who	whoever	누구일지라도
No matter which	whichever	어느 것일지라도
No matter what	whatever	무엇일지라도
No matter when	whenever	언제일지라도
No matter where	wherever	어디에 있을지라도
No matter how	however	어떨지라도

Exercise 01 다음 우리말을 제시어만을 활용하여 영작하시오.

1 당신이 지금 전 세계 어디에 있든지, 경제는 어려움을 겪고 있다.

(matter / you / in / no / the / now / are / world / where), economies are struggling.

______________________________________ ,

2 사람들이 양배추가 어떻게 요리되든지 간에 그것을 좋아하는 사람은 거의 없다.

Few people like cabbages (how / they / matter / no / are / cooked).

______________________________________ ,

3 누가 다음 대통령이 되든지, 국가가 직면한 도전은 동일하게 남을 것이다.

(who / no / the / becomes / next / president / matter), the challenges facing the nation will remain the same.

______________________________________ ,

4 어떤 장애물이 발생하든지 간에, 그녀는 프로젝트를 제시간에 완료할 결심을 하고 있다.

(obstacles / arise / what / matter / no), she is determined to complete her project on time.

→ ____,

5 그 일이 얼마나 어려워 보이든지 간에, 우리는 해결책을 찾겠다고 결심했다.

(how / difficult / task / matter / no / seem / the / may), we are committed to finding a solution.

→ ____,

Exercise 02 각 문제를 우리말에 맞게, 괄호 안의 단어를 알맞게 배열하시오.

1 지금 기차가 역에서 출발하기 시작했다. 플랫폼을 따라 뛰고 있는 저 남자는 아마도 기차를 타지 못할 것이다. 그 기차는 무슨 일이 있더라도, 결코 기다리지 않는다.

Now the train is starting to pull out. (not / will / platform / that man / probably / along / the / get / on / running). The train never waits, (what / no / matter / happens).

→ ____

→ ____

2 나는 우리가 어디에 살지라도, 우리가 무엇을 할지라도, 우리가 누구일지라도 우리 모두는 일기를 쓰도록 노력해야한다고 생각한다.

I believe that we should all try to keep diaries – (matter / where / are / no / we / living), (what / are / matter / we / doing / no), (we / are / no / matter / who).

→ ____

→ ____

→ ____

3 많이 배우면 배울수록, 어떠한 일을 하기엔 좀 더 수월해진다. 그래서 아무리 적은 능력을 가지고 있다 할지라도, 그가 하려고 노력만 한다면, 어떤 일을 한다는 것이 불가능하지는 않다.

The more one learns, the easier one can do things, so (how / no / little / ability / has / mater / a man), (to / tries / really / if / it / do / him / to / he / is / something / not / impossible / for).

→ ____

→ ____

4 우주 어디를 보든지, 우리는 더 많이 탐구할수록 존재와 존재의 본질에 대해 우리가 진정으로 아는 것이 얼마나 적은지 깨닫게 된다.

(matter / the / universe / in / look / where / no / we), the more we explore, the more we realize (and / existence / how / nature / know / truly / we / being / little / of / about / the).

→ ____

→ ____

5 정치 시스템에 대한 비판이 얼마나 깊이 있든지 간에, 사회적 불평등에 대한 논의에서 소외된 사람들의 목소리는 계속해서 무시된다.

(system / is / no / criticized / the / how / political / deeply / matter), (be / the voices / of / to / ignored / of / discussions / continue / in / social   inequality / the / marginalized).

→ ____

→ ____

Exercise 03 각 지문을 읽고, 물음에 답하시오.

1

The driving force behind any future international order must be a belief, (a) (no / it / expressed / matter / is / how), in the value of individual human beings irrespective of national affinities or allegiance and in common and mutual obligation to promote their well-being.

1 양보를 나타내는 부사절의 형태에 맞게 괄호 (a)의 단어를 글의 흐름에 자연스럽도록 배열하시오.

→ ______________________________

2 본문의 내용을 재진술 할 때 괄호 안의 단어를 바르게 배열하여 문장을 완성하시오. (단, 필요시 단어의 형태를 변형할 것)

The foundation of any future international order must be the belief (every / individual / in / the / of / inherent / worth), regardless of their nationality or allegiance, and (to / commitment / shared / a / their / advance / well-being).

→ ______________________________

→ ______________________________

2

(인생은 우리가 생각하는 그것이 그래야 한다고 생각하는 것만큼 흥미롭지 않습니다.) (나) (The other fellow's life seems full of adventure). No matter what your profession, or (다)(그 직업에서 얼마만큼 만족을 하는지), (라)there are moments when you wish you choose some other career.

1 괄호 (가)의 우리말을 아래 제시어만을 사용하여 영작하시오.

> think / to / ought / life / exciting / it / as / is / be / seldom / we / as

→ ____

2 괄호 (나)의 문장에서 밑줄 친 단어를 강조하는 강조구문을 만들려고 한다. 〈보기〉를 참고하여 전환하시오.

―| 보기 |―

Jane broke the glasses in the room.
• broke가 과거시제이므로, 강조구문 시제 또한 과거 〈was〉
→ It was Jane that broke the glasses in the room.

→ ____

3 괄호 (다)의 우리말을 아래 제시어만을 모두 활용하여 영작하시오.

> you / be / may / how / happy / in / no / matter / it

→ ____

4 밑줄 친 (라)의 문장에서 어법상 어색한 것을 골라 바르게 고치시오.

틀린 표현		바른 표현
_____________	⇨	_____________

MAGNUS 서술형 시리즈
고등영어 서술형 **기본편 8주완성**

2025년 1월 30일 초판 발행

지   지   박지성, 이진희
발 행 인   김은영
발 행 처   오스틴북스
주   소   경기도 고양시 일산동구 백석동 1351번지
전   화   070)4123-5716
팩   스   031)902-5716
등 록 번 호   제396-2010-000009호
e - m a i l   ssung7805@hanmail.net
홈 페 이 지   www.austinbooks.co.kr

ISBN   979-11-93806-59-3(53740)
정   가   18,000원

MAGNUS
서술형 시리즈

고등영어 서술형

기본편

8주완성

박지성 이진희 공저

정답 및 해설

오스틴북스
AUSTIN BOOKS

고등영어 서술형

기본편

8주완성

박지성 이진희 공저

정답 및 해설

도서 출판 오스틴북스

MAGNUS
서술형 시리즈

MAGNUS

정답 및 해설편

Unit 01 배수사 + as 원급 as 구문

Exercise 01

1 The prices of the land have risen twice as high as 10 years ago.
2 The wrestler is three times heavier than I.
3 You are not half as clever as you think you are.
4 Yumi has twice number of my books.
5 This street is half the width of that one.
6 of a prehistoric origin, but was commercialized by the Romans
   some of whom had as many as 10,000 slaves
7 has twice as much chance as a similar child in Detroit of ending up in the top 20% as an adult or has twice as much chance of ending up in the top 20% as an adult as a similar child in Detroit

Exercise 02

1 It has about three times as many people as the United States / it has only half as much land
2 The earth is millions of times heavier than any object
3 The pipes made of lead / lead is eleven times as heavy as water / It is so soft a metal that it can be hammered into various shapes
4 towns on the seashore do not suffer from extreme cold as much as do those

Exercise 03

1

1 If(When) all other things were equal,
2 earning
3 What a completely illogical decision

4 earn → earns
5 relative

해석 다른 사람들이 1년에 2만 5천 달러를 버는 동안에 5만 달러를 벌고 싶은가? 아니면 다른 사람들이 25만 달러를 버는 동안에 10만 달러를 벌고 싶은가? 상품과 서비스의 가격은 똑같다. 다시 말해 모든 다른 것들이 똑같으면 다른 사람들보다 두 배를 벌고 싶은가 아니면 당신 자신보다 두 배를 벌지만 다른 사람들의 반 이하를 벌고 싶은가? 놀랍게도 연구는 대다수의 사람들이 첫 번째 것을 선택한다는 것을 보여준다. 사람들은 다른 사람들보다 두 배를 버는 것이 그들이 가질 수 있는 것의 반을 번다는 것을 의미한다 해도 다른 사람들보다 두 배를 벌고 싶어 한다. 얼마나 완전히 비논리적인 결정인가! 그러나 H. L.Mencken이 비꼬듯이 "부자란 그의 아내의 여동생의 남편보다 1년에 100 달러를 더 많이 버는 사람이다."

2

1 ③ (one or more laborers 그 이상이 필요할 수 있다.)
2 ⑧ which → where ⑩ fraught → is fraught
3 ⑤
4 with at least three people watching
5 The cost could be four times what it could be

해석 원가견적은 시간견적에 필요 시간과 필요 노동력을 곱한 것을 의미한다. 다만 다수의 사람이 필요한 협동 문제를 조심해야 한다. 예를 들어, 한 회사에서 전기 모터를 제거하는데 아래와 같은 사람들이 필요하다. 커버를 제거할 양철공과 전기 공급을 중단할 전기 기사, 마운트를 풀어줄 기계 수리공 그리고 마운트에서 모터를 제거해줄 한명 혹은 그 이상의 사람이 있다. 이러한 상황은 비효율과 고노동력으로 가득차있다. 왜냐하면 모든 네 명의 사람들이 일정을 잡고 한명이 일하는 동안 세 명은 넋 놓고 지켜만 봐야하기 때문이다. 비용은 가능한 것의 최소 4배가 될 것이며 거래 중 하나가 제 시간에 나타나지 않으면 종종 더 커집니다.

Exercise 04

1 occupies / resulting in / being full
2 as in raisins / water / than in raisins
3 filled up / grapes / raisins

4 That water makes a big difference in how much they fill you up

🔍**해석** 물은 칼로리가 없지만 위장에서 공간을 차지하여 그것이 포만감을 만든다. 최근에 한 연구는 식사 전에 물 두 잔을 마신 사람은 더 빨리 배가 부르고, 더 적은 칼로리를 먹으며, 더 많은 몸무게가 빠진다는 것을 밝혀냈다. 수분 함량이 더 적은 음식보다 수분 함량이 더 많은 음식을 선택함으로써 바로 그 전략이 작동하도록 할 수 있다. 예를 들어, 포도와 건포도의 유일한 차이는 포도가 약 여섯 배 더 많은 수분을 함유하고 있다는 것이다.

어휘 take up (공간을) 차지하다 strategy 전략 water content 수분 함량 raisin 건포도 lettuce 상추 cucumber 오이

Unit 02 가정법 과거(완료) 구문

Exercise 01

1 If he heard of your marriage, he would be surprised.

2 If I had known the news, I should have told you.

3 If he had not been killed in the war, he would have been alive

4 If the sun were to rise in the west, I would not change my mind.

5 Had she known the importance of grit
she would have approached her career with more perseverance and passion

Exercise 02

1 If only people in the world could understand / there would be a better chance

2 Were it known that / I might lose my position.

3 I should have been a better writer / if I had devoted my whole life to literature

4 If Socrates had not questioned conventional wisdom
we might not have developed the critical thinking skills that are fundamental to modern philosophy

5 Had Morpheus not believed in Neo
the prophecy about the One might never have been fulfilled
humanity could have remained enslaved by the machines

Exercise 03

1

1 As he went mad, he was not easily forgotten.

2 madness

3 the hidden poet that was in him

🔍**해석** 그는 가난하여 항상 빚지고 있었다. 만약 그가 미치지 않았다면 그는 세인들 간에 쉽게 잊혀 졌을 것이다. 그러나 그가 미쳤기 때문에 안에 숨어있던 시적 소질이 풀려났다. 그는 다시 태어났다. 그의 영혼 깊은 곳에서부터 노래가 샘물처럼 솟아올랐다.

2

1 the folk songs

2 if we would know its basic desires and character traits

3 the evidence **that** we obtain from its folk songs

4 reflection

🔍**해석** 민요는 한 국가의 소박한 사람들로부터 유래해서, 평범한 사람들의 감정과 관심을 표현하기 때문에 사람들의 일상 생활의 한 부분이 되었다. 우리가 한 민족의 본질을 연구하기를 원한다면, 그 민족의 기본적인 욕구와 특징적인 특질을 연구하기를 원한다면, 민요로부터 얻는 흔적에 의해 많은 도움을 얻을 수 있을 것이다.

Exercise 04

1 No sooner had I started middle school than I realized that most of my fellow students had the idea that we Asian students are all smart.

2 If I were a genius, I would not mind being treated like one.

3 (a) smart   (b) painful

해석 중학교 생활을 시작할 무렵, 나는 대부분의 동료 학생들이 우리 아시아 학생들은 모두 똑똑하다는 생각을 가지고 있다는 것을 알게 되었다. 몇몇 학생들이 그렇다는 것은 사실이다. 그러나 우리 가운데 그렇지 못한 학생들은 어떻게 되는 것인가? 똑똑한 학생인 것처럼 행동해야만 하는 것은 고통스러운 일일 수 있다. 내 급우들이 대답을 얻으러 나에게 왔지만 어떤 경우에는 나는 그들을 도와주지 못한다. 그러면 그들은 나를 이상하게 쳐다본다. 내가 천재라면, 천재처럼 취급되어도 괜찮다. 그러나 나는 천재가 아니기 때문에, 천재처럼 취급되는 것이 꺼려진다.

Exercise 05

1 **Without** the body's effective compensatory mechanisms,

= **But for** the body's effective compensatory mechanisms,

= **If it were not for** the body's effective compensatory mechanisms,

= **If we were not equipped with** the body's effective compensatory mechanisms,

2 balance (또는 homeostasis도 정답 인정)

This is because pain is actually an essential component of our ability to maintain a neutral state, and allowing it will in turn reset our internal scale back to balance.

해석 뇌 과학의 발견들에 따르면, 고통과 쾌락은 뇌의 같은 영역에서 형성되고 처리된다. 우리 몸은 끊임없이 항상성을 추구하는데, 그것은 몸의 기능들의 균형이라고 정의된다. 잠재적인 변동을 완화시킬 수 있는 몸의 효과적인 보상 기제가 없다면 우리는 생존할 수 없을 것이다. 쾌락과 고통은 동일한 동전의 두 면과 같아서 그들은 함께 작동하는 것 같으며 서로 상당히 의존하고 있고 균형을 유지한다. 만약에 여러분이 쾌락과 고통을 저울 위의 두 반대 지점으로 상상한다면, 여러분은 두 지점 중 한 지점이 올라가면 다른 한 지점이 상응하여 틀림없이 내려갈 것임을 쉽게 이해할 수 있을 것이다. 우리는 '고통 없이는, 얻는 것도 없다.'라는 표현을 모두 들어본 적이 있다. 자, 정신과 의사인 Dr. Anna Lembke에 따르면, 이 말에는 어느 정도의 진실이 있을 수 있다. 그녀는 우리가 비참함에서 벗어나려는 우리의 시도가 사실 우리를 훨씬 더 비참하게 만들고 있다고 말한다. 이는 고통이 실제로 중립적인 상태를 유지하기 위한 우리 능력의 필수적인 구성 요소이기 때문이고, 그것을 허용하는 것은 결과적으로 우리의 내부 저울을 균형 상태로 다시 맞출 것이다.

Unit 03 가정법 미래 구문

Exercise 01

1 Should Bill call you, tell him he can come at any time. / 만일 Bill이 너에게 전화한다면, 언제든지 오라고 그에게 전해줘.

2 Were the Pacific Ocean to dry up, he would never change his habit of thinking. / 태평양이 마른다 하더라도 그는 결코 생각하는 습관을 바꾸지 않을 거야.

Exercise 02

1 If you should find any problems, please call me.

2 Should I die tomorrow, I will have no regrets.

3 If he should become a singer, his mother will be happy as well.

4 Should they get a score of 100, their teacher will give them prizes.

5 If Buffon were to observe today's biodiversity, he would likely find that his theories on species adaptation are still relevant

1 If you should land on the moon / you would find yourself / You would hear no sound there / nor could you smell anything

2 It would be terrible / if all the elevators/ should stop running

3 If the world were to be run / the democracy would, in fact, cease to be one

4 If international sanctions were to be lifted
it would open up new trade opportunities and economic growth for the country

5 Were David Bordwell to analyze why people watch horror movies
he would likely suggest that viewers seek out these films to experience intense emotions in a controlled environment

Exercise 04

1

1 Should the new French Republic fail
2 미국의 자유와 정의의 새로운 이상은 그 주된 지주를 잃을 것이다
 support는 "지주, 지지자, 의지가 되는 것"와 같은 명사형의 의미로 해석해야 한다.
3 success, crucial, reinforcing
4 republic

🔍해석 이 세상에는 왕이 너무 많다. 그래서, 모든 새로운 공화국들은 서로 도와야 한다고 Jefferson은 생각했다. 만약 새로운 프랑스 공화국이 실패하면, 미국의 자유정의의 새로운 이상은 그 주된 지주(支柱)를 잃을 것이라고 그는 말했다.

2

1 If one were to attempt to write a book
2 Ⓑ which → in which Ⓓ left out → were left out

🔍해석 만약 누군가가, 젊은 연구가들이 이룩한 발견들이 모두 생략된 과학의 어느 분야에 관해 책을 쓰려고 시도한다면, 쓸 것이 거의 남지 않을 것이다.

Unit 04 | I wish 가정법 구문

Exercise 01

1 I am sorry he is not here to help us. / 나는 그가 우리를 도와주러 여기에 있었으면 좋았을 텐데/ 그가 우리를 도와주러 여기에 없어서 유감스럽다.

2 I am sorry I was not with you on the train. / 나는 기차에 너와 함께 탔었더라면 좋았을 텐데/ 나는 기차에 너와 함께 타지 않아서 유감스럽다.

3 I am sorry I cannot be a little younger. / 나는 좀 더 어렸다면 좋았을 텐데/ 나는 좀 더 어릴 수 가 없어 유감스럽다.

4 I am sorry I did not know her phone number. / 나는 그녀의 전화번호를 알았었더라면 좋았을 텐데./ 나는 그녀의 전화번호를 몰라서 유감스럽다.

5 I am sorry he did not send me an email. / 나는 그가 나에게 이메일 한 통 보냈었더라면 좋았었을 텐데/ 나는 그가 나에게 이메일 한 통 보내지 않아서 유감스럽다.

Exercise 02

1 I wish I had been kinder to her
2 I wish I could run away/ I would give all my fortune/ if I could know how to get rid of the rats
3 the job is often determined / what you know and how much you know / I wish I had learned that in school/ I wish I had had more education
4 the media focused on factual reporting rather than sensationalizing conspiracy theories about Trump's assassination
5 governments recognized the potential of Bitcoin to provide an alternative to traditional fiat currencies and reduce reliance on centralized financial systems

Exercise 03

1

1 wish they could do better in school

2 Two fifths, come true, grown-ups

[해석] 4학년부터 8학년까지의 10명의 학생들 중 4명은 그들이 성장했을 때 무엇이 되어 있을까를 걱정하고 있다. 그들은 교육이 나중에 그들이 하고 싶은 것을 실현시키는 열쇠라는 것을 알기 때문에 역시 학교에서 공부를 더 잘하고 싶은 것이다.

2

1 (b) which → where (c) began → beginning
(e) suspected → was suspected

2 I am sorry I left home.

3 heavily, overnight, regret leaving home,
get arrested

[해석] 그 날은 하루 종일 비가 몹시 왔다. 나는 완전히 흠뻑 젖어 정오까지는 매우 피곤했다. 그래서 어느 초라한 여인숙에 들러 하룻밤을 묵었는데, 이제 나는 집을 떠나지 말았으면 하고 바라기 시작했다. 또한 나는 너무 비참한 몰골이어서, 나에게 물어 온 질문을 통해, 내가 도망친 머슴으로 의심받고, 이런 의심으로 인해 잡혀갈 위험에 빠졌다는 것을 알았다.

Exercise 04

1 What would happen if we were to start thinking about food as less of a thing and more of a relationship?

2 whatever digestive tools it needs to make optimal use of the plant

3 nutritious / tasty / evolved

4 Food / relationships

[해석] 우리가 식품에 대해 그것을 하나의 물건으로 덜 생각하고 하나의 관계로 더 생각한다면 어떻게 될까? 물론 자연에서 먹는다는 것이 항상 그래왔던 것이 정확히 그것이었는데, 줄곧 내려가 토양에까지 이르는, 우리가 먹이 사슬이라고 부르는 체제 속에 있는 종들의 관계였다. 종들은 그것들이 먹는 다른 종들과 공동으로 진화하며, 매우 종종 상호 의존의 관계가 발달한다. 상호 적응의 점진적인 과정은 조악한 식물을 동물을 위한 영양가 있는 맛있는 식품으로 변화시킨다. 시간이 지나면서 그리고 시행착오를 통해 식물은 동물의 필요와 욕구를 충족시키기 위해 더 맛있어지고, 한편 동물은 그 식물을 최상으로 이용하기 위해 필요로 하는 소화를 돕는 도구는 무엇이나 점진적으로 획득해 간다.

Unit 05 — as if 가정법 구문

Exercise 01

1 She talks as if she were a princess.

2 The boy looks as if he lost his way.

3 He talked about Hawaii as if he had been there many times.

4 He talked as if he had known everything.

5 He analyzed the film's narrative structure as if it were a complex puzzle to be solved.

Exercise 02

1 as if they had not a moment to lose

2 as though he had been running

3 it seems as if the courts were organized

4 She changed her lifestyle dramatically, as if every choice she made could either feed or starve the cancer cells.

5 The two parties debated the issue of climate change legislation as if the future of the nation depended on this single point

Exercise 03

1

1 Books on the shelves

해석 책은 책꽂이에서 볼 때는 사실 말이 없다. 그러나 내가 서재에 들어갈 때 나는 마치 죽은 자들이 거기에 있는 것 같은 느낌이 든다. 그리고 내가 질문을 그들에게 하면 곧 대답할 것이라는 것을 나는 알고 있다.

2

1 as something more than a public calamity

2 news

📄해설 information도 같은 뜻이지만, 철자 n로 시작하는 단어는 news이다.

3 as if they had heard of the loss of a dear friend

4 how deep → how deeply

🔍해석 Nelson의 죽음은 영국에서 사회적 재난 이상의 것으로 느껴졌다. 사람들은 그 소식에 깜짝 놀랐다. 그리고 마치 사랑하는 친구를 잃은 소식을 들은 것처럼 얼굴이 창백해졌다. 마치 그 때까지 얼마나 깊이 우리가 그를 사랑하고 존경하고 있었는지 모르고 있었던 것 같았다.

Unit 06 도치구문

Exercise 01

1 Little did I dream that I should never see her again. / 나는 그녀를 다시 만날 수 없을 거라는 것을 거의 꿈도 꾸지 못했다.

2 Here and there stood high buildings. / 높은 건물들이 여기저기에 서 있다.

3 Only then did I know that she had told a lie. / 나는 딱 그 때 그녀가 거짓말을 했다는 것을 알게 되었다.

4 That mountain we are going to climb. / 우리는 그 산에 올라갈 예정이다.

5 He didn't like music, nor did I. / 그는 음악을 좋아하지 않았다. 나도 그랬다.

Exercise 02

1 after the snow came the frost, The streets looked as if they were made of silver

2 seldom did her high school classmates think of her as different.

3 Going by jumbo jet I do not consider as traveling at all, this is very little different from becoming a parcel sent by air mail

4 have medical breakthroughs had such a significant impact on patient survival rates

5 Never before has a single election stirred such profound debate and division among the populace.

Exercise 03

1

1 If we do not remove ourselves from our own natural station.

2 never can we survey our own sentiments and motives 또는 we can never survey ~

3 never can we form any judgement concerning them

🔍해석 우리는 만약, 말하자면, 우리 자신의 자연적인 위치에서부터 스스로를 제거하지 않는다면, 그리고 어느 정도 떨어져서 그것들을 보려하지 않는다면, 결코 우리 자신의 감정과 동기를 조사해 볼 수 없으며 그것들에 관한 어떤 판단도 형성할 수 없다.

2

1 (that) in my youth I did not have someone of good sense to direct my reading.

2 wasting → wasted, that was → that were

3 What little guidance I had I owe to a young man 또는 I owe what little guidance I had to a young man

4 ⑤

5 Ⓐ regret not having had a wise mentor

Ⓑ that ultimately did not benefit me greatly

Ⓒ The only substantial guidance I received on reading

🔍해석 나는 어렸을 때 독서를 지도해 줄 좋은 분별력을 가진 누군가가 없었다는 것이 너무나 유감스럽다. 그다지 이롭지 않았던 책에 소비했던 시간들을 생각해보면 절로 한숨이 나온다. 그나마 받았던 독서에 대한 지도방법 모두는 내가 Heidelberg에서 함께 살고 있었던 바로 그 가족과 살기 위해 왔던 한 젊은이 덕택이었다.

Exercise 04

1 Much has been written of late about

2 (a) household tasks

(b) what people say should happen / what they actually do

3 genders, gender-specific chores, notable disparity, ideals, advocate for, reflected in reality

🔍해석 남자와 여자 사이에 집안일을 분담할 것에 관하여 최근에 많은 것이 쓰여 왔다. 예를 들면 남자가 차를 고치거나 여자가 요리를 하는 것 같은 한 성에만 속하는 것으로 한 때 여겨졌던 일들이 지금은 때때로 공유되고 있다. 그러나 사람들이 해야 한다고 말하는 것과 실제로 하는 것과는 차이가 있다. 비록 대부분의 사람들이 집안일이 공유되어야 한다고 생각하지만 많은 보고서들이 이것이 일어나고 있는 것이 아니라는 것을 보여 준다.

🔴어휘 **of late** 최근에 **chore** 집안 잡일 **fix** 고치다, 수리하다

Unit 07 생략구문

Exercise 01

1 To some life is pleasure, to other (**life is**) suffering. / 삶이란 누군가에게는 기쁨이며, 다른 사람에게는 고통이다.

2 When (**I was**) young, I used to go fishing with her. / 내가 어렸을 때, 나는 그녀와 낚시를 하러 가곤 했었다.

3 Look at the pictures (**which were**) painted in different colors. / 다양한 색들로 칠해진 그림들을 보아라.

4 I do not care if they go or (**they**) do not (**go**). / 나는 그들이 가든 안 가든 신경 쓰지 않는다.

5 I believe (**that**) Bitcoin's decentralized nature could potentially disrupt global financial systems. / 나는 비트코인의 분산된 특성이 글로벌 금융 시스템을 잠재적으로 혼란에 빠뜨릴 수 있다고 믿는다.

Exercise 02

1 the French love France and the Americans America

2 looks into a mirror and becomes too optimistic

3 Lost wealth may be regained by industry and economy/ lost health by temperance and medicine

4 While the rise in Bitcoin prices makes investors excited, the market volatility (**makes them**) anxious. *생략표현에 주의할 것.

5 While (**they were**) examining the cosmic microwave background radiation, scientists discovered crucial evidence supporting the Big Bang theory.

1

1 When (they were) asked in the survey what would make them happier in the year of 2010
2 When, put, before(또는 above)

🔍해석 조사에서 2010년에는 어떻게 하면 행복해 질것이냐는 질문을 받았을 때, 응답자들은 돈을 훨씬 앞질러 가족과의 보다 많은 시간, 좋은 건강, 일에 대한 여러 가능성과 기회를 꼽았다.

2

1 other books are to be swallowed
2 ③
3 little → few
4 Ⓐ the different ways in which books can be read and appreciated
Ⓑ different books require different levels of engagement and attention (또는 attention and engagement)

🔍해석 음미해야 하는 책도 있고, 통째로 삼켜야 하는 책도 있고, 꼭꼭 씹어 소화시켜야 하는 책도 몇몇 있다. 다시 말하자면, 부분적으로만 읽어야 하는 책도 있고, 읽기는 하지만 호기심을 가지지 않고 읽는 책도 있고, 몇몇은 근면함과 주의력으로 전체를 읽어야 한다.

Exercise **04**

1 They were brought into a room where four lines of unequal length were displayed
2 vote for the wrong line
3 peer pressure / making / wrong / decisions

🔍해석 1951년에 사회심리학자인 Solomon Asch는 12명으로 구성된 사람들과 한 실험을 실시했다. (그들은 동일하지 않은 길이의 네 개의 선이 제시된 방으로 인도되었다. 이들은 어느 두 선이 동일한 길이 인지 판단하고, 공식적으로 자신의 선택에 투표해야 했다. 한 사람씩 전체 중에 11명은 틀린 선에 투표를 했는데, 이는 이들 모두 미리 그렇게 하도록 지시를 받았기 때문이었다. 아무것도 몰랐던 단 한 개인은 도대체 어떻게 이 모든 정상적으로 보이는 사람들 모두가 틀린 선을 고를 수 있는지 상상할 수 없었다. 투표할 자기 차례가 되었을 때, 그는 "나의 판단이 나에게 말해 주는 것으로 가야 할 것인가? 아니면 무리를 따라 갈 것인가?"를 결정해야 했다. 실험에 참여했던 사람들 중 3분의 1이 집단압력에 굴복하고는 다른 동료와 일치하기 위해 자신의 투표를 바꾸었다.

Unit 08 현재완료 + since 구문

Exercise **01**

1 has been/ parted
2 have passed / began
3 have known/ was
4 have worked
5 has lived / was

Exercise **02**

1 I have played the piano for 3 years.
2 It has rained for a week.
3 She has learned Spanish since 2012.
4 He has been making the special chair since last year.

Exercise **03**

1 It has already been one year/ since I gave up smoking
2 About four years have passed/ since I came to live in Seoul/ I have come to love
3 It has been more than twenty-seven years/ since windsurfing was introduced

4 Medical technology has recently advanced to the point where robotic surgeries are becoming routine, significantly reducing recovery times for patients.

5 AI researchers have recently made significant breakthroughs in natural language processing, enabling machines to understand and generate human language with greater fluency.

Exercise **04**

1

1 It has been a hundred years since Henry Rousseau was born

2 the greatest master → the greatest masters

3 has passed, birth, spent, was mostly mocked by, is now celebrated as

🔍해석 헨리 루소가 태어난 지 백년이 지났고 평생을 가난 속에서 살았고 동시대 사람들로부터 거의 조롱만 받았던 이 사람은 이제 19세기의 위대한 거장중의 하나로서 존경받고 있다.

2

1 (a) tried → have tried

(d) so is universal → so universal is

(e) has at times been treating → has at times been treated

2 has for centuries been regarded as such a key

3 have sought, be fixed, understanding, such, that

4 widespread, as well as

🔍해석 그리스 철학의 초창기 이래로, 만약 예술은 조화이고, 조화란 비율에 대한 합당한 준수라면 이러한 비율은 고정되어 있을 것이라고 가정하는 것은 틀리지 않은 것처럼 보였기 때문에, 사람들은 예술에서 기하학적 법칙을 찾아내려고 애쓰고 있다. 황금분할이라고 알려져 있는 기하학적인 비율은 수세기 동안, 예술의 불가사의를 푸는 그러한 열쇠로 간주되어지고 있고, 그것의 적용은 예술에서 뿐만 아니라 자연에서도 매우 보편적이어서, 가끔은 종교적인 숭배를 받기도 한다.

Exercise **01**

1 Ⓐ It will take you one hour to walk to the station.

Ⓑ It will take one hour for you to walk to the station.

2 Ⓐ It cost me 100 dollars to buy the telescope.

Ⓑ It cost 100 dollars for me to buy the telescope.

3 Ⓐ It took three days for me to read through this book.

Ⓑ It took me three days to read through this book.

4 Ⓐ It takes her two hours to do her homework.

Ⓑ It takes two hours for her to do her homework.

5 Ⓐ It took me four months to master English grammar.

Ⓑ It took four months for me to master English grammar.

Exercise **02**

1 the number of boys and girls who go on to college has been increasing, it costs them a lot of money to send their children to college

2 With an iron bar he had to cut his way through ice walls, it took him a full day to cover

3 it took their forefathers months to cover

4 It costs companies millions in legal fees and settlements when they fail to safeguard customer information.

5 It costs millions of dollars to develop and bring to market a new pharmaceutical drug, taking over a decade to complete the necessary clinical trials and regulatory approvals.

1

1 This applies to the choice of spouses as well as to the selection of university departments. / 이것은 대학의 학과를 선택하는 것뿐만 아니라 배우자를 선택할 때도 적용된다.

2 it takes a lot of courage to choose a road one likes

3 sees → see

🔍해석 이것은 대학의 학과와 직업을 선택하는 것뿐만 아니라 배우자를 선택하는 데에도 적용된다. 말할 필요도 없이, 자신이 좋아하는 길을 선택해서 그것을 관철해 내는 데에는 많은 용기가 필요하다.

2

1 It takes approximately eight hours for a ship to complete the trip through the Panama Canal.

2 cost → costs

3 one-tenth of what it would cost an average ship to round the Horn

🔍해석 배가 파나마운하를 통해 여행을 끝내는 데에는 약 여덟 시간이 걸리며, 평균적으로 15,000 달러의 비용이 드는데, 그것은 보통의 배가 케이프 혼을 돌아서 가는 데에 드는 비용의 십분의 일이다.

Unit 10 목적어의 소유격을 대신하는 the

Exercise 01

1 she leaned in and kissed me softly on the cheek

2 Tom quickly reached out and firmly caught his friend by the hand.

3 John looked his father directly in the eye, conveying his earnest intentions without uttering a word.

4 He seized me by the collar, pulling me closer with an intensity that caught me off guard.

5 he patted me on the shoulder

Exercise 02

1 she patted her little postman on the head

2 He grasped me warmly by the hand

3 My uncle looked the toad straight in the eye/ The toad also gazed my uncle straight in the eye

4 Tim looked his father in the eye, his gaze filled with a mixture of respect and determination

5 Tom caught his friend by the hand, they made their way through the bustling crowd

Exercise 03

1

1 she slapped him on the face and hit him in the belly

2 It was in my room **where** Susan helped me with my homework.

🔍해석 그러나 그녀가 가만히 않아서, 그가 자기를 껴안는 것을 내버려 두는 동안은 그는 매우 만족했다. 그가 완전히 불쾌해 진 것은 그녀가 그의 얼굴을 찰싹 때리고 주먹으로 그의 배를 친 때였다.

2

1 confusion

2 I was going to kiss her on her lips or the cheek

3 she didn't know which way she should turn her head

she didn't know which way to turn her head

🔍해석 언젠가 나는 첫 데이트 상대에게 "너에게 goodnight 키스를 해도 될까?"라고 말했다. 그녀는 잠시 당황스런 표정을 하더니 "응"이라고 말했다. 나는 그녀의 뺨에 키스를 하기 위해 다가섰는데, 순간 그녀의 입술에 키스를 할지 아니면, 뺨에 키스를 할지 혼란스러웠다. 그리고 그녀는 어느 쪽으로 고개를 돌려야 할지를 몰랐다.

Unit 11 — used to (would) ⓡ 구문

Exercise 01

1 She used to walk along the shore every Sunday.
2 The Tower of London used to be a prison.
3 I would sometimes travel alone when I was a college student.
4 I used to get up early.
5 I used to go fishing on Sundays.
6 I used to call on her every Friday.
7 She used to be a teacher.
8 There used to be a tall tree here before the war.

Exercise 02

1 he would tell us tales of the little sea-maid/ used to sit on a rock
2 used to be open only in summer
3 She used to be an actress
4 Historically, schools used to emphasize the reproduction of existing social structures through curricula and pedagogical practices that favored the knowledge and cultural norms of the dominant social groups.
5 used to rely heavily on the concept of nuclear deterrence, the possession of such weapons would prevent potential adversaries from initiating conflicts due to the fear of mutually assured destruction

Exercise 03

1 It seemed that his patients recovered quickly.
2 ⑤
3 would soon go back to a previous condition or into a worse state

🔍해석 1950년대의 심리학자인 Milton H. Erickson이 직면한 주된 문제들 가운데 하나는 그의 환자들이 빠르게 회복되는 것처럼 보이다가 이전의 상태로 되돌아가거나 좀 나아진 후에 더 나쁜 상태로 돌아가곤 것이었다. 그것은 그들이 치료에 대해 깊은 저항심을 갖고 있었기 때문이다. 그들은 금방 예전 습관으로 되돌아가서 의사를 비난하곤 했다.

2

1 more → less
2 voted, do not (vote for fair) anymore
3 this trusting view has been slipping down steadily

🔍해석 시카고 대학교의 National Opinion Research Center에 따르면, 미국에 사는 사람들은 점차 서로를 덜 신뢰하고 있다. "사람들이 기회가 있으면, 당신을 이용하려고 할 것이라고 생각하십니까, 아니면 공정하려고 노력할 것이라고 생각하십니까?"라는 질문에 대한 응답에서, 상당히 많은 다수가 예전에는 "공정하다"에 투표했었는데, 이런 신뢰하는 관점이 꾸준히 하락하고 있다.

Unit 12 — 조동사 + have p.p 구문

Exercise 01

1 He must have done his best to solve the problem.
2 She may have read the book to know the story.
3 She cannot have met him not to know his name.
4 The bridge should have been repaired a long time ago.
5 They may not have moved from their old house.

Exercise 02

1 You cannot have felt the earthquake yesterday
2 It must have been a very brave man
3 it may have been, in part, man's better memory

4 Aquinas must have been influenced by Aristotle's philosophy when developing his theory of natural law, the clear parallels between their concepts of purpose and order in the universe

5 would rather have established a government based on the consent of the governed, he strongly believed that legitimate political authority arises from the voluntary agreement of the people

Exercise 03

1

1 꽁꽁 얼어붙은 남극은 항상 냉혹한 것만은 아니었다.

2 it must have had plenty of sunshine and a warm, humid climate

3 have discovered → have been discovered

🔍 **해석** 꽁꽁 얼어붙은 남극이 언제나 그렇게 냉혹하지는 않았다. 오래오래 전에, 빙하기가 오기 전에는 남극 땅도 많은 태양빛과 따스하고 습기에 찬 기후를 가졌음에 틀림없다. 삼림과 늪지대에서 자라는 양치식물의 정글이 무성하게 자랐다. 우리는 이것을 그 곳에서 발견된 화석과 석탄 매장물로써 알 수 있다.

2

1 the girl cannot have bought these things out of her proper earnings

2 be a really bad person

3 cannot be → cannot have been

🔍 **해석** 나는 그 여자가 자기의 정당한 수입으로 이런 것들을 샀을 리가 없다는 것을 안다. 나는 그녀가 정말 나쁜 사람이라고 생각한다. 나는 그렇게 생각하고 싶지는 않지만, 분명 그런 것임에 틀림없다. 그에게 주의를 시켜 놓았으니 그는 그렇게 어리석었을 리가 없다.

Exercise 04 

1

1 has to do with

2 (b) had performed   (c) would perhaps have won

3 might have happened

4 bronze, happiness, regret, bronze, close, winning, relieved, alternative, emotional

🔍 **해석** 대부분의 우리는 선수들이 올림픽에서 동메달을 따는 것보다 은메달을 따고 더 행복할 것이라고 생각한다. 그러나 동메달을 딴 선수들이 은메달을 딴 선수보다 실제로 더 행복하다는 연구가 나왔다. 이러한 이유는 선수들이 자신들의 경기 내용을 생각하는 방식과 관련 있다. 은메달리스트들은 자신들이 약간만 더 잘했더라면 금메달을 땄을지도 모른다는 생각에 초점을 맞춘다. 반면에 동메달리스트들은 자신들이 약간만 더 잘못했더라면 수상권 안에도 들지 못했을 거라는 생각에 초점을 맞춘다. 심리학자들은 실제로 일어났던 일보다 일어났을지도 모르는 일을 상상하는 능력을 '반-사실적 사고'라고 부른다.

2

1 should have seemed → must have seemed

2 paper

3 economic

🔍 **해석** 전자 문서의 모든 단점과 약점을 고려할 때 왜 그냥 종이를 계속 사용하지 않을까? 이 질문에 대답하는 가장 좋은 방법은 인류의 역사에서 필기도구가 교체되었던 또 다른 하나의 경우를 되돌아보는 것이다. 돌이나 점토에 쓰는 것이 익숙했던 사회에서 종이는 불과 물에 취약하고 쓰인 자국이 너무 쉽게 번지거나 흐려져 없어지는 지극히 수명이 짧은 재료처럼 분명 보였음에 틀림없다. 그렇지만 종이는 보편화되었다. 모세의 십계명판은 돌이었지만 모세의 이야기는 종이로 전해졌다. 종이를 사용하면 정보를 기록하고 보관하고 옮기는 데 비용이 훨씬 적게 들게 되었다. 바로 그런 동일한 고려가 종이 없는 전자적 필기로의 전환이 이제 불가피 하다는 것을 입증한다.

Unit 13 should have p.p

Exercise 01

1 당신은 상사에게 나를 소개시켜줬어야 했다.
2 당신은 그녀가 당신에게 썼었던 그 편지를 읽어봐야 했었다.
3 당신은 내가 당신에게 말했었던 그 남자를 만날 필요가 없었다.
4 당신은 내가 생각했던 것 보다 좀 더 일찍 그것을 말했어야했다.
5 그는 그때 사우디아라비아에 가지 말았어야 했다.
6 그녀는 우산을 가져갈 필요가 없었다.
7 나는 Jane이 떠나기 전에 그녀를 만났어야 했다.

Exercise 02

1 The plan to educate more students in science and technology, It should have been undertaken earlier.
2 You ought to have sent her the letter, You should have taken into account recent delay in mail delivery.
3 He needn't have worried about being seasick, for the ocean was as calm as a lake
4 should have predicted the 2008 financial crisis with more accuracy to mitigate its devastating effects on the global economy
5 need not have dismissed the ethical dilemmas, if they had considered the deeper implications of utilitarian philosophy

Exercise 03

1 (a) sent → was sent
  (b) enough old → old enough

(c) found → found it
(f) must have been studying → should have been studying

🔍해석 Schweitzer는 소년 시절 학교 갈 나이가 되자 마을 학교에 갔다. 그는 읽고 쓰기가 어려웠다는 것과 당연히 공부하고 있었어야 할 때 몽상에 잠겨 앉아 있던 일이 흔히 있었다는 것을 자서전에서 말하고 있다.

2

1 ③, ④
  (c) enhances → enhancing
  (d) will likely second-guess
  → would likely second-guess
2 ④
3 whether we should have chosen Greece over Thailand,

🔍해석 선택을 한 후에, 그 결정은 결국 우리가 추측하는 즐거움을 변화시키며, 그 선택한 사항으로부터 얻을 것으로 기대되는 즐거움을 향상시키고, 거부한 선택사항으로부터 얻을 것으로 기대되는 즐거움을 감소시킨다. 우리가 선택한 것과 일치하도록 옵션의 가치를 재빨리 새롭게 하려 하지 않는다면, 우리는 뒤늦게 자신을 비판하여 미칠 지경으로 몰고 갈 가능성이 있다. 우리는 태국보다는 그리스를, 커피메이커보다는 토스터를, Michele보다는 Jenny를 선택해야 했었던 것은 아니었는지 자신에게 계속 되풀이하여 물어볼 것이다.

Unit 14 have to 구문

Exercise 01

1 You have to think twice before you buy anything.
2 You don't have to speak so loud.
3 You have only to ask for it, and it will be given to you.
4 I have to do my homework in the afternoon. I have something to buy at the supermarket.

5 We have to stop throwing trash on the street, for we have to conserve nature.

Exercise 02

1 You don't have to attent the party tonight.
2 You have to serve in the army in Korea.
3 She has to study hard for the finals.

Exercise 03

1 a guest has to leave the table during a meal, Will you please excuse me for a minute
2 they have a book which informs them all about the lighthouses / they have but to open it to find out where it is
3 Every motorist dreams of a car that does not have to be refueled

Exercise 04

1

1 the efforts of children who are starved of love
2 Because the young who <u>are starved of</u> affection is the same <u>as starved bodies</u>
3 how desperately is their need → how desperate their need is

🔍해석 어떤 작가가 말하길, "사랑은 어린이들에게 필요한 음식물이다. 그들이 사랑을 필요로 하는 것이 얼마나 필사적인가를 깨닫기 위해서는, 사랑에 굶주린 어린애들이 어떤 방법에 의해서든지 주의를 끌려고 하는 그들의 노력을 그저 보기만 하면 된다. 왜냐하면, 굶주린 애정은 굶주린 육체처럼 커다란 비극이기 때문이다.

2

1 the radio waves we've been leaking into space for the past 80 years
2 ④

3 We have no idea what form these signals might take

🔍해석 멀리 떨어져 있는 어떤 문명이 지구에 있는 생명의 흔적을 찾고 있다면, 우리를 찾는 가장 쉬운 방법은 우리가 지난 80년 동안에 우주로 누출해 온 전파로부터일 것이다. 만약 어떤 외계의 문화가 우리의 것과 유사하다면, 그것 또한 전파를 방출하고 있을지도 모른다. 그리고 그것들이 우리가 찾고 있는 것이다. 만약 우리가 그것들을 발견한다면, 그것들은 먼 생명체의 기술에 대한 증거일지도 모른다. 그러나 우리는 이 신호가 어떤 형태를 취하고 있을지 전혀 알지 못하므로, 제거의 과정에 의해 찾아야 한다.

Exercise 05

1 equal, equalize
2 which is being drawn / being drawn
3 hydrated, lower
4 (a) balance (b) osmosis (c) drink water

🔍해석 비록 물고기가 물을 마실지라도, 물을 얻는 기본적인 방법은 삼투를 통해서이다. 물은 그것의 피부에 있는 작은 구멍을 통하여 몸으로 스며들어간다. 삼투는 용액의 농도가 세포막의 양쪽에서 같아질 때까지 물고기의 피부 같은 세포막을 통한 소금물 같은 용액의 단순한 이동이다. 물고기가 소금물에 살 때, 바닷물은 물고기 속에 있는 액체보다 더 많은 소금을 함유하고 있다. 그러므로 삼투는 물고기의 밖으로 물을 끌어내고 그 물고기는 그것의 몸 밖으로 빠져나가고 있는 액체를 보충하기 위하여 물을 지속적으로 마실 필요가 있다. 물고기가 소금기 없는 물에 살 때, 그 물은 물고기 속에 있는 액체보다 소금을 적게 가지고 있고 물은 물고기의 피부를 통하여 그것의 몸속으로 들어오게 된다. 따라서 민물에 사는 물고기는 물을 마실 필요가 없는 것이다.

🔴어휘 **osmosis** 삼투 **solution** 용액

Unit 15 — without ~ing, 유사보어

Exercise 01

1 He died young.
2 She died a beggar
3 They ran out of the building screaming for help.

Exercise 02

1 The letter fell into her hands without Tom knowing what was in it.
2 She slipped out of the room unnoticed by anyone.
3 He came home very depressed.
4 The old man sat surrounded by his grandchildren.
5 Bottles can reveal their contents without being opened.

Exercise 03

1 without all the villagers seeing her coming to my house
2 without people expecting them or knowing that they are going to happen
3 down the stairs and out at the front door undetected
4 unnoticed by the majority of citizens who were preoccupied with other issues

Exercise 04

1

1 A person who is called upon to act
2 we must avoid the danger of rushing into action without thinking about what we are doing
3 meditate / upon / previous / dangerous

🔍해석 행동하도록 요청받는 사람은 만약 그가 전에 비슷한 종류의 행동에 대해 곰곰이 생각해 본적이 있다면 보다 좋게 행동할 가능성이 더 크다. 만약 우리가 한 공동체의 구성원으로서 효과적인 한 부분을 담당하기를 원한다면 우리는 우리가 하고 있는 것에 대해 생각 없이 서둘러 행동하는 위험을 피해야 한다.

2

1 As they are always with us,
2 The wearer has the glasses on their nose so often that they simply exist unobserved.
3 effect / unnoticed (또는 unremarked)
 * unobserved를 쓰지 않도록 할 것.

🔍해석 한 시대의 지배적인 가정은 그 시대 속에 살아가고 있는 사람들의 생각과 믿음, 기대감과 상상력을 물들인다.[영향을 미친다.] 우리와 항상 함께 하고 있기 때문에, 이러한 가정들은 아주 자주 착용하는 사람들의 코에 있기 때문에 결코 관측되지 못하는 안경과도 마찬가지로 대개 인식되지 못한 채로 지나쳐버린다.

Unit 16 — whose (소유격관계대명사) 구문

Exercise 01

1 People whose dogs get lost make every effort to find them.
2 Hand me the book the cover of which is frayed.
3 I saw a mountain whose top was covered with snow.
4 I picked a flower whose name I didn't know.
5 I was helped by the boy whose father is a doctor.

Exercise 02

1 bike accidents are mainly caused by biker's

carelessness, by a biker who does not stop at a stop sign, by a biker whose pants' legs get caught in the bike chain

2 the branches of which are almost bare

3 the theories of whom have revolutionized the field, was awarded a prestigious prize

Exercise 03

1 compete(또는 collide), adopts

2 Nor is it always the nation whose culture is superior

3 An industrial society has its vital organs **the destruction of which** (whose destruction) paralyzes the whole organism.

4 Not until she called me could I see her.

🔍**해석** 어떤 나라나 타국들로부터 전적으로 고립되어서는 살 수 없으며, 국가 간의 접촉은 항상 그들의 언어에 영향을 미치는 결과를 가져온다. 두 언어가 경쟁 할 때, 승리가 반드시 가장 완전한 언어에 떨어지는 것은 아니다. 또한, 문화가 떨어진 나라에게 그 언어를 채용케 하는 것은 반드시 문화가 우월한 나라는 아니다.

2

1 Ⓐ The pauses <u>which</u> we make in speaking
   Ⓑ at a loss for word

2 of which the commonest is that the supply of air from the lungs becomes exhaust**ed**

3 separate, we run out of breath, unsure of what to say

🔍**해석** 우리가 말을 할 때 잠깐 멈추는 것은 각각의 단어 하나하나를 개별적으로 독립된 것으로 단절해야 할 필요성이 존재하기 때문이 아니라, 그와는 아주 다른 이유 때문인데, 그 이유들 중에서 가장 일반적인 것은 폐로부터의 공기의 공급량이 고갈되어 호흡을 하기 위해 잠깐 쉬는 것이다. 또 한편으로는, 어떠한 말을 해야 할지 당황하거나, 특히 강조하기를 원할 때 잠깐 정지할 수도 있다.

Exercise 04

1 those whose income are now at that higher level are not more satisfied with their lives

2 that's because the new level of income becomes the standard against which we measure our achievements

3 <u>with</u> the happiness from an increase **being** short-lived

4 satisfying / last

🔍**해석** 대부분의 사람들은 만약 그들이 10퍼센트 더 많은 수입을 올린다면, 그들의 삶에 훨씬 더 만족할 것이라고 믿는다. 그러나 현재 수입이 더 많은 사람들이 자신들의 삶에 더 만족하는 것은 아니다. 수입의 변화는 잠깐 동안 우리의 행복감에 영향을 끼친다. 수입의 증가가 우리를 행복하게 해 주는 것 보다 수입의 감소가 우리를 더 고통스럽게 한다. 그러나 수입의 증가로 오는 행복조차도 오랫동안 지속되지는 않는다. 이것은 얼마 지나지 않아 새로운 수입의 수준이 우리의 성과를 평가하는 표준이 되어 버리기 때문이다.

📕**어휘** **healthy** 건전한 **matter** 실용적인 **mate** 동료 **practical** 실용적인 **look after** 돌보다 **child care** 육아 **logically** 논리적으로 **appreciate** 식별하다, 인식하다

Unit 17  as (유사관계대명사) 구문

Exercise 01

1 Choose such friends as will listen to you quietly.

2 We are given as much food as we can barely live on.

3 This is the same wallet as I bought in London.

4 The streets of London were narrow and muddy, as was often the case at that time.

5 He is as hard a worker as has ever been employed.

Exercise 02

1 be contented with such foods as could be found or cultivated
2 All human beings have equal rights from the time they are born, the people of other countries have the same rights as we have
3 As many vegetables as were brought to the market, were sold out in a matter of two hours
4 Such a world as I was speaking of can exist
5 such academic research as will contribute significantly to the understanding of climate change and its global impact

Exercise 03

1

1 make more money than was needed
2 such modest returns of hospitality as might be possible for a poor bachelor

 해석 나는 옷을 입고, 먹고, 따뜻하고 청결히 사는 데 필요한, 그리고 가난한 독신 남자가 할 수 있는 일은 적은 자선 행위나 혹은 선물을 주고, 남한테 받은 후대에 적당한 보답을 하는 데 필요한 그 이상의 돈을 모으는 데는 거의 아무런 흥미도 없다.

2

1 was → had been
2 **as is often the case with** very clever young people
3 그녀는 자라서 자신의 세대에 속한 구성원들보다는 그녀보다 나이가 많은 사람들과 어울리는 것이 보다 흥미롭다고 느꼈다(여겼다).

해석 그녀는 그녀의 어머니가 전에 그랬던 것처럼 마찬가지로 완고했고 아주 똑똑한 젊은이들에게 종종 있는 것처럼, 그녀는 자라서 자신의 세대에 속한 구성원들보다는 그녀보다 나이가 많은 사람들과 어울리는 것이 보다 흥미롭다고 느꼈다.

Unit 18 but, than (유사관계대명사) 구문

Exercise 01

1 There are few books but have some misprints.
2 He couldn't bring himself to accept more money than he actually needed for his expenses.
3 There is no mother but loves her children unconditionally.
4 The work turned out to be much more difficult than had been expected.
5 I have no choice but to go abroad due to unavoidable circumstances.
6 There was no one left in the room but me after everyone had gone.
7 No man is so old but he may continue to learn and grow intellectually.

Exercise 02

1 an act done by a human being but carries with it a train of consequences
2 I found the first two years of the curriculum very dull, more attention than was necessary to scrape through the examinations
3 no event in financial history but has been influenced by the 1929 stock market crash

Exercise 03

1

1 (c) which → that
2 the end of which we may never trace

 해석 인간이 하는 행동 하나에 혹은 말하는 말 한 마디에도 그 끝을 쫓을 수 없는 일련의 결과를 수반하지 않는 것이 없다는 생각을 하면, 무엇인가 엄숙하고 무서운 것이 있다

1 which was

2 (b) approached → approaching

   (d) storing → stored

   (e) have been → has been

3 memory

해석 원래는 비효율적이라고 간주되었던 인간의 기억장치는 실제로 컴퓨터의 메모리보다 훨씬 더 정교하고 복잡하다. 다양한 관점으로 이 문제에 접근하는 연구자들이 모두 일치된 결론을 도출했는데 우리의 정신 속에는 일반적으로 생각하는 것보다 훨씬 많은 것들이 저장되어 있다는 것이다.

Unit 19 이중관계대명사 구문

Exercise 01

1 이건 오랫동안 사달라고 졸랐던 것 중 가장 필요하지 않았던 것이다.

2 이것은 내가 읽으라고 추천받았던 책 중에 정말로 쓸모 있는 유일한 가이드북이다.

3 네가 가지지 말았어야 한 것 중에 구입한 것이 있어?

4 네가 할 수 있는 것 중, 할 만한 가치가 있는 것이 많다.

5 살면서 필요한 것 중에 우리가 오랫동안 사고 싶어왔던 많은 물건들이 있다.

Exercise 02

1 There is no one that you know who can do such a thing.

2 There is not a man who lives in Seoul who does not know his name.

3 There is something that passes for heroism which is not heroism at all.

Exercise 03

1 There is no man that carries, him who does not receive a sting into his soul

2 they can be as strong or as clever as a character in film, which James Bond does in a film, that are very exciting

3 that has captured the imagination of generations as intensely as Romanticism, which rebels against reason and embraces the sublime

Exercise 04

1 which objectively means the same as 'a dog of mixed breed' but which also reveals a negative feeling we have about that particular dog

2 object, attitude

해석 만일 우리가 어떤 동물을 잡종이라 불렀다면, 객관적으로는 '잡종 개'와 같은 뜻을 지닌 말을 사용한 것이지만, 이는 또한 그 특정한 개에 대해 우리가 가지고 있는 부정적인 감정을 드러내는 것이다. 그러므로 말이란 어떤 대상을 가리킬 뿐만 아니라 그 대상에 관한 감정적인 태도도 암시할 수 있다.

1 nor is it incompatible

2 the pattern of development that physical optics acquired after Newton and that other natural sciences make familiar today

해석 그러한 방식은 오늘날의 수많은 창의적 분야에서 낯선 것이 아니며, 또한 중요한 발견과 발명과도 상충되지 않는 것이다. 그러나 그것은 뉴턴 이후 물리과학이 이룬 학문의 발전 방식도 아니고 오늘날 다른 자연과학들이 익숙한 발전방식도 아니다.

Unit 20 · who[m]ever (복합관계대명사) 구문

Exercise 01

1 이 사무실을 떠나는 누구든지 사무실의 스위치를 꺼야한다. (명사절)
2 당신이 요청하는 사람이 누구일지라도, 당신은 그 대답을 얻지 못할 것이다. (부사절)
3 당신이 사랑하는 사람이 누구일지라도 나는 그가 보고 싶다. (부사절)
4 Formula English를 마스터한 누구든지 영어를 매우 잘 말할 수 있다. (명사절)
5 그 칼럼니스트는 선거에 당선된 사람은 누구든지 그 정당의 지지를 받을 거라는 것이 확실하다고 느낀다. (명사절)

Exercise 02

1 Whoever has to deal with children
2 I resolved to find out where I belonged, whichever society they would bring me
3 whatever it is
4 Whenever we destroy beauty / whenever we substitute something artificial for a natural feature of the earth
5 Whatever criticism she wrote / whose stories had been marginalized in the literary canon

Exercise 03

1

1 Whoever came up with this idea should be given a large pension
2 No matter what / anything that
3 stand out (or to stand out)
4 the whiskey version of what Europeans have christened oenotourism

 **해석** 이 아이디어를 생각해낸 사람이 누구이든 그에게는 큰 장려금이 지급되어야 한다. 왜냐 하면, 이 아이디어가 Fortune Brand 소유의 Maker's사가 유럽인들이 '이너투어리즘'(포도주 관광업)이라고 명명한 성장일로의 거대 사업과 같은 위스키 분야의 투어리즘(위스키 관광업)에 있어서 다른 경쟁업체들을 제치고 두각을 나타내는데 도움을 주기 때문이다. (oen = wine)

2

1 ⑤
2 (b) wherever (d) whomever
3 neither can men kill
4 to collapse
5 much → little

해석 사람이 공동 사회에서 살 때 자기 멋대로 행동할 수 없다. 가령, 자동차를 운전하는 사람이 자기 좋은 대로 아무 데로나 차를 운전하면 반드시 혼란이 일어난다. 또한, 사람들이 자기 멋대로 서로 죽이고 빼앗으면 반드시 사회의 붕괴를 야기 시킨다. 이와 같이 행동에 제한을 받지 않는다면, 비록 명목상으로나마 그들이 좋아하는 것을 무엇이나 할 수 있는 자유를 갖게 된다고 해도, 사실 그들은 거의 자유를 소유하지 못할 것이다.

Unit 21 · whenever, wherever (복합관계부사) 구문

Exercise 01

1 No matter where / 당신이 어디 있을지라도, 우리가 당신을 생각하고 있다고 기억해라.
2 At any time when / 당신이 편할 때 언제든지 방문해 주세요.
3 No matter how / 그가 아무리 많이 먹을지라도, 그는 결코 살이 찌지 않는다.
4 No matter how / 아무리 많은 돈이 TV광고에 쓰이더라도, 질이 좋지 못한 상품은 팔리지 않을 것이다.
5 at any time when / 이 근처에 올 일이 있으시면 언제든지 들려주세요.

1 Whenever I drove my old car over 55 miles per hour
2 whatever you do, wherever you live, whether you like it or not, whether you know it or not
3 however wise or eminent, are human and can make mistakes
4 However far we advance our technology, we will still need to know how to think and read
5 Whenever Darwin observed nature, he noticed the endless variety of species adapting to their surroundings

Exercise 03

1

1 (b) who → which
  (d) expecting → to expect
  (e) satisfied → satisfying

어휘 saintly 성스러운, 성자 같은

2 compensations
3 unreasonable / excessive compensations / selfishness / parenthood / satisfy

해석 사회가 그녀의 아이에게 이성을 넘어선 정도의 어머니로서의 희생을 요구할 때마다, 그 어머니는, 특별나게 거룩한 존재가 아니라면, 자신의 아이로부터 그녀가 기대할 권리를 가지고 있는 보상을 넘어서는 보상을 기대할 것이다. 전통적으로 자기희생적이라고 불리는 어머니는 대다수의 경우에 있어서, 자신의 아이에 대해 매우 이기적인데, 왜냐하면, 부모로서의 도리라는 것이 인생의 한 요소로서 중요하기는 하지만, 그러한 상황이 평생 해야 하는 것이라면 만족스럽지 못한 것이기 때문이다.

2

1 (b) known → knowing (d) imposes → to impose
  (e) qualifies → is qualified
2 (f) the rights (of the commonplace)
  (g) the commonplace mind

3 Whoever
4 runs the risk of being eliminated
5 ordinary / common(또는 commonplace) / rights / accept / qualified

해석 현 시대의 특징은 평범한 사람이 자신이 평범하다는 것을 알고 확신 있게 평범함의 권리를 선언하고 자신이 원하는 어디서나 그 권리를 강요한다는 것이다. 일반대중은 남과 다른 모든 것, 뛰어난 모든 것을 부숴버린다. 모든 사람과 같지 않고, 모든 사람과 같이 생각하지 않는 사람이면 누구나 제거될 위험에 처하게 된다. 오늘날 '모든 사람'은 곧 대중일 뿐이다.

Unit 22 whatever, whichever, however (복합관계대명사) 구문

Exercise 01

1 Any / 그가 변명하는 어느 것이든지 믿질 못할 것이다.
2 No matter what problems / 당신이 무슨 문제를 가지고 있을지라도, 당신은 도움을 얻으러 나에게 항상 와도 좋다.
3 any / 나는 당신이 선택한 어느 것이든지 즐길 수 있다고 생각한다.
4 No matter which / 그가 켰었던 TV채널이 어떤 것일지라도, 그는 그림 외에 아무것도 보지 않았다.
5 No matter which / 당신이 어떤 것을 선택할지라도, 당신은 그것에 대해 지불할 필요 없다.

Exercise 02

1 Advertisers use whichever means, or media, they think will work best for them
2 whatever strength there is in its members to bring out
3 Whatever geopolitical crises may emerge / Bitcoin's reputation as a hedge against traditional financial systems remains strong

Exercise 03

1

1 no matter what

2 ④

3 **the last part of the pleasant walk** took him across open country to a large building set off quite by itself in a broad meadow.

4 standing alone (문법적으로 맞고, 문맥적으로 set off quite by itself와 같은 뜻이면 정답인정)

해석 매일 아침, 날씨에 관계없이, 그는 집을 나서서 마을 끝자락을 향해 걸어서 출발하곤 했다. 점점 인가가 드문드문 해졌고 즐거운 산책의 마지막부분은 그를 탁 트인 시골을 가로질러 넓은 초지에 덩그러니 혼자 떨어져 있는 한 큰 건물로 데려다 주었다.

2

1 (a) persuading → persuade

(b) than → to

(e) one → ones

2 whatever part of the world we come from

3 adjust / mak**ing** out / demerits / trivial

해석 우리 모두는 세상의 어떤 지역 출신이든 간에, 우리 자신의 나라가 모든 다른 나라들 보다 우월하다고 믿고 있다. 각각의 국가가 그 특징적인 장점과 단점을 가지고 있는 것을 감안하면, 우리는 우리나라가 소유하고 있는 장점이 정말로 중요한 것인 반면, 그 단점은 비교적 사소한 것이라고 이해하기 위해 우리자신의 가치기준을 조절한다.

Exercise 04

1 No matter how many times the results of experiments agree with some theory

2 you can disprove a theory by **finding** even a single observation that **disagrees** with the predictions of the theory

3 Ⓐ Each time new experiments are observed to agree with the predictions

Ⓑ if ever a new observation is found to disagree

해석 어떤 물리학 이론도 언제나 잠정적인데, 이는 그 이론이 단지 가설이라는 의미에서이다. 여러분은 절대로 그것을 증명할 수가 없다. 실험 결과들이 아무리 여러 번 어떤 이론에 부합한다 해도, 여러분은 다음번에 결과가 그 이론에 모순되지 않을 것이라고 절대로 확신할 수 없다. 반면에, 여러분은 어떤 이론이 예측하는 것과 부합하지 않는 단 하나의 관찰 사실을 찾아내어도 그 이론이 틀렸음을 입증할 수 있다. 과학 철학자 Karl Popper가 강조했듯이, 훌륭한 이론은 그 이론이 원칙적으로 관찰에 의해 틀렸음이 입증될 수 있는 수많은 예측을 한다는 사실에 의해 특징지어진다.

어휘 hypothesis 가설 contradict 모순되다 falsify 위조하다

Unit 23  what little 명사 (관계형용사) 구문

Exercise 01

1 He spent what little money he had.

2 He sold what little property he had, bought a boat and set off.

3 He sometimes speaks Spanish, which language I can't understand.

4 He told me to take a rest, which advice I followed.

5 I will give you what few books he has.

Exercise 02

1 whenever you are in trouble, I'll give you what little help I can

2 What little we know, what little power we possess, we owe to the accumulated endeavors of our ancestors

3 your neighbors have informed me of your illness, I have come to offer what little service I can

4 Scientists are utilizing what knowledge they have about the virus to develop effective treatments

5 Geologists studied what information they had about subduction zones, to better understand and predict the potential tsunami risks associated with these tectonic processes

6 Helen Keller made the most of what little faith society had in the abilities of people with disabilities

Exercise 03

1

1 The affectionate son used what little strength he had

2 the medicine that he had received from the doctor

3 medicine

🔍해석 그 효자(孝子)는 얼마 안 되는 모든 힘을 다하여, 의사로부터 받은 약을 개의 목에다 묶어, 그 개를 집으로 보냈다

2

1 I am sorry that I did not have

2 What little guidance I had

3 the same family in Heidelberg as I was living with

🔍해석 나는 어렸을 때 독서를 지도해 줄 좋은 분별력을 가진 누군가가 없었다는 것이 너무나 유감스럽다. 그다지 이롭지 않았던 책에 소비했던 시간들을 생각해보면 절로 한숨이 나온다. 그나마 받았던 독서에 대한 방법 모두는 내가 Heidelberg에서 함께 살고 있었던 바로 그 가족과 살기 위해 왔던 한 젊은이 덕택이었다.

Unit 24 To one's 감정명사 (독립부사구) 구문

Exercise 01

1 To my surprise, she accepted my marriage proposal without any hesitation.

2 To his great sorrow, leaving a void that could never be filled.

3 To her relief, despite the intense storm that had caused significant damage to other vehicles in the area.

4 To my regret, there's nothing I can do to change the unfortunate outcome.

5 To their delight, which sold a wide variety of fresh produce and groceries that they hadn't been able to find anywhere else.

6 To my shock, even though the doctors had initially thought he was on the road to recovery.

Exercise 02

1 To my surprise, I found / the house where I had been born and brought up had been pulled down

2 To my great sorrow my father died / my grief and remorse that I did not go to Dublin to see him for so many years

3 to our utter dismay / we would no longer be permitted to run wild

Exercise 03

1

1 to their embarrassment

2 may apply it on occasion to any male it sees

3 As soon as it learns to use "Kitty" for a cat, the baby is apt to apply it to a dog.

4 extend / physically similar

🔍해석 대부분의 엄마들이 알고 있는 것처럼, "아빠"라는 단어를 사용할 수 있는 어린아이는 가끔 그 말을, 당황스럽게도, 아이가 보는 어떤 남성에게도 사용할 수도 있다. 고양이를 "Kitty"라고 부르는 것을 배우고 나면, 아이는 그 말을 개에게도 사용하는 경향이 있다.

2

1 will find out → will be found out

2 takes, win it back

3 every question a child asks should be answered to his complete satisfaction.

해석 아이의 신뢰를 잃는 가장 확실한 방법은 사실은 알지 못하면서 아는 척하는 것이다. 한번은 넘어갈지도 모른다. 그리고 두 번째도 효과가 있을지는 모르지만 결국에는 발각될 것이고 오랜 시간이 걸려서야 아이의 신뢰를 회복할 것이다. 아이가 물어보는 모든 질문에 아이가 완전하게 만족하도록 대답해주어야 한다는 의미는 아니다.

Unit 25 — when, before (시간의 부사절) 구문

Exercise 01

1 I had not gone very far when I was caught in a shower.

2 It was five years before I met him again.

3 When she comes here tomorrow, I will buy her dinner.

4 Before they get home, they are going to drop by Jane's house.

5 Joe said he will give a call to you before he finishes his work.

6 Please let us know when you are done with your work.

7 There was no one living when the first immigrants arrived in Canada.

Exercise 02

1 He had not gone far when he came upon an old dog, as if it had been running a long way

2 It was half an hour before the fog began to clear up, a strange scene presented itself

3 He had not gone a mile before he came across four strangers, resting in the shade of a big oak by the side of the road

Exercise 03 

1

1 It was many days when the cat allowed me to come near him

2 Not for two or three weeks would he allow me to put a hand on him

해석 여러 날이 지나고서야 고양이는 멀리 도망가서 사라지지 않고 내가 자신에게 가까이 가는 것을 허락했다. 그리고 이삼 주 동안은 그는 내가 손을 올려놓는 것도 허락하지 않았다.

2

1 before it reached even as far as the city of Baghdad

2 It was not until the twelfth century that the new invention was introduced into Europe.

해석 비록 중국 전 지역에서 종이가 사용되고 5세기에 다른 재료 대신에 사용되기는 했지만, 삼백년이 지나고서야 멀리는 바그다드까지 퍼지게 되었다. 12세기가 되고서야 그 새로운 발명품은 유럽에 소개 되었다.

Exercise 04

1 resulting in one part's appearing in excess

2 the particular disease depending primarily upon which substance has gained the ascendancy

3 Ⓐ disturbed   Ⓑ restore   Ⓒ equilibrium(balance)

해석 히포크라테스 시대의 의사에게, 의술의 근본 원리는 자연이 안정의 상태를 유지하려고 하며 자연의 힘은 신체의 정상적인 부분들이 그들 사이에서 (서로) 균형을 유지하도록 그들을 끊임없이 조정하고 재조정하고 있다는 개념이었다. 이 균형이 존재할 때, 우리는 건강하다. 여러 가지 영향 중 그 어느 하나에 의해, 평형 상태는 방해받을 수 있고, 이것은 한 부분이 과도하게 나타나는 결과를 초래한다. 이것이 일어날 때, 병이 생기는데, 그 특정 질병은 주로 어떤 물질이 우위를 점했느냐에 의해 좌우된다.

Unit 26 — until, since (결과, 시간의 부사절) 구문

Exercise 01

1 그 소리는 점점 더 희미해졌다. 그리고는 그 소리가 사라졌다.
2 우리가 헤어진 지 10년이 지났다.
3 내가 런던으로 이사 간 이후로, 방문객이 온 것은 그 때가 처음이었다.
4 그들은 2002년에 여기로 이사 왔다. 그때까지 그들은 항상 런던 지역에 살았다.
5 그녀가 말하기 전까지 나는 그녀가 영국인이 아닌 줄 몰랐다.(그녀가 말을 해서야 비로소 영국인이 아닌 줄 알았다.)
6 그가 2주전에 집을 떠났고 그 이후로 그의 소식을 듣지 못했다.

Exercise 02

1 until at last it came to a distant country
2 The mouse begin nibbling and cutting the ropes of the net with her sharp teeth, until there was a large hole in the net
3 Our world has changed a lot since you grew up

Exercise 03

1

1 whether there is reason for it or not
또는 whether or not there is reason for it
2 too short or too homely or too unsuccessful tortures you.
3 until it flares into hostility toward the world
4 inferior / stance / negative / hostile

🔍해석 당신 자신을 정직하게 사랑하지 않는다면 다른 사람들을 사랑할 수 없다. 그에 대한 이유가 있든 없든, 당신 자신에 대해 열등한 의견을 가지고 있는 것은 당신 주변의 사람들에 대한 당신의 태도에 반영될 것이다. 당신이 너무 작거나 세련되지 못하거나 성공하지 못한 것에 대해 괴로워한다면 당신의 그러한 분개가 밖으로 드러나 마침내 세상에 대한 적개심으로 타오르게 될 것이다.

2

1 has been/ lived / received / is now honored
2 living / being ridiculed / considered

🔍해석 헨리 루소가 태어난 지 백년이 지났고 평생을 가난 속에서 살았고 동시대 사람들로부터 거의 조롱만 받았던 이 사람은 이제 19세기의 위대한 거장중의 하나로서 존경받고 있다.

Unit 27 — when (관계부사) 구문

Exercise 01

1 The time will come when you will need my help.
2 The meeting will be over by the time when you get there.
3 when he will be at home.
4 He wants everything done by the time he comes back from this vacation.
5 a time when many people feel happier than other days
6 By the time he graduates, he will have spent four years in college.

Exercise 02

1 the days have passed away, when the majority of people thought
2 He will have seen, by the time he returns home next spring
3 by the time we reached the top of the mountain

4 By the time the hero reached the castle, which stood ominously against the dark sky, the dragon had already vanished into the mist

5 the era when existentialism, a philosophy that questioned the very essence of human existence, gained popularity among thinkers who sought new meaning in life

Exercise 03

1

1 ⑤

2 It seems that the great civilizations of all time arose.

3 made it necessary for man to work

4 save up for the time when he could not produce

5 to avoid

6 연중 한 철에 착실히 일하는 것

해석 문명은 역경의 소산물이다. 모든 시대의 위대한 문명은 자연환경에 의해 연중 한 철밖에 농사지을 수 없고, 그리하여 그가 농사지을 수 없는 때를 대비하여 저축해야 하는 곳에서 일어났던 것 같다. 사람은 본디 꾸준히 계속하여 일하고 싶어 하지 않는다. 만약 자연 환경으로 인해 착실히 일하는 것을 면할 수만 있다면, 사람은 대개 일하여 진보하는 것보다는 차라리 게으르게 시간을 보내는 데 만족하는 것처럼 보인다.

2

1 by the time you have begun your conversation

2 somebody who is **impatient** to take your place

 공중전화 부스로 들어가서 꿉꿉한 냄새와 환기되지 않은 공기에 의해 거의 질식할 것 같은 느낌을 받을 때, 그리고 통화를 시작했을 때, 당신은 조급한 마음으로 자기 차례를 기다리는 누군가의 싸늘한 표정에 의해 당신의 등골이 서늘해짐을 느낀다.

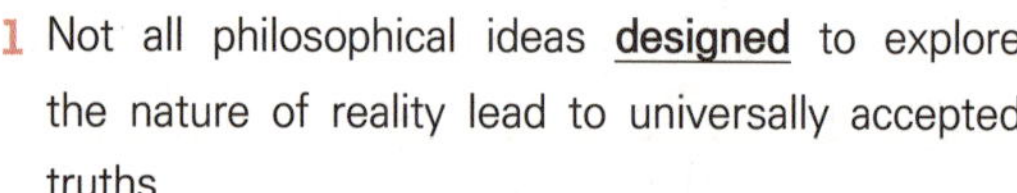

Unit 28 부분부정 구문

Exercise 01

1 Not all philosophical ideas **designed** to explore the nature of reality lead to universally accepted truths

2 Not every musical piece **composed** with great skill becomes a timeless masterpiece

3 Not every scientific theory **aiming** to explain natural phenomena is proven correct over time

4 Not all political strategies **created** to gain power result in long-term success

5 Not every social norm **intended** to guide behavior is accepted by all members of society

6 Not every AI system **designed** to improve efficiency operates without errors

Exercise 02

1 not all boys and girls like to read, those who always have "their noses in a book."

2 Most poets are said to write poetry because they are unhappy, this is not altogether true

3 Not every medical advancement developed to save lives is accessible to all patients

Exercise 03

1

1 something fittest means merely fittest for the given condition.

2 understanding → understood

해석 생존하는 최적자가 어떤 절대적인 기준에서 볼 때 반드시 가장 최고이거나 가장 우수한 것은 아니며, 단지 어떤 주어진 조건에 대해서만 가장 적합할 뿐이라는 사실을 명백히 이해하여야 한다.

1 No nation lives entirely isolated from others
2 the victory does not always fall to the most perfect language.
3 whom → whose / to adopt → adopt

해석 어떤 나라나 타국들로부터 전적으로 고립되어서는 살 수 없으며, 국가 간의 접촉은 항상 그들의 언어에 영향을 미치는 결과를 가져온다. 두 언어가 경쟁 할 때, 승리가 반드시 가장 완전한 언어에 돌아가는 것은 아니다. 또한, 문화가 떨어진 나라에게 그 언어를 받아들이게 만드는 것이 반드시 문화가 우월한 나라는 아니다.

Exercise 04

1 in different ways
2 the art of storytelling involves finding good ways to express one's experiences in a way appropriate to the listener
3 cannot → can

해설 unless는 if ~ not의 표현으로 그 자체로 부정의 의미를 지니며, unless절 내 부정을 사용하여 두 번 부정할 수 없다.

4 own(또는 first-hand) / liven up / interesting

해석 사람들은 자기 자신의 경험에 대해 항상 이야기하지만 똑같은 경험에 대해 매번 똑같은 방식으로 반드시 말하지는 않는다. 말하기 과정은 직접 체험에서 얻는 경험을 말할 때조차도 매우 창의적인 과정이 될 수 있다. 즉 이야기하기 기술은 자신의 경험을 청자에게 적합한 방식으로 표현하는 좋은 방법을 찾는 것을 포함한다. 따라서 지어낸 이야기와 직접한 경험을 말하는 것은 종이 한 장 차이이다[차이가 거의 없다]. 오락요소는 이야기를 지어내는 것에 존재하는 것과 꼭 마찬가지로 직접 체험에서 얻은 경험을 말하는 것에도 존재한다. 여러분이 일어난 일을 흥미롭게 보이게 만들 수 없다면 아무도 오늘 여러분에게 일어난 일에 귀 기울이기를 원하지 않는다. 어떤 경험을 생동감 있게 만드는 과정은 가장 지루한 부분을 없애 버리는 것과 같은 방식으로 단순히 그 경험을 말하는 것을 포함하거나, 그것은 또한 사실을 여러모로 활용하여 지루한 부분을 '개선하는 것'을 포함할 수 있다.

어휘 not necessarily 반드시 ~은 아닌 process 과정 firsthand 직접 (체험에서) 얻은 inventive 창의적인 involve 포함하다 appropriate 적합한 a fine line 종이 한 장 차이, 미세한 차이 liven up ~을 생동감 있게 하다 eliminate 없애다 play with ~을 여러모로 활용하다

Unit 29 이중부정 구문

Exercise 01

1 I never see you but I think of your mother.
2 He was so clever that there was hardly any reason why he couldn't solve the easy problem.
3 No one knows what will happen tomorrow.
4 This kind of misunderstanding is not uncommon.
5 She cannot see you unless she is done with it.
6 It never rains but it pours.
7 I cannot find any one who does not know his name.

Exercise 02

1 I never look at him but I think of my father
2 you cannot put on others, without getting a few drops on yourself.
3 You cannot have a man paint pictures, without instantly waking in him a pleasure
4 No discussion about global economic growth is complete but for the potential of the semiconductor industry
5 I never read a novel by a 19th-century female author without discovering a new perspective on society

Exercise 03

1

1 feel uneasy / accompanying (또는 attendant)

2 without

해설 never A without B B하지 않고는 A하지 않는다

해석 사람들은 항상 유별나게 다가오는 행운은 반드시 불운이 수반된다는 꺼림칙한 감정을 가지고 있었던 것 같다. 즉, 그 와중에 마가 끼지 않고서는 좋은 일이 생기지 않는다는, 즐거움이 있는 반면에 괴로움도 있다는 것과 같은.

2

1 ⓐ: making it the most universal form of reading
ⓑ: everyone finds time to read it despite their busy schedules

2 (a): lack → lacks (b): with that → with which
(e): reading → to read

해석 학문의 한 형태로서 신문에는 영원성이 결여되어 있는 것은 사실이지만, 그것이 독자들에게 불어넣으려고 하는 사상은 오래도록 영향을 미친다. 신문이야말로 누구라도 읽는 오직 하나의 읽을거리다. 사람이 아무리 자기의 직업에 바빠도 신문 읽을 시간을 낼 수 있다.

Unit 30 — not only ~ but [also] 구문

Exercise 01

1 This book covers not only history but also science,

2 praised for not only its sleek design but also its powerful performance.

3 by focusing on not only environmental issues but also social justice.

4 famous for exhibiting not only modern art but also ancient artifacts.

5 Joining the club will help you improve not only your physical fitness but also your mental health.

6 Not only does carbon capture reduce greenhouse gas emissions, but it also helps combat climate change effectively.

7 Not only has Bitcoin revolutionized the financial market, but it has also introduced a decentralized way of conducting transactions.

Exercise 02

1 not merely for making laws, but also for obeying them

2 I am doubtful whether he will be able to fulfil his literary ambitions, it requires good luck as well as talent and effort

3 it goes without saying that you need not pay more than you are obliged to

4 care not only about their absolute status but also about their status relative to other people's status.

5 Not only should we jettison the junk that weighs us down, we also need to get rid of anything that is not essential.

6 lies not only in understanding the known risks but also in preparing for the unpredictable and potentially lethal unknowns that may lie ahead.

Exercise 03

1

1 ②

2 whether for the purpose of defending himself against enemies or dangers of nature

3 in order that he may be able to work and produce

4 **But for him**, he would not only have become insane but would actually have died.
If it had not been for him, he would not only have become insane but would actually have died.
Had it not been for him, he would not only have become insane but would actually have died.

해석 생각할 수 있는 어떤 종류의 문화에 있어서도, 적 또는 자연의 위험으로부터 자신을 방어하기 위해서든 일을 하여 생산할 수 있도록 하기 위해서든, 인간이 생존하려면 타인과 협력할 필요가 있다. Robinson Crusoe 조차도 자기의 일꾼 Friday와 같이 있었다. Friday가 없었다면, 그는 아마 미치광이가 되었을 뿐만 아니라 정말로 죽어 버렸을 것이다.

2

1 two ideas which seemed to be in opposition
2 It is needless to say that injustice is a commonplace.
3 injustice / accept / commonplace / fight

해석 사람은 서로 상반된 것으로 보이는 두 개의 생각을 항상 염두에 두어야 하는 것처럼 보이기 시작했다. 첫 번째 생각은 있는 그대로의 삶과 있는 그대로의 사람들을 받아들이는 것이었다. 이러한 생각에서 보면 불의가 평범한 것이라는 것은 말할 필요가 없다. 그러나 이것이 그냥 스스로 만족하고 있을 수 있다는 것을 의미하지는 않았다. 왜냐하면, 두 번째 생각도 똑같이 강력하기 때문이었다. 즉, 사람은 결코 불의를 평범한 것으로 받아들여서는 안 되며 자기의 모든 힘을 다해 불의에 맞서 싸워야 한다는 것이다.

Exercise 04

1 ④

해설 본문에서 "rub off on"은 다른 사람에게 영향을 미친다는 의미로 사용되었으나, 좋은 방식이라기보다는 부정적인 영향을 준다는 의미로 쓰이고 있다. 해당 표현 자체는 긍정적이거나 부정적인 영향을 모두 포함한다.

2 **Not only can** bank tellers and retail staff lift the mood of customers by smiling at them, **but** they **can also do so** by asking them how they are.
3 contagious (같은 뜻의 단어이면 정답처리)

어휘 **progressively** 계속해서 **pick up** 배다, 들다, (습관·재주 등을) 들이게(익히게) 되다 **vibe** (보통 pl.) 분위기, 모양, 기분, 느낌 **teller** (은행의) 금전 출납원 **retail staff** 소매 직원 **in kind** 현물로, 동일한 것으로, 같은 방법으로, 마찬가지로 **rub off on** (습관·생각 등이) 남에게 영향을 미치다

a virtuous circle of reciprocated jollity 주고받는 즐거움(명랑함)의 선순환 **reciprocate** 주고받다, 교환하다, 보답하다, 보복하다 **more to the point** 더 중요한 것은 **take ~ to heart** ~을 마음속 깊이 새기다, ~을 진지하게 생각하다 (깊이 고려하다) **high-end** (동종의 제품 중에) 최고급인

해석 만일 당신이 경미한 우울증을 앓고 있는 사람과 주거 공간을 공유하고 있다면, 당신은 점차적으로 당신이 그들과 더 오래 함께 살수록 더 우울해지게 될 위험에 놓여서, 당신은 그들의 부정적인 기분(vibe)을 익히게 된다. 이와 마찬가지로, 은행 출납원들과 소매점 직원들은 그들에게 미소를 짓고 그들에게 안부 인사를 물음에 의해서 고객들의 기분을 진정으로 높일(lift) 수가 있다. 보통 그렇지만 고객들이 동일하게(in kind) 반응할 때, 그것은 직원들에게 영향을 미친다(rubs off on). 그것으로 인해서 상호 주고받는 즐거움의 선순환이 생겨나게 되고, 또 더 중요한 점은(more to the point) 만일 당신이 은행 혹은 상점 매니저라면 증가된 판매고를 낳는다. 일부 소매상들은 이런 사실을 명심하고, 그래서 어느 고가(고급) 패스트푸드 체인은 그런 기분들은 단지 이 사람에게서 저 사람에게로 전달될 수 있을 뿐만 아니라 친구들과 업무 동료들로 이루어진 전체 사회적인 세상들을 가로질러 전달될 수 있다는 것을 보여준다.

Unit 31 부정주어 비교 구문 (의미상 최상급)

Exercise 01

1 No discovery in history has been more groundbreaking than the theory of relativity.
2 No novel has been more influential in modern literature than "To Kill a Mockingbird."
3 No player in basketball has ever been more dominant than Michael Jordan.
4 No environmental issue is more urgent than climate change.
5 No invention has had a greater impact on communication than the smartphone.

Exercise 02

1 Nothing is more absurd than, someone who hasn't the least intention of listening to you.

2 No people talk so much about the weather as the British, you will never fail to keep up the interest of your British friends.

3 No subject has so many superstitions as the weather, because the weather is so important to us.

4 Not many authors can weave elements of surrealism and existential questions into a story as effectively as Haruki Murakami.

5 Not even the most thorough historical analysis can fully capture the complexity of the American Revolution as McCullough does in his writings.

6 Not a single gesture in Han Kang's writing goes unnoticed, every small movement reveals deeper layers of her characters' psychological struggles.

Exercise 03

1

1 has been destroyed → has destroyed

2 have less impact on man's life than what his intolerance imposes on it

🔍해석 홍수와 번개에 의한 어떤 손실도, 자연의 거친 힘에 의한 도시와 사원의 어떠한 파괴도 인간으로부터 인간의 무관용이 파괴시킨 것들만큼 많은 고귀한 생명을 앗아 가지는 않았다.

2

1 It is said that nothing is more vivid than a picture.

2 No visual image is so vivid as the image created by the mind in response to words.

🔍해석 사람들은 그림보다 더 생생한 것은 없다고 이야기 하며, 우리는 그에 동의하지 않는다. 단어에 반응하여 정신세계에 의해 창출되는 이미지보다 더 생생한 시각적 이미지는 없다.

Exercise 04

1 It's frustrating when that driver will neither speed up nor pull over.

2 ⓐ On highways where there are more lanes
ⓑ let the faster drivers pass them
ⓒ there's no room to get around him
ⓓ That's what causes road rage and accidents

3 driving(traveling) at a snail's pace

🔍해석 제한속도가 40mph인 2차선 도로에서 25mph로 가고 있는 사람을 지나서 가려는 운전보다 더 나쁜 것은 없다. 당신은 속도를 꽤 늦춰야 하고, 그 운전자가 속도를 내지 않거나 차를 길가에 대지 않을 때에는 짜증이 난다. 더 많은 차선이 있는 고속도로에서는 운전을 천천히 하는 사람은 오른쪽 차선으로 옮겨야 하고 빨리 가고자 하는 사람들이 자신의 차를 지나가도록 해야 한다. 당신이 달팽이와 같은 속도로 가는 누군가의 뒤에 있고, 그를 지나갈 공간이 전혀 없을 때 그런 상황은 사고를 일으킬 수도 있다.

Unit 32 비교구문 (의미상 최상급)

Exercise 01

1 This invention is as remarkable as any other achievement in modern science.

2 Jane is more diligent than any other student in her class.

3 His argument was as persuasive as any other proposal we've heard.

4 The athlete ran faster than any other competitor in the race.

5 This painting is as beautiful as any other masterpiece in the museum.

Exercise 02

1 Inflation is more detrimental than any other factor in destabilizing an economy.

2 The policy is as effective as any other measure introduced to stabilize the economy.

3 This study is more comprehensive than any other research conducted in the field of psychology.

Exercise 03

1 he was as respectable a gentleman as I ever met

2 are as easily digested as any other

3 Happiness and success in life depend upon good health more than any other single thing, where there are few trees, where there is little fresh air and grass, he is subject to many disease

Exercise 04

1 He was one of the greatest novelists of our day

2 His novels have as good a chance of surviving as any

해석 그는 우리 시대의 위대한 소설가들 중의 한 사람이었다. 그는 거대한 인물이었다. 그의 소설들은 지난 100년 동안 쓰인 어느 소설 못지않게 후세에 남을 가능성이 많다.

2

1 has spent → has been spent

2 I have lived about as solitary a life as any modern man has experienced.

해석 나의 인생은, 내가 아는 어느 누구의 인생보다도, 고독과 방황 속에 보냈다. 15세 때 부터—한 번의 기간을 제외하고는—나는 현대인이 경험한 아마 가장 고독한 생활을 했다.

Exercise 05

1 the crop yields of organic farms are much lower than those of conventional farms

2 democratic

3 <u>fields suffer from weeds and insects</u> (, thus reducing the yields of the crop)

4 productive / starvation

해석 유기농 식품의 생산이 대폭 증가하고 있다. 많은 소비자들은 그들이 지구를 돕고 있고, 더 건강하게 먹고 있다고 확신하기 때문에 유기농 식품에 기꺼이 높은 가격을 지불한다. 하지만 몇몇 전문가들은 유기농업이 단점을 가지고 있다고 말한다. 가장 빈번한 비판 중 하나는 유기농의 작물 생산량이 전통 농업보다 훨씬 적다는 것이다. 그것은 유기농 농경지가 전통적인 농경지보다 잡초나 해충으로부터 더 피해를 당하기 때문이다. 종종 전문가들이 제시하는 또 다른 주장은 유기농이 부유한 소비자들의 틈새시장을 위해 식량을 공급할 수 있지만 전 세계의 수십억의 굶주린 사람들을 먹일 수 없다는 것이다. 값비싼 유기농법이 아닌 오직 화학 물질 투입을 신중하게 하는 것이 기아에 직면한 나라들에서 식량 생산을 상당히 증가시키는 도움을 줄 수 있다.

Unit 33 · The 비교급, the 비교급 구문

Exercise 01

1 The more effort you put into your studies, the greater your chances of success will be.

2 The faster technology advances, the more complex our societal issues become.

3 The longer you wait to make a decision, the more difficult it becomes to choose the right option.

4 The harder you work to improve your skills, the more confident you will become in your abilities.

5 The more you learn about history, the clearer it becomes how past events shape our present world.

Exercise 02

1 As a film is to produce expensive more, it is likely to make money more.
2 As a hospital had devices more, its care was thought to be more advanced.
3 As the infant morality rate is higher, the need for public health services is greater.
4 An animal is higher in the evolutionary chain, it depends less on instinct.

Exercise 03

1 The more air we can take into the lungs, the better it is for our health
2 stirs him all the more deeply
3 Tom loves Sally the better of the two
4 The more social mobility is allowed in democratic societies, the more individuals strive for social distinction.
5 The more celebrities interact with their followers on social media, the more fans expect personal involvement and accountability from them.

Exercise 04

1

1 The older he grew, the more he suffered, the more he came to understand her.
2 simple → simplicity
3 such as he had never encountered in any other person.

해설 He understood that she had had a simple and an integrity, **such** as he had never encountered in any other person. 여기서 such는 동격명사임.

해석 그리고 그가 나이가 들수록, 더욱 고통을 당할수록, 그는 그 여자를 더욱 이해하게 되었다. 그가 어느 누구에게서도 만나지 못한 그런 소박함과 고결함을 그 여자가 지니고 있었다는 것을, 그는 이해했다.

2

1 (b): most of it → most of which / (d) which nonetheless wear → which nonetheless wears / (e) effort involving in → effort involved in
2 noise / subconscious / attempt

해석 도시의 노동자는 소음에 노출되어 있다. 그런데, 그 소음의 대부분을 그는 의식적으로 듣지 않게 된다. 그러나 소음은 그럼에도 불구하고 그를 지치게 한다. 듣지 않으려는 [듣지 않으려는데 내포되는] 무의식적인 노력 때문에 더욱더 그렇다.

Exercise 05

1 The harsher the wind become, the stronger a tree must be in order to withstand it
2 A forest that has been subjected to storms is much sturdier than woodlands in protected areas
3 A law of survival of the fittest
4 adversity / adverse

해석 폭풍이 분 다음에는 가장 튼튼한 나무들만이 계속 서 있다. 바람이 거셀수록 바람에 잘 견딜 수 있기 위해 나무는 더 강해져야 한다. 가장 불리한 날씨 상황에서 살아남은 나무들은 깊은 뿌리를 성장시킨다. 폭풍우를 겪었던 숲은 보호받는 지역에 있는 삼림보다 훨씬 더 튼튼하다. 더 약한 나무들은 제거되어 더 튼튼한 나무들이 번창할 공간을 더 많게 해준다. 나쁜 날씨로부터 보호받는 숲은 양분과 햇볕을 갖기 위해 모두 경쟁하는 가늘고 약한 나무들로 지나치게 붐비게 된다. 이 지역이 결국 폭풍에 노출될 때 거의 모든 식물들이 쓰러질 것이다. 역경에 의해 끊임없이 시련을 받는 숲은 자라서 견딜 것이다. 어려운 상황에 좀처럼 노출되지 않는 보호받는 지역은 약해져서 거의 장수하지 못한다.

어휘 sturdy 억센, 튼튼한 harsh 호된, 모진, 가혹한 withstand 잘 견디다, 버티다 adverse 반대하는, 불리한 subject 겪게 하다, 당하게 하다 nutrient 영양소, 자양물 vegetation 식물, 초목 level 쓰러뜨리다 longevity 장수

Unit 34 If절 대용 구문

Exercise 01

1 A man of sense would be ashamed to do so.
2 To hear him talk, you would take him for a girl.
3 In your place, I would not employ him.
4 Without music, the world would be a dull place.
5 Had he known her phone number, he would have given a call to her.
6 Take your umbrella, or you will get all wet.

Exercise 02

1 would have treated such a student
2 is believed to be the largest practical telescope, would not allow astronomers to see farther, because the earth's air clouds the view
3 I could have written the history of my school days, with an accuracy which would be quite impossible now

Exercise 03

1

1 ⓐ The reason the free nations strive to settle international disputes
ⓑ one more great war could sweep both the victor and the vanquished equally
2 (가) mean → means (나) like → alike

 **해석** 자유국가들은 국제분쟁을 해결하는 평화로운 수단을 찾기 위해 최선을 다하고 있다. 그들은 한 번 더 전쟁이 일어나면 승자와 패자 둘 다가 멸망할 것이라는 것을 알고 있다.

2

1 (a): watching → to watch
(b) to perform → perform or performing
(e): amazed → amazing
2 If there had been a slight slip of his hand, it would have meant an instant death for the patient.
or If his hand had slipped slightly, it would have meant an instant death for the patient.

해석 얼마 전에, 나는 한 의사가 정교함을 필요로 하는 뇌 수술을 하는 것을 볼 기회가 있었다. 손이 조금만 미끄러졌다면 환자가 바로 죽을 수도 있는 상황이었다. 그 의사에 대해 감명 받았던 것은 그의 기술이 아니라 놀라운 침착함이었다.

Unit 35 양보(이유)를 나타내는 도치 구문

Exercise 01

1 Young though he is, he has remarkable leadership skills.
2 Challenging though the task was, she completed it successfully.
3 Tired though the team was, they refused to give up and achieved their goal.
4 Improbable though the solution seemed, it worked perfectly.
5 Against them though the odds were, they remained optimistic.

Exercise 02

1 Important as women's role in business and community life is in America, a great many women see themselves primarily as housewives
2 Brave boy as he was. when he was told to go up the snowy mountain with his father

3 Great inventor as he was, He achieved a great fame, but never took pride in it

4 Significant as the challenges he faced in his personal life and career were, made groundbreaking contributions to the fields of computation and artificial intelligence

5 Challenging as carbon capture technology is to implement on a large scale, it remains a crucial tool in combating climate change

Exercise 03

1

1 Much as we may pride ourselves on our good taste

2 ⑤

🔍해석 비록 우리가 우리의 좋은 취향에 대해 자부심을 가진다 할지라도, 광고가 우리에게 미묘한 영향을 미치기 때문에 더 이상 원하는 것을 자유로이 선택하지 못한다.

2

1 Great physicist as he is

2 Indifferent as he is about publicity and so uncomfortable with fame

3 fame

🔍해석 그는 비록 대단한 물리학자이지만, 한 인간으로서 여전히 더 위대하다. 비록 그가 공적 관심에 무관심하고 명성에 불편해하더라도, 그는 다른 어떤 과학자보다 더 큰 명성을 얻었다. (그러나) 명성이나 외부 환경은 그를 거의 변화시킬 수 없다.

Unit 36 양보를 나타내는 부사절 구문

Exercise 01

1 No matter where you are in the world right now

2 no matter how they are cooked

3 No matter who becomes the next president

4 No matter what obstacles arise, she is determined to complete her project on time.

5 No matter how difficult the task may seem, we are committed to finding a solution.

Exercise 02

1 That man running along the platform will probably not get on, no matter what happens

2 no matter where we are living, no matter what we are doing, no matter who we are

3 no mater how little ability a man has, it is not impossible for him to do something if he really tries to

4 No matter where we look in the universe, how little we truly know about existence and the nature of being

5 No matter how deeply the political system is criticized, the voices of the marginalized continue to be ignored in discussions of social inequality

Exercise 03

1

1 no matter how it is expressed

2 in the inherent worth of every individual. a shared commitment to advancing their well-being

 미래 국제사회의 질서를 이끌어 갈 기저에 깔려 있는 추진력은 그것이 어떤 식으로 표현 되든 간에, 국가적 동질성이나 신의에 관계없이 각 개개의 인간의 가치에 대한, 그리고 그들의 복지를 촉진시키는 상호 공통적인 책임에 대한 믿음이어야 한다.

2

1 Life is seldom as exciting as we think it ought to be.
2 It is the other fellow's life which seems full of adventure.
3 No matter how happy you may be in it
4 choose → had chosen

 삶은 좀처럼 우리가 그래야만 한다고 생각하는 것만큼 흥미진진하지는 않다. 모험으로 가득 차 있는 것처럼 보이는 것은 다른 사람들의 삶이다. 직업이 무엇이든, 또는 그 직업에 얼마나 만족하든, 다른 직업을 선택했으면 하고 바라는 때가 있다.

MAGNUS
서술형 시리즈

고등영어 서술형

기본편 8주완성

저자운영카페

N | 공유의 기쁨

http://cafe.naver.com/chongjee 보충자료다운로드